THE
GENESIS
PLAGUE

†THE
GENESIS
PLAGUE

MICHAEL BYRNES

SIMON &
SCHUSTER

London · New York · Sydney · Toronto

A CBS COMPANY

First published in Great Britain by Simon & Schuster UK Ltd, 2010
A CBS COMPANY

1 3 5 7 9 10 8 6 4 2

Simon & Schuster UK Ltd
1st Floor
222 Gray's Inn Road
London WC1X 8HB

www.simonandschuster.co.uk

Simon & Schuster Australia
Sydney

A CIP catalogue record for this book
is available from the British Library

ISBN 978-1-84737-239-0

Typeset by M Rules
Printed in the UK by CPI Mackays, Chatham ME5 8TD

For Caroline, Vivian, Camille, and Theodore

'He that is in the field shall die with the sword; and he that is in the city, famine and pestilence shall devour him'

– The Book of Revelation

†HE GENESIS PLAGUE

PROLOGUE
MESOPOTAMIA,
4004 BC

Nightfall was darker now, more ominous, thought Enliatu. The unrelenting cloud cover choked the moonlight to a dull glow and blotted out every celestial light in the heavens. And with the darkness had come great misfortune for his people. It was not that Nahna, the illuminator god of the night sky, purposely hid from the earth. All of it, Enliatu was certain, could be attributed to a malevolent *earthly* force: the outsider who had mysteriously emerged from the forbidden realm over the eastern mountains; the beautiful woman who was now being marched to her death.

The captive was flanked by eight warriors carrying spears and bitumen torches. Two of the men tightly gripped the ropes fastened to the leather collar cinched around her neck. Her hands were unbound so that she could carry the mysterious clay jar that had been in her possession since her arrival six moons ago. She cradled the vessel as if it were her child.

Her exotic fair skin and gem-like eyes were nothing like those of the dark-coloured tribes that inhabited the known lands. The women of the village were captivated by her. They'd competed to stroke her strange soft hair and smooth skin. To them, the unknown words that she spoke sounded like music, and her scent – sweet and spicy – seemed from another world. They'd prepared for her the finest foods, even braided her hair with beautiful flowers.

The men shared in the seduction, though their attraction was far more feral. Never had they laid eyes upon such an alluring female. As Enliatu had feared, they could not restrain themselves. They had vied for her attention, and her fierce indifference merely intensified the rivalry. Eventually the men agreed surreptitiously to share the prize.

On the third moon the conspirators – led by the two men whom Enliatu had designated to watch over her – crept into the hut where she slept. They covered her mouth, restrained her limbs, stripped away her coverings. Then, in predetermined order, they had their way with her until each man's carnal appetite had been sated.

The men later confided to Enliatu that she had not fought their advances. There had been no screams, no tears, no struggle. With flaccid repose she had stared at each aggressor with vacant eyes as he defiled her, a thin grimace twisting her soft lips.

By sunrise the first man had fallen ill. First came sweating, then chills and quaking limbs . . . and the blood. So much blood.

All were dead before sunset.

If only the tragedy – the punishment – had stopped with them, lamented Enliatu.

As the procession moved swiftly along the bank of the swollen river, Enliatu noticed that the flood had swallowed the circular granaries up to their rooftops. Soon the mud bricks that formed their walls would soften and dissolve beneath the churning water, the straw roofs carried downstream to rot. Not a trace would remain.

Surely a cleansing was under way. Perhaps the creator, Enlil, was seeking to reclaim mankind itself, for just as men had formed bricks to build dwellings, the gods had moulded men from earthen clay.

The procession broke away from the riverside and disappeared through a line of towering cedars. Beneath the dense forest canopy the torchlight illuminated only the nearest tree trunks against a perfectly black background. Soon the roiling river could no longer be heard. The warriors carried on in silence, while the prisoner began to softly hum a sensual melody. Overhead, the night owls, otherwise passive creatures, screeched in unison as if in response to her call. This caused the men to stop suddenly. They held the torches high and, with terror-filled eyes, searched the darkness with spears at the ready.

'*Il-luk ach tulk*!' Enliatu screamed out in frustration.

The handlers tugged the ropes, choking the prisoner back into submission. When she fell silent once more, the unearthly chorus above abruptly ceased.

The ground rose sharply; the cedars thinned and yielded to the scrubby foothills leading up to the stark, jagged mountains. The procession paused as Enliatu made his way forward to lead them up a scree-covered slope towards a fire pit flickering bright orange. The two boys he had sent ahead in daylight to prepare the site knelt beside the pit, stirring two clay bowls that simmered over the low flames.

The handlers goaded the prisoner ahead.

Keeping a safe distance, Enliatu instructed the boys to confiscate her burden. When they advanced towards her, she pulled the jar close to her breast, screaming wildly as they tried to tug it free. The handlers yanked back on the ropes until veins webbed out over her face and her eyes bulged. Finally the boys stripped the jar from her. She fell limp to the ground, retching.

'*Ul cala*,' Enliatu instructed the older boy. *Open it.*

The boy was not keen on carrying out the task, for he was certain that the jar itself might contain the woman's evil spells.

'*Ul cala!*'

The boy curled his trembling fingers under the lid, swiftly pulled it away. Immediately the dancing fire glow captured movement deep inside the vessel. He recoiled and stumbled backwards.

Undeterred, Enliatu stepped forward and extended his torch over the opened jar. Upon seeing the hideous form nestled within the jar, he scowled in revulsion.

The warriors exchanged uneasy glances and awaited the elder's instruction.

It would end here, tonight, Enliatu silently vowed. He instructed the boys on what to do next.

The older boy returned to the fire pit and slid wooden rods through the handles on the simmering clay bowls. Then his partner helped him to lift out the first bowl. Steadying it over the woman's jar, they decanted the glutinous, steaming liquid – kept pouring until the resin bubbled over the jar's rim.

The prisoner shrieked in protest.

Again the owls screeched from the dark forest.

Enliatu studied the concentric ripples billowing across the resin's shimmering surface. The wicked dweller was trying to emerge.

The petrified older boy replaced the lid, held it firmly in place until the thumping within the jar slowed, then ceased. He allowed a long moment to pass before pulling his hands away.

Satisfied, Enliatu turned his attention once more to the prisoner. On hands and knees, she was growling like a wolf, tears cutting hard lines down her dusty cheeks. Their eyes locked – two stares searing with determination. He was convinced that this was certainly a beast in disguise, a creature of the night.

Through bared teeth she hissed gutturally, spittle dribbling down her chin. All the while she kept her fingers wrapped around her beaded necklace – an object from her native land. Was this how she communicated with the other realm? Enliatu wondered. Regardless, he was certain that she was cursing him, summoning her demon spirits to destroy him.

The time had come.

He signalled to the warriors. They forced her to the ground, face up, and restrained her splayed limbs. The largest warrior came forward, tightly gripping the haft of a formidable axe, its bronze blade glinting orange in the firelight. He crouched beside her, grabbed a fistful of hair at the crown, and yanked her head back to expose the smooth flesh of the neck. A momentary assessment just before he raised the axe high, then brought it down in a precise arc aimed directly above the collar.

The blade split the soft skin and muscle to bring forth a rush of blood that seemed to glow in the firelight. A second fierce chop sank deeper into the gaping muscle to separate vertebrae – the vile blood splashing up, painting the warrior's face and chest. He delivered two more blows, until the head was cleanly separated.

Grunting with satisfaction, the warrior tossed the axe aside and grabbed the severed head by its soft locks. But his smile vanished when he looked into the glowering eyes that still seemed alive. Even the soft lips remained frozen in a taunting grimace.

Enliatu went to the fire pit. '*Eck tok micham-ae ful-tha.*' He pointed to the second simmering clay bowl.

Extending the ghastly head away from his body, the warrior dropped it into the boiling resin. Enliatu watched it sink lazily into the opaque sap amidst a swirl of blood – its dead eyes still glaring defiantly, as if to promise that the stranger's curse had only just begun.

1

NORTHEAST IRAQ
PRESENT DAY

'I'm empty!' Jam called over to his unit commander who was four metres away, crouched behind a massive limestone boulder.

Keeping his right eye pressed to the rifle scope, Sergeant Jason Yaeger reached into his goatskin rucksack, pulled out a fresh magazine, and smoothly tossed it to Jam. Hot metal intermingled with the discharge gases blowing downwind from the muzzle vent on Jam's rifle. 'Slow it down or you're going to lock it up!' Precisely the reason Jam had earned his nickname, he thought.

Jam ejected the spent clip, snapped in the new one.

The unit's mishmash of Russian weapons, scrounged from a wandering Afghani arms dealer, gave each man's rifle a unique report that helped Jason to roughly keep a count on expended rounds. Jam was heavy on the trigger of his Cold-War-era AK-74 – more pull than squeeze. The others in the unit were far more judicious with their shots.

Though the ten remaining Arab militants had superior numbers and a high-ground advantage, the art of the kill was heavily weighted in favour of Jason's seasoned team. The dwindling ammo supply, however, couldn't have come at a worse time. If the bad guys were to call for backup, Jason's unit could be attacked from the rear in the open flatlands leading to the foothills. Worse yet, the enemy might slip through the nearby crevasse and head deeper into the Zagros Mountains – a rebel's paradise filled with caves and labyrinthine, rugged passes.

Over the border and into Iran.

He whistled to Jam, made a sweeping hand motion that sent him scrambling up the hill and to the right. He fought the urge to scratch at the prickly heat beneath his scruffy beard, which, along with contact lenses that transformed his hazel eyes to muddy brown, a deep tan that could be the envy of George Hamilton, an unflattering galabiya robe, vest, and loose-fit pants combo, a keffiyeh headwrap with agal rope circlet, and sandals – had respectably passed him off as a Bedouin nomad. The other unit members had donned similar dress.

It took less than a two-count before a red-and-white chequered keffiyeh popped up over the rock pile, a Kalashnikov semi-automatic sweeping into view an instant later. Sliding his index finger off the trigger guard while matching crosshairs to chequers, Jason squeezed off three successive shots that would've left a perfect dime grouping on a bullseye. Through the scope he saw a pink mist and red blobs spit out behind the headscarf.

He adjusted the remaining target tally downward: nine.

Ducking from sight, he grabbed his rucksack and scrambled away just as a pomegranate-shaped grenade arced over the boulder, landed in the sand and popped. A ten-metre uphill dash brought him to a rocky hillock covered in scrubby brush. More automatic gunfire burst in his direction as he dived for cover.

While the militants screamed back and forth to one another in Arabic – not Kurdish? – Jason brought out his Vectronix binoculars and scanned the two enemy positions. The device's laser automatically calculated GPS coordinates while recording live images on to its micro-sized hard drive.

Dipping beneath the hillock, he flipped open a laminated field map to verify the correct kill box on the grid. From his vest pocket he fished a sat-com that looked nearly identical to a civilian cell phone. He placed a call to the airbase at Camp Eagle's Nest, north of Kirkuk. A barely perceptible delay followed by a tiny digital chirp confirmed that the transmission was being securely encrypted, just before the command operator responded with the first authentication question: 'Word of the day?'

He pressed the transmitter button. 'Cadillac.'

Chirp. Delay.

'Colour?'

Chirp. Delay.

'Magenta.'

Chirp. Delay.

'Number?'

Chirp. Delay.

'One-fifty-two.'

Pause. Chirp.

'How can I help, Google?'

Even under fire, Jason had to smile. He'd earned his new nickname a few months ago, after joining the boys at the airbase for a drink-while-you-think version of Trivial Pursuit. Jason had circled the game board and filled his pie wheel without ever cracking open a beer. The other players weren't as fortunate, but maybe that was their intention. Obtuse facts – 'things no self-respecting 29-year-old should know' – were

3

Jason's forte. What he wouldn't do to have that beer right now . . .

'We're low on ammo. Copy,' Jason reported loudly over the persistent rat-a-tat-tat-tat in the background. 'Nine militants pinned down. Some light artillery. Need a gunship ASAP.' He provided the operator with the kill box and INS coordinates. 'Have the pilot call me on approach.'

'Roger. I'll have Candyman there in four minutes.'

Noting the time on his no-frills wristwatch, he slid the sat-com back into his vest and mopped the sweat from his eyes with his sleeve.

He needed to make sure that the others weren't too close to the intended strike zones.

First he glanced over to Jam, who was now a good fifteen metres further up the slope, curled up in a gulch, cursing at his weapon's stuck slide bolt. Vulnerable, but he was adequately covered.

Along the roadway at the hill's base, Camel was still dug in behind a felled, bullet-riddled Arabian one-humper. For the past few months, former marine sniper Tyler Hathcock had shared a strange – at times, disturbing – bond with the beast, which, coupled with his preferred cigarette brand, helped to inspire his nickname. Earlier, Camel had used the beast as a decoy by riding it bareback down the narrow roadway to block the approaching enemy convoy. When the ambush began, he'd been trapped in the open. So he'd dismounted, shot his humped buddy through the ear and used it as a surprisingly effective shield.

Crazy bastard.

Not far from Camel's position, he spotted Dennis Coombs – dubbed 'Meat' for his imposing stature that was pure Oklahoma farm boy muscle – still pinned down behind the severely strafed

Toyota pickup that had been the convoy's lead vehicle. In the driver's seat was the slumped body of an Arab male, back of the head blown open, brain matter and gore smeared throughout the cabin, compliments of Jason's opening three rounds delivered from fifty metres to the mark's left eye.

Behind the Toyota were three more trucks left abandoned by the enemy. Eight dead Arabs littered the ground around them. Bobbing in and out of view over the hood of the second truck was the red turban marking Jason's last man, Hazo. The 42-year-old Kurd acted as the unit's eyes and ears: translator, facilitator, go-to man. Hazo was simultaneously their best asset and worst liability, since, like most Kurdish Christians, he refused to handle a weapon. All brain, no brawn – but a helluva a nice guy. Jason guessed that Hazo was in the fetal position reciting a few novenas. If he didn't move, he'd be perfectly safe.

Jason low-crawled further up the rise. When he peeked up to survey the enemy again, he didn't like what he saw. Behind a formidable rock pile, three white-turbaned Arabs had unpacked a long polyethylene case they'd hauled out from the Toyota before taking off for the hills on foot. The sand-coloured weapon they were now assembling had a long fat tube with Soviet markings. A fourth man wearing a black keffiyeh was readying its first mortar shell.

'Damn.'

Jason used his binoculars to scout the airspace above the western plain, until he found the black bird twelve klicks out over the horizon, closing in fast. Two minutes away, he guessed. He'd need to buy some time before the guys with the rocket launcher got busy.

He positioned himself behind a natural V in the rock. Not the best sight line and only the targets' headscarves were visible . . .

but he'd make it work. With the stock of his SVD sniper rifle nestled comfortably on his right shoulder, Jason stared through the scope and took aim at the black keffiyeh. Then he sprang up slightly until the target's angular, bearded face panned into view.

Pop-pop-pop.

The rounds hit home and pink mist confirmed the kill.

The mortar fumbled out from the dead man's hand, rolled out of view. The three white turbans retreated from his crosshairs as they scrambled to recover it. Jason sank back below the ridge. The sat-com vibrated in his vest pocket. He pulled it out and hit the receiver.

'It's Candyman. Talk to me, Google.'

'Three targets remaining in position one . . . guns and an RPG. Copy.'

'Roger. And position two?'

'Five gunmen. Copy.'

'You're getting soft on me. I thought we were gonna see some real action.'

'Sorry to disappoint, Candyman.'

After pocketing the sat-com, Jason took up his rifle and rucksack then kept moving further up the hillock, hoping to get a better angle on the white turbans. But only arms and legs occasionally came into view. With limited rounds to spare, it was headshots or nothing at all. He only hoped the men wouldn't succeed in loading the RPG-7 before the air strike commenced.

His new vantage point did, however, let him monitor the gunmen who were pinned down in the second position: four men surrounding one tall guy in the centre. Jason swung the rifle in their direction and steadied the crosshairs over a chunky Arab who was all cheeks beneath a patchy grey beard. Patchy made an abrupt move that granted Jason a clear facial on the central figure nestled in the ring's centre. The sinister portrait Jason captured in the crosshairs made his heart skip a beat.

'Can't be,' he murmured.

That hard dark face, however, and the incredible death toll associated with it, was unmistakable. What the hell was *he* doing here? The visceral urge to pull the trigger was overwhelming. But if he knowingly took down terrorism's newest most-wanted man, he'd whip up an unimaginable shit storm. Directives were black and white for a reason, he reminded himself. Not yet. Let it go. He quickly zoomed in on the face with his binoculars and recorded the images.

Snatching up the sat-com, he used the analogue walkie-talkie channel to radio the other unit members: 'Nobody fire on position two. I repeat: hold your fire on position two.'

The thumping rotors of the AH-64 Apache were getting louder by the second. Dropping back, Jason watched the gunship sweeping in on a direct line.

A second later, the sat-com vibrated on its digital channel and he hit the receiver.

'That you, Candyman?'

'Roger, Google. You ready for me?'

'Yes, but do not, I repeat, do not fire on position two. Over.'

'Got it. How 'bout position one?'

Jason peeked up over the rocks, saw one of the white turbans pop up then disappear. Then the rocket tube came in and out of view. No clear shot for Jason.

'Hydras on position one. Have at it,' Jason replied urgently.

'Roger that. Stay low and cover your ears.'

Fifteen seconds later, the Apache was in strike range. The laser sensor on its nosecone locked on the rock pile's GPS coordinates. An instant later, a pair of Hydra 70 missiles launched from the chopper's stub-wing pylons.

Jason stole a final glimpse of position one. The RPG-7 launch tube jutted out from the rock, this time with a mortar securely affixed to its tip. It was going to be close.

Ducking down, he tossed his rifle to the ground, covered his ears, and pressed his back against the mound. He watched the missiles stream in along sharp trajectories that laced the crystalline blue sky with two crisp lines of exhaust smoke – a fearsome sight.

Then Jason witnessed an equally remarkable sight: as the tandem missiles hissed overhead, the rocket launcher's mortar sliced upward and glanced one of them – not hard enough to detonate the Hydra's warhead, but enough to push it off its intended path.

The first Hydra slammed position one and threw a reverberating blast wave over the mound that made Jason's teeth rattle. A rush of intense heat came right behind it.

A split second later, the second Hydra struck and the ground quaked even harder. The explosion echoed off the mountains.

Jason watched the chopper bank hard to avoid the wobbling mortar, which stayed airborne for five seconds before plummeting into an orchard of date trees and exploding in a tight orange fireball.

As he pulled his hands from his ringing ears, a tattered white turban covered in red splotches came fluttering down from the sky and landed at his feet. With it came the smell of burnt flesh.

Snatching up his rifle, Jason flipped the selector to burst. Then he scrambled down the slope, careful not to let his sandals slip on the gore blanketing the hillside. With the rifle high on his shoulder, he swept the muzzle side to side, waiting for any movement near the decimated rock pile. The smoke and dust made it impossible to see what was happening behind the second position, so he eased back, took cover behind a boulder, and waited. He scanned the area through his gun scope. No activity.

A westerly wind quickly thinned the smoke.

Down below, Camel broke cover and sprinted up the slope. Jason covered him with suppressive fire until he did a home-plate slide through the gravel and came to a stop at Jason's feet.

'Safe!' Camel called out, grinning ear to ear like a school kid out for recess.

Some guys are born for this. Then Jason got a good look at Camel's face. It appeared as if he'd stuck his head in a bucket of gore. 'You all right?'

'*I'm* fine. My camel's fucked. Why the ceasefire on the second position?'

'Fahim Al-Zahrani is with them.'

'*What?!*' Camel's brow crinkled, cracking the congealing camel blood like dry clay. 'Can't be. Intel said he's in Afghanistan.'

'Intel's wrong. Wouldn't be the first time.'

'You sure about this?'

'Show you the pictures later,' he said, tapping his binoculars. 'He's the tall one in the middle. Remember, the Pentagon wants him alive. So try not to shoot him and we'll get home a lot faster.'

Suddenly, Jam screamed over to Jason: 'They're heading uphill!'

Jason and Camel went storming out on opposite sides of the boulder with weapons drawn.

The black smoke was still thick enough to provide cover for the Arabs, but Jason was relieved to see Al-Zahrani's awkward, tall form being pulled up the slope by a pair of cronies. The remaining two Arabs trailed behind them, hauling a second polyethylene case.

As Jason and Camel closed in behind them, Meat broke cover to pull up the rear.

Then Jam popped out from the gulch and began sprinting along the ridge in a perpendicular intercept. He had his now-useless AK-74 clutched menacingly in his right hand, knowing the best he could do was intimidate the Arabs, maybe slow their advance.

The dragnet was closing.

When Jason broke through the smoke, he saw that the Arabs had decided against the crevasse and were instead heading for a sizable opening in the cliff face that looked like a cave. Judging by the flames licking the rocky outcropping above the opening and the fresh scars above it where an entire section of the mountain had sheared away and tumbled down the slope, Jason figured that it had been the impact point for the deflected Hydra missile.

Once the Arabs had funnelled into the opening and disappeared from sight, Jason slowed his advance and signalled to the others to take cover. No telling what the Arabs were planning, and chasing after them into a cave wouldn't be smart.

Could the blast hole be that deep? he wondered. And why would they corner themselves like that?

2

From behind a boulder, Jason scanned the opening with his binoculars. No sign of the jihad quintet, but when he zoomed in, he did notice something peculiar: about two metres into the opening the black void was framed by a rectangular enclosure – like an open doorway. Tighter magnification revealed bolt heads lining the hard, unnatural lines.

'What do we have here?' he muttered.

Someone whistled loudly.

Lowering the binoculars, Jason peered over to Meat, who was pointing to a smoking object that lay not far from where he'd taken cover. Even from a distance, Jason could tell that the mangled and blackened rectangular hulk of metal was the door that had been blown clear off the frame he'd just spied. Scoping the object, he determined it to be roughly one by two metres, fat as a phone book, with a wide circular turn-crank like he'd expect to find on a submarine hatch. The door's unmarred sections showed that it had been painted to match the mountain's earth tones. Around its edges were remnants from military-grade camouflage netting. Must have been quite effective, he thought, if no one had spotted it earlier. The opening was certainly positioned high enough to trick the naked eye.

Maybe the militants hadn't intended to slip through the mountains. Maybe they were heading to this place all along. Perhaps it was a bunker.

Then again, Jason had seen the Arabs do a double-take before running into the opening – like they were equally surprised to see it there. Either way, since this was no mere blast hole, there was a strong possibility that whatever had been protected behind that security door ran deep – *really* deep; the snaking cave systems running beneath these mountains could put Rome's most impressive catacombs to shame.

He'd read in his field manual that the Zagros Mountains were formed from the ancient tectonic collision between the Arabian and Eurasian plates. The jagged range stretched 1,500 kilometres from northern Iraq down to the Straits of Hormuz in the Persian Gulf, with peaks reaching 4,500 metres (even taller than Colorado's Pikes Peak, he'd noted). Caves and tunnels resulted from the erosion of the softer mineral-laden rocks inside the mountains. The Zagros's most bittersweet contribution to the region, however, was the sedimentary deposits trapped beneath its eastern foothills – Iran's massive oil fields.

From out of the cave came a muffled fizzy sound, like a freshly cracked bottle of pop releasing its carbonation. Just as Jason's eyes found the opening, a blinding glow flashed in the black void beyond the doorframe . . . the silhouette of a projectile . . . a resounding *whump*. In the next instant, a roiling fireball billowed out from the opening, throwing heat waves that rippled down the slope. Huge rock fragments shot out in all directions.

The Americans went for cover as the debris came raining down around them.

A softball-sized stone plummeted down and struck Jason squarely between the shoulder blades, knocking him flat to the ground. The wind heaved out from his lungs in a heavy gasp. Pain jolted up his spine, down his arms. He rolled on to his back, arcing his spine, groaning in pain, seeing nothing but white for a five-count. Had he not been wearing a Kevlar vest under his robe, the stone might have paralysed him.

Fast footsteps crunched along the gravel and came to a stop next to him.

'You okay, Google?'

He blinked his eyes and drew a steady breath. 'Yeah, I'll live.'

Jam helped him to his feet and Jason squeezed his shoulder blades together to coax the pain away.

'That's gonna leave a mark,' Jam said.

Jason noticed that Jam's left cheek was red and blistered, the curly black scruff sizzled away.

'You should talk,' he replied with a wince.

'I was a bit too close when the missile went off.' He stroked the tangle of toasted hairs. 'I needed a shave anyway.'

Jason looked up at the grey smoke cloud spewing out from the ridge. The doorframe was lost behind the collapsed cliff face. He shook his head in disbelief.

'That was an RPG . . . right? I mean I barely saw it.'

'Yeah, it was.'

He shook his head and put his hands on his hips.

Meat, Camel and Hazo jogged over to join them.

'Everybody all right?' Jason asked the trio.

'Super,' Meat grumbled. When he got a good look at Jam, he stepped closer and cringed. 'What's with your face?' Then he got a whiff of the singed beard and said, 'Aaah. I hate that smell . . . burnt hair. Shit, I'm gonna vomit.' He shook his head violently.

'You're one to talk, Dracula. That blood mask really brings out your eyes.'

'Ha, ha, very fun—'

'All right fellas,' Jason cut in. For frontline fighters, adrenaline surges always came with euphoria – at least if you were still standing when the bullets stopped flying. It was the junkie high that kept them coming back for more. But it also made the hyped-up men tougher to rein in. 'Good to see that everyone's all right. I'm sure you've noticed that we've got a new problem on our hands.' He motioned to the smoking cliff.

Camel pulled out a small round tin from his vest, opened it, and pinched out some chewing tobacco. In passing himself off as an abstaining Muslim, a nicotine patch would have been far subtler, but the chew sure beat puffing away on cigarettes. 'Looks good to me. The rag-heads went and buried themselves.' He began stuffing his cheeks full of tobacco.

Jam pulled a hunting knife off his belt and began cutting the singed beard away, since it did stink something fierce. 'Seems to me they don't want us coming in after them.'

'I'd go with that,' Meat agreed.

'These caves . . .' Hazo chimed in, his tone level and one notch too low. 'The tunnels can lead anywhere. It's no good. They could find a way out. Maybe on the other side of the mountain . . . maybe a kilometre away.'

'Or they went and buried themselves,' Camel reiterated before hawking a brown gob on to the rocks. 'Crawled into a hole. Just like your buddy Saddam.'

The Kurd frowned.

Jason was inclined to agree with both assertions. 'Let's have a closer look at that door.' He waved for them to follow, then strode over to it.

Kneeling beside the door, Jason could feel heat radiating off the blackened metal. He carefully hunted the surface for any telling marks: manufacturer's stamps, engraved plates, painted emblems or Arabic scrawls, anything. He found nothing. 'Let's flip it,' he told the others. 'Cover your hands. This thing's smokin' hot.'

It took all five men to heave the thing up and over. It landed on the gravel with a crunching thump.

'Weighs more than my wife,' Camel grumbled.

'Nah, she's got a few more L-Bs on her,' Meat said, as if to imply intimate knowledge. 'More to love.'

The others chuckled. Camel's chewing came to grinding halt.

'Cool it,' Jason said as he squatted to resume the analysis. The door's reverse side was clearly what would have faced inward. The twisted hinges looked like they'd been lifted from a bank vault. The turn-crank was bent into a pretzel shape. No telling marks. Not even on the edges.

'That's definitely military construction,' Meat observed.

'You're a genius,' Camel said under his breath.

Meat ignored him. 'I'm guessing that's one of the old regime's hideouts. A fallout shelter, maybe.'

'Shit, maybe we'll finally find some WMDs squirrelled away up there,' Jam added.

Jason got to his feet. 'Whatever's inside that mountain must be mighty important to have been covered up like this.'

'Hey wait. You missed something there, Sarge,' Jam said, pointing to the corner where some camouflage netting had melted into the metal. 'Here . . .' He moved closer and tapped it with his knife. Then he stood and began cutting away the good half of his beard in large tufts.

Jason crouched and leaned in for a better look. Sure enough, there was a rectangular object caught up in the netting, slightly bigger than a credit card, thicker too. 'Good eye.'

Whatever it was, it had taken a beating, just like the door. Curling his fingers under its edges, Jason tried to pry it free. But it had a plastic casing that had glued to the hot metal. He felt a tap on his shoulder.

'Here,' Jam said, handing over his Rambo-sized beard trimmer.

'Thanks.' Working the blade under the object, Jason managed to cut it away. Strings of melted plastic stretched behind it – like a shoe stepping off a wad of gum on a hot day. He let the strings cool before shaving them off.

'You should put that stuff on your face, Jam,' Camel said. 'Be a good look for you.'

Handing the knife back to Jam, Jason turned the object over a couple of times. It was taupe, lightweight, with a now indiscernible picture on its topside – what might have been a passport photo. There was a long keyhole slit centred on its short edge where a clip or strap could be affixed. 'Looks like a library card, or something.'

'ID badge,' Meat said.

Jason nodded. 'Um.'

'There's probably a chip inside that casing,' Meat added. 'You know, like a swipe card.'

Jason proffered the card to Meat, who moonlighted as the group's all-round techie. 'Think you can open it up . . . see if there's any useful data that might tell us who this belonged to?'

Meat took the card, flipped it over a couple of times. 'Looks fried. I'll see what I can do,' he replied non-committally.

'Make it happen,' Jason said. 'Now, we need to get into that cave. Fast. Unfortunately, as I see it, we're going to need some help to make that happen.'

16

Everyone knew what he meant. None was thrilled about the proposition, yet no man could find adequate reason to oppose it. Autonomy went only so far.

Reluctantly, Jason pulled out his sat-com and radioed the command operator with instructions to immediately dispatch a marine platoon to his position.

3

LAS VEGAS, NEVADA

Wrapping up a business call, Pastor Randall Stokes discreetly passed his eyes over the attractive female reporter from the *Vegas Tribune* who was seated on the guest side of his mammoth mahogany desk. Ms Ashley Peters was too busy taking inventory of the inner workings of Our Savior in Christ Cathedral to take notice. Late twenties, he guessed. A bit conservative with high-lighted reddish brown locks pulled back in a tight bun, designer eye glasses whose lenses seemed strictly cosmetic.

'Look, a cathedral without a carillon is like an angel without wings . . .' he told the caller '. . . or a four-cylinder engine in a Corvette.' Pause. 'I know, I know. We've been through all that . . .'

He noticed that Ms Peters was jotting copious notes with a mother-of-pearl pen as her shrewd gaze swept the bookshelves on one wall that brimmed with treatises on world peace and Evan-gelicalism, biographies of military generals including Alexander the Great and Genghis Khan, Napoleon, Patton. When she spot-ted *Guns, Germs, and Steel* among the collection, her meticulously groomed eyebrows tilted up. Then her attention shifted to the opposite wall where Stokes's diplomas, certificates, citations and war medals hung in neat frames together with a display of photos. When he saw her squinting, he snapped his fingers to get her attention, then motioned for her to get up and have a closer look.

Smiling, she stood up and went to take a look at the impressive photo montage. It took only a moment before the pen began moving rhythmically across the notepad.

'You tell the architect that's how it's going to be. Remind him that *we're* the client.' There was plenty of biographical material on that wall to please any reporter, Stokes thought: Randall Stokes front and centre with international dignitaries; Randall Stokes rubbing elbows with Hollywood power brokers; Randall Stokes shaking hands with secretaries of state, presidents and generals spanning three presidential administrations. He noticed that Ms Peters paused longest on the shot of Stokes striking a pose alongside the Pope.

She continued along the wall to the portrait of a teenaged marine cadet in dress blues. Then came the photos of a twenty-something, more fit Randall Stokes with his war buddies, grinning and armed to the teeth amid the ravaged backdrop of half a dozen battle zones – Kuwait, Bosnia and Baghdad among them. She admired his glinting marine officer's Mameluke sword mounted on a hook, then finished with the impassioned stills capturing Stokes in his most familiar role: preaching to the masses – his ever-swelling evangelical flock. In two other frames, those photos had morphed into *Time* magazine covers.

'Don't be afraid to use a little backbone, all right?' Pause. 'God bless you too.' As he cradled the phone, he let out an exasperated sigh and folded his hands over his chest. 'My apologies,' he said to the reporter. 'Been wearing too many hats lately.' He rolled his eyes.

'Not a problem,' she said, and made her way back to the chair. 'Still okay to use this?' She pointed to the slim digital micro-recorder she'd set on the end of his desk.

'Sure.'

She hit the device's record button.

'Where were we?' Stokes asked.

'The megachurch,' she reminded him, pointing with her pen out the wide plate-glass window at the nearly complete gleaming glass, steel and stone construction superimposed over the distant backdrop of the Mojave Desert Valley's sprawling casino metropolis. 'How most confuse it for a sports arena,' she reminded.

Stokes chuckled. 'There will be no monster truck rallies or hockey games here, I assure you.'

'Many call you a modern-day Joseph Smith – the proselytizing, the temple in the desert . . .' she said, almost accusatorily with a tip of her left eyebrow.

Stokes made a dismissive gesture and grinned. 'Ms Peters, I didn't transcribe the Word of God from golden tablets scrawled in hieroglyphics.' Not exactly the truth, he thought. 'We'll let the Mormons make those proclamations.'

The interview continued with innocent questions about the church's tremendous growth and Stokes's ambitious mission to transform faith not only in America, but in countries around the world – to 'baptize the world in the name of the saviour, Jesus Christ – the only path to redemption and salvation'. She then asked probing questions about his 'retirement' from the military, which went largely unanswered. Next, the reporter tact-fully solicited his perspective on the motivational lecture series he'd parlayed into a global ministry, and why his fresh message of revelation proved so timely for Christians who saw the US invasion of Iraq as fulfilment of End Times' prophecy heralding Christ's return.

As Stokes anticipated, things soon turned serious when Ms Peters turned her queries to the contributions that funded both his global mission and this extraordinary construction project. Venturing into the minefield, the reporter had smartly turned up her charm. It began with some innocent nibbling on the tip of her pen – a mildly seductive act that Stokes had to admit was a potent distraction.

'As you know, your past and current political affiliations have many speculating as to how the church raises its funds. There's rumours that a major network is producing a scathing primetime exposé which suggests that large transfers have been deposited into your accounts. Transfers that can't be traced –'

Stokes held up a hand. 'Ms Peters, let *60 Minutes* speculate all it wants. Success always draws detractors. But I suggest *you* stick to the facts.'

'Which are?'

Feisty, he thought. He sighed, tapped his thumbs together. 'Our major contributors and benefactors choose to remain anonymous,' Stokes simply replied, 'just how Christ himself would have wanted it.'

'I see,' she relented. Some more notes. She paused the micro-recorder. 'Off the record . . . do you miss all that?' She pointed with the pen at the military photos. 'The action, the glory?'

Spoken like a true civilian. 'Memories of war aren't like fond recollections of one's first love.'

'True. An ex-girlfriend might take your favourite sweatshirt and CDs . . . but not your leg.'

It was common knowledge that Stokes's military career derailed in 2003 when a bomb in the road outside Mosul had claimed his right leg just below the knee. However, Stokes could tell by her reddening cheeks that she was well aware that the thin line of etiquette had just been crossed. Smiling tightly, he replied, 'I suppose you're right. Every soldier leaves a piece of himself on the battlefield. Some of us, more literally so.'

She nibbled the pen with more zeal and back-pedalled with, 'It's just so amazing how after all of that . . . with all that you saw . . . you found God. I've read that it was after your . . .' a pause to hunt for the right word '. . . accident . . . that He began speaking to you. Is that true?'

'That's right. And I have no doubt you've also read that my critics attribute my revelation to post-traumatic stress disorder.' Stokes's pundits didn't merely cite the mental and physical trauma he'd suffered from his violent disfigurement. They even went as far as to blame the drug pyridostigmine bromide, or PB, which had been given to US troops during the 1st Gulf War to counteract the effects of chemical agents, such as nerve gas. By the way she smiled, he could tell he'd stolen some of her thunder. 'Utter nonsense,' he said loudly for the micro-recorder.

'So you *were* chosen by God? You're a prophet?'

'Something like that, I suppose.' His posture became more guarded.

The manner in which she now set down her pen implied that her next question would be off the record. 'But you hear Him? When He talks to you, I mean.'

'Loud and clear,' Stokes soberly confirmed, casting his eyes heavenward.

She stared at him in wonderment for a long moment. 'Wow.'

Now he could see her feline eyes subtly assessing him in impure ways. Charisma was like catnip for ambitious women like Ms Peters. Despite forty-six years and his mild 'handicap', he'd vigilantly maintained a physique that was nothing but lean muscle stretched over a wide six-foot frame. Strong jaw, a full head of hair that was still cropped into a high-and-tight, and a smooth bronze tan that made his green eyes flash. No doubt Ms Peters's article would make note of his commanding presence. After all, there was no denying that the right image had buttressed his star power.

She snatched up the pen again, turned on the micro-recorder, her starry gaze turning clinical once more. 'How about all this recent economic and political turbulence? Do you think it benefits the Christian Evangelical movement?'

Stokes shrugged. 'Certainly humbles even the non-believers . . . forces introspection.'

'Are the End Times here? Are scripture and prophecy being revealed?'

He swivelled his chair, peered out the window to the distant city centre where construction cranes hung motionless over the skeletons of unfinished casino resorts. Though not in a literal sense, sulphur and fire were raining on Sodom and Gomorrah. 'Best to assume that judgement can come at any day, any hour.'

'Do you think God's judgement will fall on terrorists, like Fahim Al-Zahrani, for past atrocities and the recent attacks orchestrated against religious monuments around the world?'

The preacher's expression turned severe.

Two months ago, Fahim Al-Zahrani – Al-Qaeda's newest top lieutenant and the man rumoured to be Osama Bin Laden's heir-apparent – had claimed responsibility for the most fearsome terror attacks since 9/11. With the industrialized nations still in the throes of global economic crisis and waning political support for an increased military presence in the Middle East powder keg, his timing had been perfect. He'd masterminded wide-scale attacks on soft targets with the express intent of unravelling the fabric of Western society. Al-Zahrani was like a patient *torero* weakening the bull for a final thrust of the sword.

Stokes's voice went down an octave as he replied, 'Any man who sends suicide bombers into holy places like St Peter's Basilica and Westminster Cathedral should expect eternal punishment beyond human comprehension. To murder innocents on such a grand scale is unconscionable, even by the standards of fundamentalist Islam. Regardless of what happens here, on this earth . . . whether perceived as justice or injustice . . . no manhunt, no supreme court, will ever compare to the wrath of God.'

The reporter had to catch her breath before continuing. She held up her pen, cleared her throat, and said, 'On that note . . .' She skimmed her list of questions. 'With the tide reversing on the recent troop withdrawals in the Middle East, some say we may soon embark on a modern Holy War. A new crusade between West and East. In your opinion, will military intervention ever change the dynamic in the Middle East?'

His reply was anything but direct. 'Not until every human being has accepted Christ as humankind's saviour will the war for souls end.'

Stalemate.

The desk phone buzzed quietly – a ring-tone assigned to a secure, dedicated line. 'Excuse me.' Hiding his alarm, Stokes stiffly picked up the phone. He listened as the caller calmly reported without preamble: 'They've found the cave.'

Chirp. Delay.

'I see,' he replied. 'Hold a moment.' Stokes glanced up to the reporter. He covered the receiver and said to her, 'I'm afraid we'll need to stop here.'

4

IRAQ

While Camel and Jam scoured the interiors of the four pickup trucks the Arabs had abandoned on the roadside, Jason strode towards the rectangular mobile command shelter his team had erected in east–west orientation at the bottom of the foothill. From a distance or from the sky, the structure's black goat-hair sheathing and simple wood framework were easily confused for Bedouin – a purposeful ruse since Arabs shunned nomads in much the same way as Westerners spurned gypsies.

However, nomads weren't as common in the north as in southern desert regions like the Ash Sham, the Sahara, the Sinai and the Negev. Plus a Bedouin *bayt*, or family unit, typically travelled with women, children and small livestock such as sheep or goats. So it was no surprise when four months earlier the team had been approached by an overly eager Iraqi Security Force patrol unit. Luckily, a pair of marines had been shadowing the Iraqis, and Jason had pulled them aside to explain in great detail how they were all playing for the same team. The marines quickly herded the ambitious Iraqis into the Humvee and the patrol disappeared as quickly as it had come.

Jason pulled back the door flap and dipped inside the tent's cool interior.

Provisions were stacked around its interior perimeter, leaving just enough room to accommodate three sleeping mats at night-time (two men always remained awake and rotated watch duty). A section of the roof had been peeled back to let in some light. Crammed into a camping chair, Meat sat in front of a folding table that hosted his laptop and techno gear.

Jason swilled some water from his canteen and watched Meat tap away on the laptop's keyboard. The guy looked like the ultimate terrorist, with his chequered headscarf, cocoa tan, bushy jet-black beard and eyebrows, and determined dark eyes searing with suppressed rage. But, unlike the jihadists who simmered on rigid interpretations of the Qur'an or gummy Middle East politics, Dennis Coombs struggled to reconcile an alcoholic mother, an absentee father, sibling rivalry, rural poverty and a fiancée's serial infidelity. All of which had made him easy pickings for the marine recruiters' notorious 'poverty draft'.

'Any luck?' Jason asked.

'Yeah, actually. The outside was cooked.' He motioned with his head to the cracked-open plastic casing. 'But the inside was raw.' Pinched between tweezers, he held up the extracted circular, wafer-thin computer chip that was no bigger than the fingernail on his pinky. 'Just like I prefer my steak cooked: black and blue.'

Jason smiled.

Next, Meat examined each side of the chip with a magnifying loop. 'No stamps. Nothing. The data's probably encrypted too. RSA or something similar, I'd bet.'

'What do you think it was used for?'

'It's no library card, I'll tell ya that. I'm thinking it's an IPS chip.'

The Identity and Passport Service data chip, Jason recalled, was a smart card for biometric access systems – encrypted files containing a user's retinal scan, fingerprints and other unique identifiers.

'No worries, though,' Meat said. 'I'm sure we can crack it.'

Jason watched as Meat hooked a rectangular USB device, no bigger than a deck of playing cards, into his laptop – a hi-tech data reader developed by the NSA, which Meat commonly used to skim embedded information off passports.

Meat placed the chip on the reader's flat surface.

The software interface launched on the laptop screen. It took only seconds before the chip reader identified the protocol, matched its key, and brought up the data.

'That was fast,' Jason said.

'There's good reason to be worried about cyber terrorism.' Scrolling through the biometric data, what looked like a passport photo came up on the screen – the face of an attractive, thirty-something female. Meat whistled. 'Yummy.'

Leaning in, Jason's brow rumpled with confusion. 'How can that be right?' he said. The green-eyed brunette with a flawless complexion looked like a spokesmodel for Revlon. 'That's no Iraqi.'

'Nope.' Meat scrolled the data. 'That's Ms Brooke Thompson. Sorry, make that *Professor* Brooke Thompson. Female, as you can see ... US citizen ... Born April 19, 1975 ... last clocked-in 15.02, May 2, 2003. No social security number, but her passport number's here.'

'What would *she* have been doing here?' Jason aired his thoughts aloud.

'And right after the Battle of Baghdad, in fact. This place was a battle zone back then.'

'Transmit that data to the home office and ask them to send an agent immediately to find her and vet her.'

'Got it.'

Jason waited for him to wrap up the call on his sat-com, then encrypt the data file and bounce it off a satellite to Global Security Corporation's Washington DC headquarters.

'Anything else?' Meat asked.

Jason unclipped the binoculars from his neck strap, handed them to Meat. 'Let's have a closer look at some of the video I took earlier.'

Meat patched the binoculars' hard drive into the laptop with a fire wire. A new program launched onscreen. 'Tell me what you're looking for and I'll freeze the image,' Meat said.

Jason leaned in close to review the playback. The high-resolution images were crystal clear. The frames skipped backwards until Jason spotted what he wanted. 'There.'

Meat hit a key to pause the image.

'Zoom in on the tall guy in the middle.'

'That Al-Zahrani?'

'You tell me.'

For a good minute, Meat replayed and advanced the footage. Satisfied that he'd found the best full frontal view of the guy's face, he froze the image, dragged a frame over the head, and zoomed in. The enlargement pixellated before sharpening on the screen.

Meat slumped back in his chair and gave his beard a long, hard stroke. 'Fuck me, Google. You're right. That's definitely him.'

'We need to be 100 per cent on this.'

Meat held his hand out at the laptop. 'That's not a face to forget.'

'Humour me and run facial recognition on it.'

Huffing, Meat leaned forward again to work the keyboard. He opened the biometric software in a new window, imported the picture file, and initiated the analysis. The program deconstructed the photo using virtual lines that measured eighty nodal points between the irises, the ears, the chin and nose, and various other facial landmarks. Ten seconds later, the 'face print' was complete. Using an encrypted signal, he linked to the military's satellite network and routed an inquiry to the FBI. Meat's limited clearance enabled him to pull Al-Zahrani's biometric stats from the agency's database. Then he instructed the program to compare the biometric statistics.

'As close as I've ever seen to a precise match,' Meat reported. 'See for yourself.'

As Jason verified the results, excitement and concern came in equal measure.

'Imagine if we catch this fucker alive,' Meat said. 'We'd be goddamn heroes. Not to mention the bounty. Shit. Ten mil? Forget this soldier-for-hire gig. We could all retire.' He flitted his eyebrows.

'Right. You wouldn't know what to do with yourself,' Jason scoffed. 'The hunt' gave them all purpose, and allowed them to exorcize their demons. Back home, a small fortune would do little to dispel the haunting memories that drove them here to begin with.

Meat considered the dream, then dickered it down in his mind to settle for something more realistic. 'I'd at least take some R&R . . . eat some cheese steaks instead of MREs and vermin roast. Maybe even shit in a toilet instead of a trench with sand flies nipping my ass. You know, take a dump with dignity.'

'I'd settle for a proper shower,' Jason said, scratching at his beard. Getting back to business, he asked, 'Hey, where's the Snake?'

'Over there,' Meat said, pointing to a bulky case loosely covered by a goatskin.

Jason went to retrieve it. 'Give me hand with this. I want to get up that hill . . . see if we can't peek inside the cave.'

5

LAS VEGAS

It took a lot to fluster Randall Stokes. Plenty of years spent skulking behind enemy lines to stare down the Devil made most of life's stressors seem mundane. However, when the caller had conveyed what had transpired in Iraq, a sour taste came to the back of the preacher's throat.

There'd always been the possibility that someone might accidentally stumble upon the cave installation. Precisely the reason so many security protocols had been built around the programme, including tripwires for unauthorized persons attempting to breach the main hatchway.

But what had happened just an hour ago was something even Randall Stokes could not dream up. Such an incursion fell far outside the limits of possibility – the outlier of outliers. The caller had indicated that a US helicopter gunship had misfired a missile – a freak accident. But Arab militants storming into the tunnels? Stokes thought. Certainly this was God's plan. It was the only plausible explanation. Has the time already come?

Seated at his desk and directed towards his oversized LCD computer monitor, Stokes drafted a secure e-mail. The brief message stated in cryptic terms that countermeasures were to commence immediately. Step one: a comprehensive clean-up.

There was an outside chance that some random clue left behind might trigger an investigation. Regrettably that meant that outside contractors who'd worked on the project – the most vulnerable links – would need to be eliminated, quickly and cleanly. Because if the media were to somehow get wind of what was happening at the site, one of the scientists might get cold feet and ignore the restrictive confidentiality agreement he'd signed.

Stored on his computer's encrypted hard drive were the vital statistics for each scientist – everything from birth certificates, passport information, credit history and social security numbers, to work history, credentials, family contacts and last known addresses. There were passport photos and biometric data too. Stokes attached all eight 'A-list' profiles to the e-mail.

Just as he was about to click the SEND button, the phone's intercom came to life with a small chime.

'So sorry to disturb you, Randy.'

'I'm busy. What is it, Vanessa?' he replied agitatedly.

'Mr Roselli is here,' she reported in a subdued tone. 'He's insisting on seeing you. He doesn't look so good . . . acting strange too. Should I call security?'

'No. It's fine.' Perfect, actually. 'Give me a minute, then send him in.'

'As you wish.'

Stokes focused again on the draft, removed profile number '4' labelled 'ROSELLI-FRANK'. Verifying the content one last time, he clicked a command that encrypted the message and pushed it out into the ether. He leaned back and stretched, considered how exactly to handle the surprise visitor. When he

32

peered at the open door centred in the rear wall of the office, an idea came to him. A brilliant idea.

Fifteen seconds later, the double door opened and Vanessa held it as Roselli lumbered into the room, hands stuffed in the pockets of his rumpled seersucker slacks.

'I was going to run to the Post Office,' Vanessa said. 'Need me to stay?'

'No, no. You go ahead,' Stokes said. He stood and rounded the desk. She was right: the five-foot-eight portly project manager looked even more ruddy than usual. 'Frank,' he greeted him with presidential style. 'What a surprise.'

'What's the emergency?' Stokes asked, calmly reclining in his office chair.

Roselli was huddled on the edge of the leather visitor's seat, elbows propped on knees. Sweat peppered his brow below an island of sun-bleached dirty blond hair that looked like a badly replaced divot. His round cheeks and bulbous nose were pink with sunburn, three deep worry lines cut parallel tracks across his forehead, and his dull hazel eyes, set too close together, were too small for his head.

'Haven't you heard?' he said. 'The alarm in the cave? For God's sake. They'll find –'

Stokes raised a hand to stop him. 'I've heard,' he replied levelly.

'And you're still *here*?' He spread his hands. 'Have you gone mad? What if they –'

'Calm down. Don't you see? This is better than we could ever have hoped for.'

'What? Are you insane?'

'Now, now, Frank . . .' he warned. But Roselli was inconsolable.

'I told you this might happen!' he overrode indignantly. Pointing a pudgy index finger at Stokes, he said, 'We should've permanently sealed the opening.' He shook his head with dismay. 'Christ, we *knew* that hatch might draw attention.'

'And how do you suppose what's in the cave could be released without a doorway?'

Rolling his eyes, Roselli didn't have an answer.

'Let me remind you that it was a *missile*, Frank. A missile that accidentally veered off course. Sorry, but we didn't plan for that.' Stokes got up again. 'Let's not have someone overhearing this conversation,' he said conspiratorially. He waved for Roselli to follow, led the way to the open door in the rear of the office.

Huffing, Roselli got up and went over to him, hesitated at the entry threshold to assess the keypad on the doorframe. His head tilted to calibrate the thickness of the door – five, maybe six, inches. Then he peeked inside. 'What is this place?'

'My private gallery. We can talk more freely in here.' Stokes offered a composed smile, placed a gentle hand on the man's shoulder and urged him inside.

The spacious, windowless gallery housed an impressive collection of ancient artifacts in sturdy display cases – mostly Middle Eastern, as far as Roselli could tell. No surprise since Stokes was obsessed with anything remotely linked to Mesopotamia or Persia, both past and present. Floor-to-ceiling shelves lined the walls; dozens of compact clay tablets were neatly laid out behind thick glass doors. He could also make out jewellery, pottery and Bronze Age tools and weapons stored there too.

But the room's centre featured the relics Roselli knew intimately.

Mounted atop a wide granite plinth was an enormous lime-stone slab; maybe six feet high, four feet wide, he guessed. On the monolith's face were intricate relief etchings of two winged beasts, spirits facing one another in profile, as if courting for a dance – each half human, half lion. The stone seal they'd removed from the cave entrance and replaced with a heavy-duty metal door.

In the display cases beside the seal, Roselli spotted some of the cursed artifacts they'd recovered from deep within the labyrinth: an assortment of clay tablets stamped with ancient wedge-shaped symbols and pictograms; a beautiful necklace of glossy shells; a clay jar painted in symbols and whose bizarre contents remained locked within rock-hard resin. But the most prominent display case was covered with a veil. The thought of what might be inside it made him shudder. 'You must be insane . . . keeping all these things here.'

'Do you really think anyone would know where these treas-ures came from? I'm a mere collector, Frank. Stop being paranoid,' Stokes suggested delicately.

'*Paranoid?* Do you know what will happen if anyone finds what we left behind in that cave?' Then he turned pale when he thought of the most serious consequences. 'My God . . . what if those American contractors go inside . . . what if they all die?'

With hands behind his back, Stokes paced over to the stone slab and admired it for a long moment. 'When God expelled Adam and Eve from Eden, the cherubim were posted outside the entrance so that the humans could never return to paradise. The sacred guardians . . .'

'Now is not the time for Bible-thumping,' Roselli fumed. 'We need to focus on the cave. What are we going to *do*?'

Stokes shrugged and contemplated the situation for five

seconds before responding. 'The cave being discovered like this . . . well, it can only be considered divinely inspired, wouldn't you agree?'

'Bullshit.'

'I understand you're upset,' Stokes said.

'Damn right I'm upset.'

'Let me get us drinks. Then we'll talk about this, figure things out. Scotch?' Another of Roselli's Achilles heels.

In Pavlovian fashion, Roselli licked his lips. Then he sighed and ran his fingers through the divot. 'That'd be good.'

'Neat?'

Looking wounded, Roselli nodded.

'All right.' Stokes patted him on the back. 'It'll be okay. I promise. Be back in a minute.'

Stokes pivoted on his good foot and made his way outside.

Roselli turned back to the centre of the room and stared at the veiled display case. The loose ends of the silky cover billowed against air pumping in from overhead vents. Or maybe something beneath it was stirring. Curiosity got the best of him and he stepped cautiously towards it. Cringing, he reached out and began to lift the cover. But the sudden sound of the door closing made him jump in fright. His eyes snapped to the door.

'Stokes?'

The door's locking mechanism turned over with a *clunk*.

'Stokes!'

On the other side of the door, Stokes punched a code into the keypad mounted on the doorframe and activated the hermetic seal. Roselli's screams barely permeated the dense walls. But soon, all would be silent.

6

Roselli's fists throbbed as he pounded on the door again, leaving splotches of perspiration on the cold metal. Helpless anger blinded him to the futility of escaping the vault.

He'd tried unsuccessfully to access the sealed shelving units containing the bronze tools, thinking he might somehow be able to use an axe or chisel to pry open the door lock. With every fixture in the room bolted to the floor, and no loose implement to use as a striker, however, he'd resorted to using his fists on the glass. That effort, too, proved a waste of time and energy. Even if he'd been able to get to the tools, he knew that the primitive bronze would be too flimsy to have any effect on the formidable security door.

So he'd been reduced to what amounted to a child's tantrum.

The ceiling vents steadily hummed. Instead of the climate control system scrubbing away contaminants, however, it was now sucking oxygen out from the room. The air reeked of ozone.

Finally, he turned and put his back against the door in defeat, slid down to the Berber carpet. He loosened his necktie, unbuttoned the shirt collar. Scanning the room again, he cursed the fact that there were no windows or secondary doors. Even the air ducts, he'd observed, seemed too tight for a mouse, let alone a 205-pound middle-aged man.

Each laboured breath became more shallow, more painful. It felt as if he was being slowly strangled by invisible hands. The grim reality quickly settled over him: there'd be no escape. This vault was to be his tomb. Ironically, what angered him now was that the cunning preacher had not made good on delivering the Scotch. All those years watching each other's back in the most inhospitable war zones on the planet, and it came down to this. 'If you're going to kill me, a little civility would have been nice,' he grumbled.

He wondered where Stokes would dump his body: at home, where his wife would assume high cholesterol and runaway blood pressure had finally gotten the best of him? At his office, where his secretary would grumble that he'd finally succeeded in working himself to death? Or in a Caesar's Palace hotel room, where one might think his mounting gambling losses and excessive boozing had finally taken their toll?

'Devious bastard,' he said in a thin, wheezy voice.

His starved lungs made his chest heave up and down. His senses were beginning to feel foggy.

Perhaps this was a fitting end for what he'd done to assist Stokes these past years – to enable his ambitious plan for world domination, Armageddon, or whatever moniker might be ascribed to the delusional end game. Would justice ever find Stokes for what *he'd* done? If there was a God, why would He grant victory to such an evil prick? Whatever happened to good ole wrath, retribution and smite?

Determined not to go down without a fight, Roselli tried to think of how he could warn the others whom Stokes would consider a threat. From his jacket pocket, he pulled out his BlackBerry, confirmed that not one signal bar showed on the screen.

Lethargically, he moved towards the room's centre with the PDA held close to the ceiling, hunting for a signal. Nothing. 'That's just great,' he huffed.

The room started to spin, so he sat on the floor and propped himself up against the plinth. Every breath was a struggle.

Using the PDA's stylus, Roselli navigated his address book and began drafting a mass e-mail – a warning to all who'd worked on the project, plus an admission of his participation in a most egregious act with consequences that potentially threatened humankind's existence. That should get their attention, he thought. Maybe then the scientists would learn how they'd unwittingly participated in a sinister plot that would make the Manhattan Project seem like child's play. Maybe then they would rally together and seek justice. The possibility gave Roselli hope.

Finally . . . full disclosure, he pondered.

Next, he prepared a second e-mail message, but assigned it a later delivery time. This one was meant for Stokes. What would prove to be Roselli's shocking final message from the grave. When he finished the draft and read it over a final time, he couldn't help but grin, despite the bleakness of his predicament.

Roselli edited delivery instructions for the two messages to ensure completion of two tasks: attempt delivery every minute until a signal is obtained and delivery confirmed; auto-delete the messages upon successful transmission.

The wheezing was heavier now; his vision, spotty.

From his pocket, he withdrew a tiny glass vial filled with white powder and uncapped its rubber stopper. With utmost care he sprinkled the tacky granules over the PDA's keyboard and control buttons. Then he slipped the empty vial back into his jacket pocket, followed by the powered-on PDA.

He let his arms drop limply to the floor. The room seemed to be crushing in around him.

Burn in Hell, Stokes, he thought.

A minute later, darkness crept in from the corners of his vision. Then everything slipped into oblivion.

7

IRAQ

'Keep back from the opening,' Jason reminded Jam. 'Let's not have you catch a bullet with your face.'

'Yes, mother,' Jam replied.

Having clambered to the highpoint of the rubble heap that blocked the cave entrance, Jam had pulled away enough debris and stone to enable Camel – straddled beside him – to punch five feet of three-inch-wide conduit clear through to the other side. Not hard for Jason to imagine someone on the other side attempting to put a few bullets through the PVC pipe.

'Good to go,' Camel reported. 'Pass the line up.'

The sand-coloured armoured flex cable hung in long loops from Hazo's crooked elbow. The slight-statured Kurd passed Camel the business end of the line – a shielded optical lens tip. The cable's other end connected to a toaster-sized portable command unit that was mostly lithium battery.

Camel began threading the Snake through the PVC.

'Clear?' Jason asked.

'Yeah, it's going through,' Camel said. 'Smooth as a colonoscopy. Keep it coming, Hazo.'

Meanwhile, Meat flipped back the device's lid, which doubled as the LCD viewing screen, and powered on the unit. The setup was similar to a compact laptop: full-size keyboard, touchpad mouse, some simple controls. From the carrying case, he retrieved what looked like a videogame joystick, plugged it into a port on the unit's rear panel. With the touch of a button, the halogen floodlight mounted on the Snake's tip lit up. The streaming video came through bright and clear.

'We have eyes,' Meat reported. He reached into the case again, grabbed the unit's headphones and put them on. Then he adjusted the audio level on the integrated microphone.

Jason came over and crouched beside him to get a look at the images coming back from inside the cave.

As Camel pushed more flex cable through the pipe, the camera advanced further down the bumpy slope of rocks until it found gravel.

'Hold it there,' Meat said. He pulled back on the joystick while pressing his thumb on the control button. Like a charmed cobra, the cable curled at the tip (an integrated hydraulic balance kept the camera level). The first clear pictures immediately shone bright and clear.

'We're in,' Meat said. Just behind the blocked entry, smooth parallel walls set roughly two metres apart tapered off into the darkness. 'Not your typical cave.'

'No, it certainly isn't.' Jason studied the image, saw no sign of activity. 'All right, Camel, keep it moving . . . slow and steady.'

'Hear anything yet?' Jason asked.

'Nothing,' he reported. 'It's quiet in there. Really quiet.'

Jam jumped off the pile and helped Hazo feed more loops to Camel.

A few metres in, Meat spotted something on the walls. 'Hey, see that?'

'Hold up,' Jason called up to Camel. The picture steadied. 'What is it?' he asked Meat.

'Something on the left wall,' he replied, squinting tight at the screen. He toggled the joystick to get a better angle, then zoomed out for a wide shot.

When the picture came into focus, Jason was amazed at what he was seeing: the entire left wall was filled with narrative scenes carved in pristine bas-relief. The central figure depicted in the scenes was a shapely woman holding a cylindrical object that emanated wavy lines. Assembled around her were men and women presenting gifts and food. There was even a group genuflecting as if in worship. Beneath her feet was a repeating pattern of nautilus-shaped swirls. 'Whoa,' Meat said. 'That's weird.' He panned side to side. 'Looks like a mural or something.'

'Sure does,' Jason agreed. 'Hazo, come take a look at this.'

The Kurd passed the coiled cable to Jam and joined them.

'What do you make of that?'

Hazo's brow rumpled. After ten seconds, he shook his head. 'I don't know this . . . ah . . . but this rosette here?' He pointed to a bracelet on the woman's wrist. 'This means she is like a god, or how you say . . . ?' He fished for the word.

'Divine?' Jason surmised.

'Yes, divinity. This says divinity.'

'So she's a goddess. Some kind of religious image.'

'I think so. But not Christian. And Muslims would never allow these pictures. Very blasphemous.'

Pointing to the swirls on the image, Jason asked, 'Is this supposed to be a river?'

43

'Um, yes. I'd agree with that.'

'And what's this in her hands?'

Hazo shook his head. 'A large fruit . . . um, no . . . maybe a container. These lines . . .' Hazo said, tilting his head sideways to ascertain a meaning. 'Maybe a light?'

'Or something radiating from it.'

Meat gave Jason a surprised look. 'What, like magic?'

He shrugged. 'All right, let's document everything. Meat, take some still shots, then keep the camera moving along this wall.'

'Got it,' Meat said.

For the next ten minutes, Camel worked more cable through the pipe to push the camera deeper and deeper into the passage. The images on the left wall had become progressively disturbing. The swirls rose with each 'frame', and Hazo's early guess that this portrayed rising flood waters proved correct, when later images showed bodies and animals being swept 'downstream' in elongated swirls.

Most disturbing, however, was how the story's depiction of the woman progressed. Her devotees from frame one had obviously had a change of heart, because the final frames showed men binding her, then leading her away with spears to the mountains. The final frame depicted the woman's gruesome beheading.

'She must've gotten too lippy with them,' Meat joked as he saved the image as a pix file.

Jason shook his head. 'Not funny.'

At the end of the storyboard, the wall was covered top to bottom in wedge-shaped hashes laid out in neat rows. Jason asked Hazo to take a gander at what it might mean.

This time Hazo was quick to respond: 'That looks like a very ancient alphabet. Maybe from Sumer.'

'Sumer?' Meat asked.

'The southern region of ancient Iraq,' Jason told him.

'Yes,' Hazo concurred. 'Sumerian.'

'So what is this place?' Meat asked. 'One of Saddam's old bunkers? He liked all this ancient stuff, right? Thought he was the reincarnation of a Babylonian king or something . . .'

'Correct,' Hazo said. 'King Nebuchadnezzar.'

Jason shook his head. 'We've seen plenty of bunkers. Nothing like this.' He rubbed his neck while glancing over at what remained of the optical cable. 'Let's push the camera in as far as we can. See if we can spot anything else.'

With the camera reoriented straight, the hewn passage walls abruptly transitioned to rough, uncut stone. Three metres deeper, the camera approached a split.

'Which way?' Meat asked Jason.

'Left.'

'Keep it moving . . . steady push,' Meat called up to Camel. Working the joystick, he commanded the flex cable to bend along the turn.

'How far in do you think we are right now?' Jason asked.

Meat looked over at what little flex cable remained. 'Eighteen, twenty metres maybe.'

The light stripped the shadows off the tunnel's crenulated outcroppings.

'Wait . . .' Meat said to Jason, pressing an index finger against the headphone speaker. 'I hear something.' He punched a button on the keyboard and the audio feed played over the unit's built-in speakers. Sliding the headphones off, he raised the volume some more and listened intently. Jason and Hazo crowded in beside him.

First came the distinct chatter of voices, the dialect unmistakably Arabic. Two, maybe three different men, Jason guessed.

The exchange was forceful, argumentative. To him, this was an encouraging development. The Arabs had yet to find a way out. Maybe this tunnel wasn't so extensive after all.

'They see the light,' Hazo whispered, translating the exchange. 'They don't know what to do.'

The next sounds were metallic bolts sliding and clicking – weapons being readied.

'Maybe we should pull the camera—' Meat started.

On the screen, a glossy shape poked out from around the corner and winked in the light.

'Is that a mirror?' Jason said.

'I think so,' Meat said. 'We should pull the camera out.'

'Good idea,' Jason said. 'All right, Camel,' he loudly called out, 'let's pull it back.'

But before Camel could react, the tiny flicker dropped off the unit's screen just before one of the Arabs popped into view and stormed towards the camera. His rifle was safely slung over his shoulder, but between his hands was a melon-sized rock. His dirt-smeared face twisted into a snarl as he raised the rock up high over his head and lunged at the camera. The last image was a clear shot of the man's grungy sandals. The last sound was a resounding *thwack* that rattled the unit's speakers. Then the image snapped offline and turned to snow.

'That's not good,' Hazo said.

'Ouch,' Meat said, cringing.

Camel began pulling out the flex cable in fathoms and Jam coiled the line back into neat loops. A minute later, the flattened tip popped out from the conduit, smoking and crackling.

'Sorry buddy,' Camel said to Meat in mock apology as he assessed the damage. 'That thing's toast.' He tossed it to Jam.

'At least we know they're still in there, Sarge,' Jam said.

'I was thinking the same thing.'

'Guys,' Camel said, peering off in the distance. He spit a gob of chewing tobacco on to the ground and pointed out along the flatland. They all turned in unison.

Three kilometres out, a military convoy whipped a billowing dust cloud up into the blazing orange sunset. A UH-60 Blackhawk was flying random crisscrosses above it to scout the terrain.

'Cavalry's here,' Camel grunted.

8

LAS VEGAS

Once the muted thumping inside the vault stopped, Randall Stokes sauntered to the wet bar, pulled a tumbler off the shelf, and poured two fingers of very expensive single-malt Scotch, neat. He withdrew a plastic pillbox from his jacket pocket, popped open the lid, and pinched out a pure white Zoloft tablet.

Putting the pill on his tongue, he raised the glass towards the vault door.

'Cheers, Frank.'

He nipped at the Scotch and swilled down the dose of tranquillity. Then he went and sat behind the desk.

It hurt when good men – loyal men – were sacrificed for the greater good. Military life had a way of hammering into one's head the notion that brotherhood always came first. Survival could be a singular effort, but lasting victory could never be. Fighters are made, not born. And that was certainly true with Frank Roselli.

Roselli was an extremely valuable asset. He'd perfectly coordinated the project in Iraq, which, given the mission's complex logistics and broad scope, was no easy task. Though it was Stokes's brainchild, Roselli had tackled recruiting the multi-disciplined talent who took the project from concept to reality. From around the globe, he'd assembled a team of renowned archaeologists and anthropologists and brought them into the middle of a war zone to unlock the greatest discovery in human history. It was Roselli who'd designed the ingenious security protocols and eliminated redundancies so that each scientist working on site knew only a piece of the cave's intricate puzzle. Most impressive was Roselli's brilliant handling of high-ranking members of Congress, the FBI and the armed forces, to bring together the funding and technological know-how. And as far as the stakeholders were concerned, it was all an anonymous debit against the defence budget in the name of national security. So thorough was the mission's cover that even the president's eagle-eyed Cabinet members would give the appropriations a mere cursory glance.

Stokes and Roselli had been together since the beginning: through twelve weeks of boot camp at Parris Island and the gruelling fifty-four-hour Crucible march; side by side at the Emblem Ceremony, receiving their eagle, globe and anchor pins; at Marine Special Operations School learning the tactical art of irregular warfare.

Best friends.

Brothers.

Staring out the window, Stokes lost himself in the muddled reflections that danced across the cathedral's reflective glass dome. The colours pinwheeled and shifted like a kaleidoscope. Entranced, his mind's eye brought him back to the Kuwaiti desert: distant oil fields burning like torches against a night sky as black as oil; the paradoxical bitter cold of a sunless desert set ablaze. He could still feel the sixty-five-pound field pack weighing on his back, the ice-cold fifteen-pound M40A1 sniper rifle biting into his hands; the sand creeping down into his combat boots (despite three wraps of duct tape around the boot top). Even the choking stench of smouldering crude seemed fresh in his nostrils.

And there beside him, equally vivid, he could still see Roselli – forty pounds lighter, all muscle – the runt of the litter who had the piss and vinegar of a man twice his size. He'd witnessed Roselli beat a six-foot-two recruit unconscious with a boot for calling him Napoleon. Roselli was one tough mother who never gave up the fight. He'd even saved Stokes's life by bayoneting an Iraqi soldier who tried to attack Stokes with a knife.

Now Stokes had repaid the deed by locking Roselli in an airless room, using the only viable weapon he could – one that stabbed much deeper than the bayonet: deception. Nothing noble about that, Stokes lamented.

He drained the Scotch.

Pushing down a welling sense of self-loathing, Stokes reminded himself that nothing could deter the mission's success. So much was at stake. There was a new battlefront now – a new killing field. The last generation of fanatics was mostly desperate, idealistic kids blinded by radical religious teachings with no regard for any human life – infidels and innocents alike. But the leaders now operating behind the scenes to manipulate these malleable foot soldiers were by far the most dangerous enemy he'd ever encountered – a societal cancer that strove to destroy civilization. An enemy that wasn't a country, didn't wear uniform, had no generals or central power structure, and was fuelled by an ingrained hatred that no army could ever remedy. The industrialized world lacked the resources and mettle to effect any meaningful change in the Middle East. Left to conventional tactics, this modern war could last decades, perhaps generations. When Stokes had worked as a counter-terrorist operative, he'd seen little proof that anyone knew a viable long-term solution. One thing, however, was certain: in the end, only one side would remain standing.

'It's for the best,' a soothing voice said from behind.

Startled, Stokes spun around in his chair.

There was no one in the room.

When would He present Himself?

'Yes, it *is* for the best,' Stokes agreed. 'Frank's work was vital . . . but he didn't understand the grand design to which we aspire.'

'Few do, my son.'

Stokes's eyes darted back and forth, searching for an apparition. 'They found the cave. You know that, of course. Will this jeopardize our work?'

'Have faith. All is in accordance.'

The voice came at him from every angle.

'And when will I know that it has begun?'

'It has already begun. Do you not see the signs?'

There are no accidents, thought Stokes. 'Yes, I see the signs. And the Rapture? When will it come.'

No answer.

Stokes scanned the room. He felt the presence dissipate. Gone.

9

BOSTON, MASSACHUSETTS

The snow was staging an encore as GSC Special Agent Thomas Flaherty turned his '95 Chrysler Concorde off Huntington Avenue on to Museum Road. Rounding the corner, the car caught ice and began to skid. Shit! His heart went into overdrive. Gripping the steering wheel, he compensated by tugging it hard to the right. Steer into the turn, he told himself. Finally, the tyres caught salt and asphalt and he eased to a stop. He took a moment to catch his breath. Luckily, there'd been no cars in the oncoming lane.

'Okay. Get it together.' He accelerated nice and slow. Damned snow, he thought.

The promo banners hanging along the museum's neoclassical cut-granite edifice were dusted with snow, but the words 'Treasures from Mesopotamia, Sept. 21 – January 4' were easy enough for him to make out.

The last time he'd visited the Boston Museum of Fine Arts had been during an eleventh-grade field trip hosted by the Boston Latin School. Not exactly a bragging point. Nowadays it was tough to find time for culture. At least that was the excuse he was going with.

When he steered to the kerb, his front right tyre thumped its way in and out of a pothole hard enough to make his teeth rattle. He rubbed the dashboard affectionately. 'Sorry 'bout that, sweetie,' he told the old war horse. He put the transmission in park, cut the engine.

From the centre console, he grabbed his BlackBerry, punched in the PIN code for his secure e-mail account, and accessed the urgent find-and-deliver order he'd received from Global Security Corporation's Boston office. Only ten minutes ago, he'd received a terse phone call confirming that the museum was the asset's current location.

The woman's profile was a bit lengthy, so he read aloud to himself to drive home the key points: 'Brooke Thompson. Born and raised, Orlando, Florida. Thirty-three. No children. Single . . .' He paused and looked back at the attractive photo, trying to reconcile the contradiction. 'Hmm.' *Single?* He could only assume that she came with an ex-husband, excessive emotional baggage, two cats and a worn copy of *Twilight*. Otherwise, the facts simply didn't compute.

The highly agreeable face, nonetheless, was easy enough to remember.

He continued down the bulleted list. 'PhD in palaeontology, Boston College . . . professor at same . . . Middle East antiquities curator, Boston Museum of Fine Arts . . . award, award, award . . . blah, blah, blah . . . lives in the Back Bay on Commonwealth Ave . . .' Satisfied, he dropped the BlackBerry into his coat pocket.

Bracing for the cold, he threw open the door on groaning hinges, swung his boots out into the slush, and got out from the car. The chill immediately cut into his bones. One of these days, he might remember to bring along some gloves, maybe a scarf too. If he wasn't a serial bachelor, maybe he'd have someone at home to remind him of these things.

Stuffing his hands into his pockets, he set a brisk pace towards the visitors' entrance.

Inside he headed straight for the admissions desk and discreetly asked the sixty-something female docent with a beehive hairdo where he might find museum staffer, Professor Brooke Thompson.

'You're just in time, she's just gone up to present. Here, take this.' She handed him a glossy programme. Sensing his confusion, she explained, 'Her lecture is simply fascinating. Adorable too, wouldn't you say?' she stage-whispered.

'Uh, yes, a real gem.'

'Just around the corner, in the Remis Auditorium.' She pointed and made a shooing gesture. 'Hurry now.'

Flaherty slipped through the auditorium door and a museum employee immediately came over with a finger pressed against his lip in a hushing gesture. Without a word, he waved for Flaherty to follow him and set off along the auditorium's dimmed rear to the left side aisle. He pointed to an empty end seat six rows down.

Keeping his coat on, Flaherty eased into the seat, surprised that the place was practically filled to capacity. It took some shifting around to get a clear view of the main stage, thanks to the towering guy seated directly in front of him who should have been in the Celtics locker-room at the Fleet Center.

There was a huge viewing screen above the stage that along with the tiered seating made him feel like he'd come to watch an IMAX movie. However, the still image projected on to the screen – some glossy brownish skull with a heavy brow ridge, maybe ape, maybe primitive human – wasn't exactly blockbuster material.

When Flaherty's gaze finally settled on the lecturer whose sultry voice buttered the sound system, his eyebrows went up.

'Whoa!' he exclaimed to himself.

Roaming freely in front of the stage's central podium, clicker in her hand, clip-on microphone wired to the lapel of a form-fitting navy pants suit, was Professor Brooke Thompson. What he'd seen of her on the BlackBerry was only a headshot that showed wavy hair shaped to the shoulder, a long graceful neck and a face straight off a magazine cover. The complete picture was far more impressive. She seemed taller than the five-nine indicated in her profile, lithe with a perfect blend of tight curves that suggested a conscientious diet and rigid fitness regimen. Certainly helped explain the predominantly male turnout, he thought, glancing once again at the attendees.

Finally he began to focus on what she was saying. And once again, he was impressed. Brooke Thompson was an engaging speaker. Though Flaherty thought he wouldn't give a rat's ass about the seemingly arcane topic – listed on the programme as 'Mesopotamia and the Origins of Written Language' – she immediately hooked him.

10

'So it's around 10,000 years ago,' Brooke Thompson went on, 'when the most recent Ice Age finally comes to a close. The massive glacial sheets retreat to uncover the land, while the rapid melt-off causes a dramatic rise in sea levels. The most recent cycle of global warming, not attributable to emissions from SUVs and coal-burning power plants.'

Some chuckles from the audience.

'The Neanderthals had long since vanished' – she pointed up to the skull still showing on the big screen – 'whether due to a turf war with early humans, or, as some scientists have suggested, genetic dilution through inbreeding with *Homo sapiens*. By 6000 BC, modern humans are thriving. They domesticate live-stock for food, milk and clothing. They plant seeds along the fertile river banks to grow their own food. They are the world's first farmers. Around 5500 BC they begin to irrigate the land with canals and ditches, allowing them to spread from the fertile north, to the arid south. For the first time in history, our great ancestors rely less on migratory hunting and become sedentary. This agricultural revolution spawns large organized settlements throughout the Middle East in modern Egypt, Israel, Syria and Iraq – a region referred to as the Fertile Crescent, or the Cradle of Civilization.'

She pointed the clicker and the projector brought up a detailed map centred on the Middle East.

'Surplus foods allow extensive trading over wide areas, while specialization of labour fosters hyper-speed technology. To manage this new way of life, industrious humans develop a systematic means of communication that doesn't rely on memory or oral transference. They are to become the world's first bureaucrats. Enter the first written language. Which leads us to the epicentre of it all – right here . . .'

Brooke used the clicker's laser pointer to place a bright red dot at the map's centre, just north of the modern Persian Gulf.

'Here is where archaeologists have unearthed the ruins of the world's earliest hierarchical societies. This once lush and peaceful paradise was known as the "land between two rivers", or "Mesopotamia". Hard to imagine since today it is a war-torn nation known as Iraq.'

Some quiet chatter rippled through the crowd.

'Now I'd like to focus on how written language enabled these early civilizations to develop first into agricultural cities with tens of thousands of citizens, then city states hundreds of thousands strong, and eventually . . . empires stretching across Eurasia.'

Scanning the sea of faces that filled the auditorium, Brooke focused on the intent smiles and nodding heads, blocked out the few sceptical scowls. The recent articles she'd published in the *American Journal of Archaeology* on the emergence of written language, which not-so-subtly challenged the archaeological establishment, had lured a number of detractors here today. Best to know your enemies, she thought.

'The earliest known written communication dates to around 3500 BC.'

Brooke hated snubbing the *real* truth about the ancient writings she'd uncovered in Iraq only a few years ago – the truth that would upend every established theory about the emergence of Mesopotamian culture; the discovery of an ancient language that would push back the timeline by at least five centuries. But she'd signed an airtight confidentiality agreement with that project's benefactor.

Taking a five-second break to sip some water helped her to fight the compulsion to scream out a pronouncement that would amount to career suicide. Any one of the faces staring back at her from the audience might be linked to that benefactor, she reminded herself. Someone out there is hanging on my every word.

If only she could tell the world how irrefutable evidence showed that around 4000 BC a cataclysm took place in northern Mesopotamia – an event so profound that progress and humankind itself were thrown back in time, forced to start anew. The first Dark Ages.

But instead, she forged on with the story that her esteemed colleagues expected.

'Around 3500 BC, the Mesopotamian elite began using stamped seals to identify their property. A mark of ownership. Here you have a typical cylinder seal,' she said, pointing the clicker to advance to the next image – a small stone tube covered in geometric depressions. 'Cylinders like this would be rolled on to a wet clay slab to leave artful impressions and picture stories. Fast-forward to 3000 BC and we find that scribes then begin pressing into these damp clay tablets with reeds, or stones chips, or other instruments, to create pictographs and hashes representing numbers. Our first accountants and tax collectors.'

The next slide showed an oblong clay tablet delineated into rows of boxes, which were filled with simple representations of animals. The pictographs were beset by vertical lines bisected with numerous cross hashes to resemble overlapping Ts.

'Here is a fantastic specimen that shows how the oldest Mesopotamian civilization, the Sumerians, tallied food supplies. This mushroom-shaped symbol here represents a cow . . .' she indicated it with the laser pointer, '. . . and here we have the head count.' She moved the dot slightly up and to the left to indicate symbols that looked like sideways Vs. 'At first, these simple clay tablets were left to dry in the sun. As such, few of the earliest examples remain, since over time moisture and the elements took their toll on the clay – disintegrated the tablets. Eventually, however, the scribes learned that if the finished tablets were baked at a high temperature, the record would be virtually indestructible – permanent. It's worth noting that this same technological advance was also applied to mud brick so that the ancients could construct grander, more permanent architectural structures.'

For the next few minutes, she elaborated on a series of slides that showed a steady 2,000-year evolution from crude pictographs to schematic wedge-shaped forms called cuneiform – a slow march towards standard word symbols that borrowed and refined the old elements. Next came pictures of various artifacts that chronicled 3,000 years when cuneiform reigned supreme: a clay tablet from 2300 BC Akkad which tallied barley rations; an elaborate cylinder seal whose impressions depicted the Mesopotamian pantheon of gods and goddesses alongside narrative inscriptions; a clay 'letter' circa 1350 BC sent by the

Babylonian king Burnaburiash to an Egyptian pharaoh; a stela from 860 BC, depicting the Assyrian king, Ashurnasirpal II, in full royal dress, covered in neat rows of cuneiform; an inscribed Babylonian world map from 600 BC; an elaborate clay cylinder excavated from the palace wall of Nebuchadnezzar II.

'It wasn't long before writing was used to record legends and mythology. Thousands of years before Adam and Eve appear in the Hebrew book of Genesis, Mesopotamian creation myths – the world's first true literature – featured a garden paradise, a tree of knowledge and humanity's first man and woman. Long before Noah's great flood, a cuneiform epic written in clay around 2700 BC tells the story of the Babylonian hero Gilgamesh, who'd built a boat to escape a cataclysmic flood. The tower of Babel is based on a magnificent temple pyramid in Ur – the ziggurat. And in 2100 BC Abraham leaves Ur to become the Old Testament patriarch, founder of monotheism and progenitor of the twelve tribes of Israel.'

She noticed that the few scowling faces in the audience looked visibly relieved, leading her to conclude that they found her delicate tip-toeing through the material agreeable.

'From these primitive languages emerge the early Semitic languages: Assyrian, Aramaic, Hebrew. Then come Greek, Latin, the Romance languages and English,' she said. 'Not until the Macedonian army led by Alexander the Great conquered Mesopotamia and Persia around 325 BC did cuneiform begin its rapid decline,' Brooke said. 'So be sure to visit the gallery and enjoy this most incredible exhibit – a true time capsule of human history written in clay.'

11

In a wide stance with his winter coat folded over a crooked arm, Agent Thomas Flaherty stood stage-left, patiently waiting for the last fans queued along the auditorium's main aisle to have Professor Thompson autograph a copy of her latest book, *Mesopotamia – Empires of Clay*. He couldn't help but smile as he watched the left-handed palaeolinguist grip the pen in a tight hook and press her face close to the page while scrawling personalized messages and a swooping autograph.

Flaherty carefully observed how she interacted with her admirers. A self-proclaimed master of character assessment – partly resultant from his undergrad psychology minor at Boston College – Flaherty decided that her endearing charm seemed genuine. No narcissism here. There was an air of innocence and vulnerability about her too, he decided.

Fifteen minutes later, the final fans dallied out from the auditorium and the professor sat back to flex the fingers on her left hand.

Flaherty moved in, saying, 'And I thought the Middle East was all about oil.'

Brooke smiled courteously.

'Really enjoyed your lecture,' Flaherty said. 'You know your stuff. And you actually make it interesting. Too bad I didn't have more professors like you when I was at B-C.'

'Ah, a fellow alumni. What year did you graduate?'

'A couple years ahead of you. Ninety-five. Took an extra term, but got it done.'

'Congratulations.'

'Thanks. Made the parents proud.'

'I'm sure you did.'

Sensing by her reserved expression that he was flirting with being pegged as creepy, he reached into his pocket for his credentials and skipped to the formal introduction: 'Special Agent Thomas Flaherty, Global Security Corp.' He flashed the ID. 'I know this isn't the best time, but I need to ask you some questions about your work in Iraq back in 2003.'

'Let me see that,' she said, motioning for his ID.

He gave it to her.

Brooke closely studied the laminated card: the data, the agency's sleek holographic imprint, the not-so-flattering photo of Agent Flaherty before he'd shaved away an unruly goatee. Then she passed it back to him. 'Never heard of Global Security Corporation.'

He kept it simple by replying, 'We work for the Department of Defense.'

'Sounds very official,' she said. 'So what can I do for you?'

'Actually, this might take a while. Maybe I can buy you a coffee in the café downstairs?'

'All right,' she said. 'But tea. Green tea.'

12
IRAQ

Jason used his binoculars to survey the approaching military convoy. With all the dust being kicked up, he wondered why they even bothered painting the vehicles in desert camouflage paint.

The lead vehicle was a six-wheeled, twenty-ton behemoth with a V-hull – a Mine Resistant Ambush Protected armoured transport, or MRAP. Affixed to its front end was a huge mine roller that scraped the ground to pre-detonate any pressure-triggered improvised explosive devices, or IEDs, that might be buried in the roadway. To Jason, the apparatus looked more like a colossal paint roller or something that might be used to flatten asphalt. On the MRAP's roof, he could make out a telescoping optics mast – infrared, heat sensors, the works. He suspected it had been retrofitted with metal detectors and radio frequency jamming equipment too.

Trailing like ducklings behind the MRAP were five flat-bellied Humvees.

He spied the Blackhawk again. Its side doors were open. Besides the pilot and copilot, he spied six marines inside the fuselage.

A conservative tabulation meant that twenty-five to thirty jar-heads would be arriving in the next five minutes. Marines weren't always keen on cooperating with contractors. But circumstance dictated that a team effort would be critical to getting into that cave . . . and fast. Play nice, an inner voice told Jason.

'Hey, Meat,' Jason called out.

'Yo.'

'Print out those pictures, pronto. I need to send Hazo on a field trip.'

'I'm on it.'

Hazo came over with a nervous look on his face. 'Field trip?'

'You know the locals,' Jason explained. 'I want you to take those pictures with you, show them around, figure out what those images on the wall can tell us. And I want you to see if anyone knows this woman whose ID we found melted to that door. No way she was here alone.'

Tentative, Hazo nodded. 'I understand.'

'Good. And don't be long. I'm going to need your help here.'

'But how will I get to the city?'

'You'll fly, of course.' Jason pointed to the chopper.

While the twenty-eight light infantry troops of the 5th Marine Regiment, 1st Division Expeditionary Force, busily pitched camp, Jason convened with Colonel Bryce Crawford in the makeshift Bedouin command tent. Before he set out to brief the colonel on what had transpired, Jason requested Crawford to loan out his chopper for a critical fact-finding mission. It took some convincing, but Jason was a consummate diplomat. Jason then summoned Hazo inside.

'Make it fast,' Crawford warned Hazo. 'No goofing around out there.'

Jason could tell that the forty-something, no-nonsense Texan – nothing but muscle dressed in crisp fatigues and a soft cap – intimidated Hazo. The Kurd cowered from the colonel's tough, grey eyes and jutting square cleft chin.

'Yes Colonel,' Hazo replied sheepishly. 'I promise to work quickly.'

'Then why are you still standing here? Get moving!' Crawford barked.

Jason watched Hazo scramble out from the tent, down the hill to the chopper.

'A Kurd?' Crawford grumbled, shaking his head with severe incredulity. 'You sure he's on our side, Sergeant?'

'Hazo's been thoroughly vetted. We'd be dead in the water without him.'

'You guys really do march to a different drummer. If he fucks up, it's on your head, Yaeger. Not mine. Got it?'

Jason nodded.

Crawford pummelled agitatedly to the Blackhawk pilot that the request had been granted.

They watched as the copilot helped Hazo into the fuselage jumpseat and secure his flight helmet. Then the copilot took his place in the cockpit. The rotors wound up and the chopper lifted into the air, spinning sand in its wash.

The colonel frowned as he scanned the inside of the tent. 'Christ. How long you been living like this?'

'Six months, give or take.'

'Shit, cavemen had it better.'

'We specialize in dirty work,' Jason subtly reminded him.

'Don't play the martyr, Yaeger,' he warned. 'We're all in the trenches in this shithole.'

Jason let the comment roll.

'So tell me what we've got. I see a lot of blood and meat out there. Any of it ours?'

Jason shook his head. 'No, sir. Four kills on the hill, eight more on the road. Five more holed up in that cave.' Then he took a breath and dropped the bomb: 'And we suspect that Fahim Al-Zahrani is in there with them.'

Crawford's eyebrows tipped up. 'Is that right,' he said with a sardonic grin. 'You expect me to believe that?'

'See for yourself,' Jason said, moving over to Meat's laptop and bringing up the side-by-side pictures. 'Took these myself. Ran facial rec on them. Perfect match.'

Crawford sat rigidly in the chair and gave each image a critical, dismantling stare, his sharp chin protruding outward. Finally, he said, 'Well fuck my mother. This raghead is supposed to be in Afghanistan.'

'They were trying to move him through the mountains.'

'Sure they were. Slippery bastards are probably trying to bring him over the border to his buddies in Iran. Shit.' He exhaled heavily. 'Heard you called in an air strike. You sure some of that gunk smeared over those rocks isn't him?'

'Negative. Called off the strike on his position. I saw Al-Zahrani run into the cave. I've got video of that too.'

'And he's not buried under all that stone?'

'Already pushed a Snake through the rubble. All clear on the other side. So far, we've seen no blood or bodies. And one of the hostiles managed to smash the camera. We're pretty sure they're all still trapped in there.'

Crawford nodded. 'All right, Yaeger.' His covetous eyes stayed glued to Al-Zahrani's digital portrait. 'I need this fucker alive.'

And there it was, thought Jason – the colonel's subtle jockeying for claiming the prize as his own.

Then in the reflection of the computer monitor, Jason caught Crawford staring sideways at the cracked-open ID badge casing and its extracted chip which Meat had left beside the laptop. He swore he saw the colonel's eyes go wide with alarm. It lasted only a fraction of a second.

'You should know that that's no ordinary cave up there,' Jason said.

Crawford stood up, squared his shoulders and crossed his arms tight across his chest. 'How so?'

Jason told him about the blown-out security door and the strange images carved into the entry tunnel's wall. For now, he refrained from telling him about the ID badge they'd found – a calculated, risky move.

Crawford took fifteen seconds to mull the facts. Then he said, 'All right, Yaeger. I get it. So what do you say we go ahead and plunge this toilet?'

13

Thirty kilometres south of the cave, the Blackhawk glided over a lush plain framed by the Goyzha, Azmir, Glazarda and Piramagrun mountains. Hazo peered out the fuselage window to Kurdistan's economic hub, As Sulaymaniyah. The city was a dense wheel of three- and four-storey buildings, spoked with roadways. He mused how from the air, he could see satellite dishes on practically every rooftop. Kurds loved their television, he thought.

Instead of heading for the international airport a few kilometres to the west, the pilot eased to a hover along Highway 4 and set the chopper down in a vacant parking lot. At the far end of the lot, Hazo spotted the Humvee escort the copilot had arranged while en route. Two severe-looking US marines in desert fatigues and mirrored sunglasses stood in wait, each clutching an M-16.

The pilot killed the turbine and the blades wound down.

The copilot assisted Hazo out from the chopper. As he escorted him to the Humvee, he asked, 'How long will you be in Suly?'

'Maybe forty minutes,' Hazo yelled.

'We'll wait here.' A thumbs-up and the copilot trotted back to the Blackhawk.

Hazo jumped into the Humvee with his two chaperones and provided them with the name of a restaurant located in the city centre, off Sulaymaniyah Circle. Hazo was not surprised that the marines knew its precise location. The restaurant was a hotspot for tourists and US military, thanks in part to its central location and fine Middle Eastern cuisine, but more so for its immaculate bathrooms and chic Arabian décor, which appealed to finicky Americans and Europeans. The marines got chummy when Hazo told them that the jovial proprietor and restaurant's namesake, Karsaz, was his cousin.

The Humvee zoomed through the busy streets, its massive tyres humming along the potholed pavement. The marines gave Hazo some moist towelettes so he could scrub his grungy face and hands, and blot the blood spatter off his sleeve. He did his best to pat the sand and dirt from his pants.

Hazo was delivered to the restaurant's doorstep in less than ten minutes. He hopped out and made his way into the foyer, where he was immediately overtaken by the heavenly redolence of cumin, mint, frankincense and rich tobacco. From behind a podium, a pretty hostess in a shiny taffeta dress glanced out the door to the idling Humvee then gave his attire a disapproving once-over. She offered a cautious greeting.

Hazo told her he'd come to speak with his cousin. She perked up and rounded the podium. Threading her arm through his, she proceeded to take him through a pointed archway leading off the main dining room and into the sumptuous hookah lounge.

Arabian-style arches set atop honey marble columns separated a dozen cosy seating areas adorned with Persian rugs, silk ceiling swags, and ornate Moroccan lamps set to a warm glow. Patrons lounged on plush floor cushions, puffing dreamily from hookah pipes. This was their safe zone, he thought – the womb where war and economic chaos had no place. Towards the rear of the lounge, they found Karsaz among a group of young Americans in business suits, talking in his animated, mayoral style.

The hostess led him to the service bar at the room's centre. 'Just a moment. I will tell him you are here.'

She walked over to Karsaz and waited patiently with hands folded behind her back until the rotund, moustached owner addressed her. She pointed in Hazo's direction. When Karsaz made eye contact with Hazo, his face brightened. After telling the waitress to bring his guests a complimentary dessert, he hurried over to Hazo with hands spread wide.

'*Choni*!' Karsaz greeted him with delight. He came up and wrapped his thick arms around Hazo, gave a big squeeze.

'*Bash'm supas, ey to?*' Hazo replied.

'Things are good, thank God,' he boasted. 'My cousin, why do you wait so long to come and see me! Are we not family?'

Hazo gave a boyish shrug.

'You look like hell,' Karsaz teased.

'And you still need to lose weight,' Hazo jabbed back.

Karsaz burst out laughing. 'This is true! So true! My wife, she tells me this every day.' He hooked a heavy arm over Hazo's shoulder and held him tight. He swept his hand over the lounge. 'How do you like this, eh? Finally we finished the renovations.'

'It's beautiful,' Hazo replied truthfully. 'You are a blessed man.'

'Yes. I'm very happy with this.' He gave another affectionate squeeze with his arm. 'Come, let us sit and talk.'

Karsaz kept the arm around Hazo's shoulder and towed him into the bustling dining room, stopping twice to introduce his cousin to some of the regulars. Finally, they settled into a booth set off in a quiet corner, and Karsaz asked the waitress to bring some coffee.

Under the bright light, Karsaz contemplated Hazo's languid appearance. 'Really, Hazo . . . you're not looking so good. Makes me think you're still patrolling the mountains with those American mercenaries.'

Hazo flashed a guilty smile.

Karsaz tsked in disapproval. 'I worry for you, cousin. Outsiders don't understand this place. And these foolish Americans? They think terrorism can be found on a map,' Karsaz said, 'even though it is but a few men drifting like ghosts around the world. Why do you bother with them?'

'I try to explain things to them, help them, so that innocent lives may be spared,' Hazo explained. 'It was you who said, "See with your mind, but hear with your heart."'

Karsaz chuckled. 'Ah, cousin! Remember: I also told you, "Do not shoot the arrow which will return against you."' He reached across the table and clasped the side of Hazo's neck with his meaty right hand. 'Perhaps your cause is a noble one,' he appeased. 'Though being a Christian in Iraq, I wonder if *I* understand anything that goes on here.'

They had a good laugh and Karsaz pulled back his hand.

The waitress returned and set down a saucer and mug for each of them. Hazo immediately sipped the Turkish coffee, or *qahwa*, savouring the spicy cardamom.

'I suppose no one can ever proclaim to understand our people,' Karsaz warned. He fingered his mug and sipped some coffee. 'So many conflicts. So many old scores yet to be settled. War is in our blood, is it not?'

Hazo nodded.

'We'll never cooperate,' Karsaz lamented. 'Maybe it's not so bad that you don't have a family of your own. Less grief and worry.'

The comment stung Hazo, but he managed a tight smile before moving on to business: 'I don't mean to rush, but I have little time,' he eased in. 'The reason I am here . . . I was hoping you might help me.'

Tilting his head, Karsaz replied, 'I *do* have a family, so I trust you won't put me in harm's way. You know what they do to informants?' he said in a low voice.

'I understand.' From his pocket, Hazo pulled out the photos. 'Please, if you could take a look at these pictures.' He began with the headshot of the female scientist. 'This woman was here a few years back. Perhaps with others. Do you recognize her?' If he was really lucky, the woman – like most tourists – would have walked through Karsaz's doors.

'Many, many people walk through these doors . . .' Karsaz replied with obvious scepticism. Retrieving a pair of bifocals from his suit jacket pocket, he put them on and gave the photo a cursory glance. A surprised look came over him. 'Ah . . . yes.' He held up an index finger and tapped it at the air. 'Yes, I remember this one. Years ago. She wore shorts and a teeshirt. Ooh, what a sight, I'll tell you,' he confided. 'The legs, the . . .' Midway through the vision, he cupped a hand over his chest and gave the memory a cold shower. 'Anyway, as you might imagine, the women were not pleased. The men weren't kind, either. Dangerous for such a very pretty woman who has no shame. I actually mentioned these things to her, you know, to help her. It's the way I am . . .' he said, tapping his hands to his chest.

'Of course.'

'She did eat here a few times. Very friendly, polite. Always left generous tips. Those Americans and their tips. When will they learn?' He shook his head.

'Do you remember when she was here?'

'Not long after the Texas cowboy blew up Baghdad.'

'Was she alone?'

'No, there were others too, I'm sure of it.' He took a long moment to juice the memory. 'The others were all men. Five, maybe six. Some military men, yes . . . and two wearing Levi jeans. I'd like a pair of those,' he confessed. 'I'd look like John Wayne . . . or maybe James Dean, no?'

Hazo smiled. 'Do you remember *why* they were here?'

Karsaz shrugged. 'Lots of soldiers back then. Reporters too. Nothing unusual.'

'Do you remember any talk of them going up into the mountains, excavating perhaps?'

This confused Karsaz. 'I'm sure the only digging they did was for Saddam and Osama.'

'I mean digging for artifacts.'

A look of confusion preceded another shrug.

Hazo moved on to pictures from inside the cave. 'And these . . . Any idea what these images might mean?'

'What is this?' Karsaz said to himself, as he studied the haunting images. 'Looks like something one might find over the mountains in Persepolis. Or maybe in the temple ruins of Babylon . . . or Ur, perhaps. You remember? Back in school we saw things like this on our trips, yes? Saddam was rebuilding the old empire in hopes of inciting the Jews and Christians to scream Armageddon. Thought he was the new Hitler. Brought a new Holocaust to our people. That evil man.'

Hazo tried to keep him on track. 'These etchings are different from anything I've ever seen in Babylon. See this woman?' He tapped the picture. 'This goddess figure is highly unusual.'

'Maybe it is Ishtar?' Karsaz guessed.

The Assyrian goddess of sex and war? Hazo considered, contemplating the picture again. 'It's possible.'

'What is this she carries in her hands?' Karsaz said, scrunching his eyes. 'And why does it glow like this?'

'I thought you might know, cousin.'

Karsaz shook his head. 'This is like nothing I have ever seen.' He studied the images a few moments longer, considering the connection to the American woman. 'The woman in the photo . . . did she find these things in the mountains?'

Perceptive, as always, thought Hazo. 'It would be best that I not say too much about it.'

'I see,' Karsaz said. 'There are many secrets in those mountains. I suppose if anyone were to know about them, it would be the monks. The Chaldeans know many secrets. After all, they profess to be direct descendants of the ancient Mesopotamians who once inhabited those mountains.'

'I think you're right.'

'There is that monastery in the mountain north of Kirkuk . . .' For three seconds Karsaz spun his hand to conjure the name, but came up blank. 'You know the place I speak of?'

'I do.'

Karsaz neatly arranged the photos, handed them back to Hazo. 'I would suggest you go there. See if the monks might answer your questions.'

14

LAS VEGAS

Stokes punched his security code into the keypad and the mechanical jamb bolts disengaged. He cranked down on the handle, gave a push, and the door whispered open. The fowl stench of excrement drifted out at him. 'Good lord,' he gasped, holding back his gag reflex. He set the air filtration system to the max. Then taking the handkerchief from his blazer's breast pocket, he covered his mouth and tentatively proceeded into the vault.

At the room's centre, Roselli was sprawled face up on the carpet in a spread eagle, blue complexion, murky eyes opened wide and frozen to the blank ceiling. Whatever he'd had for dinner and breakfast, both liquid and solid, had found its way into his trousers. Post-mortem bowel release; Stokes had seen it many times in the killing fields.

'Oh, Frank. Why couldn't you just keep your cool, like the old days?' he said, crouching down and rummaging through the corpse's pockets until he found a key ring and Roselli's PDA. 'All right fellas,' he called back to the door. 'Get in here.'

A broad-shouldered man came in wearing a sour expression.

Behind him a second man, shorter by at least five inches, came in pushing a heavy duty Rubbermaid tilt truck. Both men were wearing periwinkle baseball caps and coveralls embroidered with a crisp logo for a fictitious company whose speciality was document shredding. The truck parked near the service entrance bore the same insignia, along with a slogan: 'YOUR SECURITY IS OUR SPECIALTY'.

Stokes stood and stepped aside. 'It's not pretty. I'll throw in extra for your trouble.'

'How do want to do this?' the taller one asked, all business.

'Let's go with heart attack at the wheel.' Stokes tossed the keys over.

'Like a telephone pole . . . something like that?'

'Sure. Just nothing too dramatic,' Stokes reminded. On a previous assignment to eliminate a pesky senator who'd been poking around into the project's financing, this same duo had roughed up the body enough to raise a coroner's suspicion. An investigation ensued, which luckily led only to dead ends.

'And no witnesses, you hear me?' Stokes warned. He slipped Roselli's PDA into his inside breast pocket.

'No witnesses,' the taller man replied.

'All right. Get him out of here.'

The shorter man wheeled the tilt truck closer.

The two men each claimed a spot on opposite sides of the corpse, hooked an armpit and a knee, hoisted the body up on a three-count, then dropped it into the tilt truck with a thud. The taller man folded down the stiff legs while his partner got back behind the handles.

Stokes stared down at the wide brown stain left behind on the rug. A call to housekeeping would raise too many questions. He settled on cleaning the mess himself.

As he made his way out from the vault, a small ring tone chirped inside his jacket. Stokes paused in confusion and pulled out Roselli's PDA. A confirmation flashed on the display: '2 MESSAGES DELIVERED.'

Liberated from the vault's thick walls, the PDA had finally caught some airwaves.

'Great,' Stokes huffed.

Navigating the BlackBerry's menus, he hunted for the draft copy of Roselli's first message. But he found nothing. Almost immediately, however, 'undeliverable' error messages started bouncing back from the intended recipients' e-mail accounts. Stokes was relieved to see that the addressees were the scientists who'd partaken in the 2003 cave excavation. The message began with a warning about Stokes's malicious intentions. Next came a rally call for each recipient to contact authorities with all information pertaining to his or her time spent in Iraq. Also included in the e-mail were hyperlinks to classified material and documents that detailed the project's true mission. What Roselli hadn't anticipated was that Stokes's NSA contact had already deactivated and thoroughly emptied said e-mail accounts – stage one of the clean-sweep that would be complete only when each name in this e-mail wound up being the subject for an obituary. That task was well under way.

'Nice try, Frank. Always a step ahead of you.'

The PDA's grimy keyboard was making his fingers sticky; some tacky white powder that could only have come from the doughnuts that had led to Roselli's equally doughy belly. Disgusted, Stokes paused to wipe his hands with his handkerchief before hunting for the second stealth e-mail.

But sifting through the SENT and DELETED items, he could not find a second draft. If Roselli set the message to automatically delete upon transmission, there'd likely be no way of retrieving it or determining the recipient.

After two more minutes, however, Stokes did manage to determine the e-mail address to which the second message had been sent. The domain was registered to Our Savior in Christ Cathedral – Stokes's personal e-mail account. Rushing over to his computer, Stokes went into his e-mail client. Some spam about cheap health insurance and solar heating systems managed to sneak through, but nothing from Roselli.

What tricks did Roselli have up his sleeve? he wondered.

Cursing, Stokes tossed the PDA in his desk drawer.

From a utility closet adjacent to the elevator, he collected some cleaning supplies and made his way back into the vault. He began by thoroughly spritzing the air with odour neutralizer. Then off came his blazer and he got down on his knees to squirt the soiled mess with commercial-duty rug cleaner. He used a scrub brush to attack the stain, blotted up the resultant frothy goo with paper towels, and repeated the process. The heinous act reminded him of shitter detail back in the Corps. Though nothing could match that raunchy mix of kerosene and flaming excrement – truly the stuff of nightmares.

Satisfied, Stokes rounded up the supplies and filled a trash bag with the waste.

15

BOSTON

'Your green tea with honey,' Agent Flaherty said, and set a paper cup in front of Brooke Thompson, waiter-style.

'Thanks. You're pretty good at table service.'

'Got me through college.' He set down a second cup for himself – black coffee – then sat in the chair on the opposite side of the café table. He took a second to peer out the floor-to-ceiling window at the wind whipping the snow drifts that carpeted Calderwood Courtyard. 'God, I hate the cold.'

'Then you might consider moving. Because last time I checked, the Boston summer lasts about two weeks.'

He chuckled. 'I grew up in Southie, youngest of seven. Leaving isn't an option. How about you . . . leaving Florida to come here? Not exactly the picture of sanity.'

'I prefer beaches and sun, but I had to follow the work.'

Like many pallid Bostonian Irish, Brooke thought, the guy looked like he could use some time at the beach. Though it was that same UV avoidance that probably accounted for his unblemished complexion. If he'd graduated in '95, she assumed him to be thirty-six, maybe thirty-seven. But with thick black hair cropped in a short, corporate cut, he easily could pass for thirty. He was wearing a navy blazer – so trademark Boston – and she could tell by the way his arms and shoulders filled it that he was an athletic guy. Brooke was a stickler for a good nose and ears, and he had both; the right mix of pretty boy and man's man, naturally handsome, light on the manscaping. His magnetic eyes suffered an identity-crisis between blue and green. Despite the bad one-liner he'd opened with back at the auditorium, Agent Thomas Flaherty had passed her first-ten-seconds test with flying colours, she decided.

'Mind if I take notes?' he asked.

'Fine by me.'

He sipped some coffee, then took out a small notepad and a Bic pen. 'Let's talk about Iraq, starting with when you were there and why.'

'Hold on, Agent Flaherty . . .'

'Tommy.'

'Right. Tommy. First you need to tell me why I should be talking to you.'

'Fair enough.' He did his best to keep it simple. 'There was an incident in the Iraqi mountains. Some of our guys were working under cover, patrolling the area. They got into a shooting match with some, how shall we say, hostile locals. An ID card with your name on it was found in the middle of it all.'

'ID card?' She considered this. 'Oh yeah. I did lose one of those. It was more like a security badge.'

'That's a good start. So tell me how you lost it. That way I can explain to my boss how you weren't associated with the other side.'

His deadpan expression showed he wasn't joking. 'Look . . . yes, I'd received an offer to assist in an excavation in the northern mountains. I accepted. I arrived there September 2003. The four-teenth, to be exact.'

This did jibe with the passport activity provided to him. To keep her honest, he jotted down the date anyway.

'All expenses paid,' she added. 'It was a great resumé builder, an incredible opportunity . . . especially since Western archaeologists hadn't turned a shovel in that region for decades . . . thanks to politics, of course. Since this was only months after the US invasion, everything was very hush-hush. And I wasn't told anything specific until I'd arrived in Baghdad.'

'Who made you this offer . . . handled the arrangements?'

'A guy named Frank took care of everything.'

'Frank . . .?'

She shrugged. 'Just Frank. He was a middleman.'

'He funded the project?'

She gave him a confused look. 'I was never told who funded the project. Not so unusual. Benefactors sometimes want to keep a low profile. But shouldn't you guys know this? I mean, why are *you* asking *me*?'

'Sorry?'

She held out her hands. 'I thought it was you guys.'

He returned a blank stare.

'You know, the military, some obscure part of Homeland Security, the CIA, or whatever it goes by nowadays. I mean, I'd been given a military escort . . . US soldiers wearing desert fatigues with American flag arm patches, the works. You might want to ask your boss about that. Might save you some time.'

This temporarily stumped Flaherty. If his boss knew anything about it, this visit wouldn't be taking place. 'And what kind of work were you asked to perform?'

'What I do best, of course: decipher ancient languages. I was brought up north to the mountains . . . to a tunnel, or a cave actually, that dated back a few thousand years. The walls were covered in ancient picture carvings and cuneiform. Wasn't easy, either. That language predated anything I'd ever seen. In some ways, more sophisticated than what came centuries after it. Really incredible stuff.' She checked to make sure nobody was listening in then said in a low tone, 'The kind of stuff that would challenge every established theory on the emergence of writing.'

'And what did it say?'

She bit her lower lip. 'Sorry. Can't share. I had to sign a confidentiality agreement.'

'I'll need to know.'

'Then you'll want to talk to Frank. Because if I can't publish in the *American Journal of Archaeology* or *National Geographic*, you'll have to wait your turn.'

'You have a number for this middleman, Frank?'

She shook her head. 'Everything was handled by e-mail. The couple times he did call, the number came up "restricted".'

'Of course it did.'

'Cloak and dagger. Just as you guys like it.'

'You can give me this e-mail address?'

'When I'm back to my computer, I suppose.'

He dug in his pocket and pulled out a business card, slid it over to her. 'If you could forward it to me, that'd be great. And try not to lose the card, please,' he taunted.

'Funny,' she said. She dropped the card into her clutch purse and snapped it shut like a clamshell. 'I remember when I lost that ID. Frank freaked out when I couldn't find it. There was so much equipment in the cave, debris too. Lord knows where it wound up. But he got me a new card within minutes. Super-tight security there. Guys with guns outside, the works. Lots of

crazy stuff going on. I'd hear the fighter planes flying overhead . . . bombings, gunfire off in the distance. Not the safest
place to be at that time.'

'Any other scientists there?'

'A handful of others on rotation. Some coming, some going.
Archaeologists, mostly. But we were kept apart, no consorting or
information sharing. Really frustrating way to work. The others
had higher clearance than me. I was only allowed in the entry
passage – the first leg of what was probably a maze of tunnels.
There was a guard stationed where the entry tunnel forked,
scanning IDs. Like a checkpoint.'

He needed to fish for a connection to the Arabs who were now
holed up in the cave. 'Any chance it had something to do with
Islamic militants?'

'You're kidding, right?'

Flaherty shook his head sharply.

'What I saw in that cave had been there over 4,500 years
before Muhammad was even born. Terri*fying*, yes. Terror*ism*,
no.'

A few tables away, Flaherty noticed a man, with a thin face and
Dumbo ears, sipping coffee. The guy seemed preoccupied with
their discussion, but quickly diverted his attention back to a
museum map laid flat on the table. Flaherty lowered his voice.
'Anything else?'

'I was only there a few days, taking pictures, making rubbings
of the walls. Once I cracked the alphabet, I was asked to give all
the materials back. Then they put me back on a plane, no pictures, no records, no copies, nada. The most incredible thing
I've ever seen and all I've got to show for it is up here.' She
tapped her temple. 'But memories don't offer a high degree of
provenance,' she said with great sarcasm. She watched him

scrawling more chicken scratch, his fingers pinching the Bic way too tightly in a crooked grip. 'I'm not in any trouble, am I?'

Flaherty's eyes didn't move from the notepad. 'I'll need to report this all back to my boss, see what she has to say. There'll be some fact checking, of course.' He finally looked up. 'I'll keep you posted. But we'll probably need to meet again. So try not to skip town,' he said with a smile.

'Not even for some sunshine?'

'Not unless you bring me.' He said it too fast to catch himself, and he felt the blood rush into his cheeks. 'You know, because we may need you to answer more questions . . .'

'Of course,' she said, grinning.

16

LAS VEGAS

Finished with cleaning the carpet, Stokes took a breather next to a metre-high display case shaped like an obelisk. The artifact contained in its pyramidal glass tip captured his attention: a clay tablet, no larger than a hymnal, etched in lines, pictograms and wedge-shaped cuneiform. An amazing work created by the first masters of celestial study – the ancient Mesopotamians.

He'd never divulged to anyone how he'd truly procured this treasure map to the origins of Creation hidden deep within the Zagros Mountains. Even his closest confidants, like Frank Roselli, had clung to the story that he'd recovered the relic from an antiquities smuggler who'd looted it from the vaults beneath the Baghdad Museum after the capital first fell. Amazingly, everyone had accepted the story.

But that explanation – the lie – was far too simple.

This tablet represented Stokes's pledge to those who'd truly bestowed the artifact, and its secrets, upon him. The pledge that had transformed a warrior into a prophet.

And it all began on a calm day in 2003, when Randall Stokes lost his leg . . .

*

While US forces bombed Baghdad, Stokes's Force Recon unit had still been routing out Taliban from the Afghan mountains, just like they'd been doing since October 2001, when Operation Enduring Freedom responded to the terror attacks in New York and Washington. Shortly after Iraq's capital had been seized, his unit had been redeployed to northern Iraq to pursue Saddam loyalists who were fleeing Mosul and heading north over the mountains for Syria and Turkey.

The Department of Defense had issued a deck of playing cards listing Iraq's most-wanted men in four suits, plus jokers. In the first two weeks, Stokes and his six-man unit had captured two diamonds, one heart and one club. By the end of the first month, they'd hunted and killed fifty-five insurgents, without one civilian casualty. The worst injury his unit sustained was a non-lethal bite from a Kurdistan mountain viper whose fangs punctured more boot than skin.

Things had gone smoothly.

Perhaps that should have clued Stokes that his luck was sure to turn.

On an uncharacteristically mild Tuesday in late June, Stokes and fellow special operative Corporal Cory Riggins were heading south to Mosul for a weekly briefing with the brigadier general. Their Humvee was forced to a stop in a congested pass where a group of Iraqi boys had turned the dusty roadway into a soccer field. The kids made no effort to move.

'I should just run over them,' Riggins said. 'A few less fanatics in our future.'

'Never did like kids, did you?' Stokes said, hopping out from the Humvee. 'I'll take care of it.'

Stokes had made it only four paces from the truck when one of the boys scored a goal that sent the soccer ball rolling up to

Stokes's feet. He didn't think much about the fact that the kid playing goalie didn't come running after it. The kids simply jumped up and down, waving their arms for Stokes to kick it back. Grinning and shaking his head, Stokes cranked his leg back and planted a swift kick on the ball.

That was the last time he'd seen the lower half of his right leg.

What Stokes didn't know was that the soccer ball had been packed with C-4 and had been remotely armed the moment it rolled to a stop, waiting for the force of Stokes's kick to compress its concealed detonator.

The explosion was fierce, lifting Stokes into the air and throwing him back against the Humvee. He dropped to the ground at the same moment a combat boot smacked the window above him, spraying blood. The boot plunked into the sand beside him. He remembered seeing the jagged bone and stringy meat sticking out above its laces. Only when he looked down at what remained of his right leg – nothing but peeled raw flesh just inches below the knee – did he realize that the boot was his own.

There was no pain. Just the woozy haze from shock and an overwhelming urge to vomit.

The boys scattered as the trio of militants broke cover to ambush the Humvee. With their machine guns raised up, they shredded the Humvee's interior, before Riggins could escape or return fire.

Then they circled around Stokes, jeered him as he spat bile into the sand. Since his eardrums had been blown out, he couldn't hear what they were saying, and his eyes, coated in blast residue, struggled to focus.

Then came the beating.

The Arabs mercilessly kicked him about the face until he spat out teeth. Next, they simultaneously pummelled his ribs and testicles. When they began stomping on his bloody stump, Stokes passed out.

They'd done everything possible to maim him. Yet for some reason, no doubt wicked, they let him live. Perhaps they'd determined that his mutilation was punishment far greater than death.

Big mistake.

For hours he lay there, bloodied and beaten, cooking in the sun. Onlookers came and went, going about their business, some stopping to spit on him. All he could think was how he'd given his life to save these people – *the great liberator* – and not one came to his aid.

Was this how the freedom fighters were to be repaid? he'd wondered.

Finally, when he'd given up hope, one person did come for him: the man who would for ever change Stokes's life; the man who would confide in him a divine secret protected since the beginning of recorded history . . . and who would guide him down the path to ultimate retribution.

As Stokes continued to stare in wonderment at the clay tablet, he recalled a second set of playing cards issued to Iraqi ground troops by the Department of Defense – tips on how to sensitively handle Iraq's archaeological treasures.

He thought about the omnipotent words on the three-of-spades: 'To understand the meaning of an artifact, it must be found and studied in its original setting.'

Equally telling was the message from the six-of-diamonds: 'Thousands of artifacts are disappearing from Iraq and Afghanistan. Report suspicious behavior.'

But the Jack-of-hearts seemed to know his future best: 'Local elders may be a good source of information about cultural heritage and archaeology.'

Indeed, Randall Stokes's destiny certainly was 'in the cards'.

17

IRAQ

'Give it some more gas!' Jason yelled down to the driver.

The MRAP's 450-horsepower Mack diesel engine rumbled. The winch's braided steel cable stretched even tighter, straining to pull free a mammoth mountain chunk that easily weighed ten tons. The rock was wedged in tight, anchoring the debris pile that had slid down to block the cave entrance. Even larger boulders had toppled almost twenty metres down the slope before coming to a rest.

Jason's thinking was simple: pull this Big Mama out from the bottom of the heap, let gravity do the rest.

While the MRAP continued to pull, Jason monitored the two cable loops that Crawford's marines had managed to lasso around the boulder, hoping they wouldn't slip or snap under the extreme pressure.

'Come on, Big Mama . . .'

Some gritty scratching.

A sharp pop.

The marines retreated further along the slope's thin ridge.

'Come on . . .' He kept his hand raised and kept his finger

spinning in circles so the driver knew not to ease off the gas.

The first steel loop suddenly snapped and whipped out on a wide arc. Jason managed to duck and weave before it lashed his face.

'Nice move, Ali,' Camel called over. He was leaning casually against the cliff face, nipping at his canteen.

Jason flipped him the bird.

More shifting and groaning deep in the rock pile.

The second loop was starting to fray along one of the rock's sharp edges.

'Forget it, Yaeger!' Crawford bellowed up at him. From below, the colonel was monitoring the effort through binoculars. 'We'll blast it out!'

Jason had already explained to Crawford that another explosion would only exacerbate the problem by shaking free the loose stone that had yet to fall from the cliff face, compromise the tunnel itself. So he pretended to not hear him, kept spinning his finger.

The MRAP's engine revved harder.

Finally, Big Mama began to pull free. The rock did a drunken lurch then teetered forward.

'Everybody back!' Jason screamed. He motioned for Crawford and the dozen or so marines watching at the bottom to clear off to the sides. Then he yelled to the MRAP driver: 'Move out!' This could get messy, he thought.

Once Big Mama got going, the huge pile dammed up behind her erupted into a landslide – huge, sharp rocks bouncing and tumbling end over end.

Watching Big Mama curl down along the steel cable like a retracting yoyo, Jason feared she was going to gather enough momentum to vault the boulders that formed a protective wall at the slope's base and shoot straight for the plodding MRAP. Even the twenty-ton armoured behemoth wouldn't stand a chance against the huge rock.

Jason cupped his hands around his mouth and screamed, 'Move it! Go! Go! *Go-o-o-o!*' The driver was quick to respond, but Jason could tell that the MRAP wasn't accelerating fast enough.

Down bottom, Big Mama leapfrogged one of her siblings, connected with another, and did a gravity-defying flip that launched her into a rainbow-shaped arc that crested at five metres. Jason cringed. 'Oh crap . . .'

Big Mama came down like a meteor and struck the MRAP's rear with a huge clang.

When the dust settled, it was apparent that the MRAP had fortunately escaped being flattened. Jason noted, however, a sizable dent in the rear split door and fractures in its small windows too.

Clearly upset, Crawford paced over to the truck with hands on his hips, shaking his head. The driver immediately hopped out, rubbing his neck. He proceeded to the truck's rear to help Crawford assess the damage.

'You know Crawford's probably going to send you a bill for that,' Camel called over to Jason.

Ignoring him, Jason's attention went back to the cave. Despite the mishap, what he saw had him grinning. Though some smaller debris would need to be ferried away, once again a wide opening yawned in the cliff face.

18

To avoid reported mortar fire in northern Kurdistan the Blackhawk maintained a westerly flight path high above the Iraqi plain. On approach to Mosul it curled right, keeping the city comfortably to the west, then headed for its next destination, which lay thirty-five kilometres northeast.

As he gazed out towards the distant city, a great sadness came over Hazo. It had been over thirty years since Saddam Hussein's regime had forced hundreds of thousands of Kurds – Hazo's family among them – to relocate from Mosul to camps in the desolate southern deserts. Those who hadn't cooperated were attacked with Sarin nerve gas. Following the first major waves of ethnic cleansing, the fascist Ba'ath Party then seized the tribal lands in a bold attempt to 'Arabicize' the region.

While in the resettlement camp, Hazo's asthmatic mother had been denied access to critical medicine. She subsequently died from the desert's oppressive dry heat. His father, once a robust, jovial man, and, prior to the displacement, Mosul's most industrious carpet retailer, had been executed by a firing squad and tossed into a mass grave. Hazo's two older brothers had been killed by a suicide bomber while travelling by car together to seek work in Baghdad, shortly after the US invasion. Their wives and children moved in with Hazo's oldest sibling, his sister Anyah.

Now Mosul's streets were once again filled with Kurds. The tide of discontentment, however, had merely reversed with resettled Kurds staging violent reprisals – restaurant bombings, car bombings, shootings – against resident Arabs. After all that Hazo's family had endured, how could Karsaz question the fight for a new Iraq? Otherwise how would the cycle of violence ever end? *Could* it ever end? Hazo wondered. The grim truth, he feared, was that Iraq's history would continue to be written in blood.

His sombre gaze traced the wide curves of the Tigris to the outskirts of Mosul where mounds and ruins scattered over 1,800 acres marked the site of ancient Nineveh. The Bible said that the prophet Jonah had come here after being spat out from the great fish's belly to proclaim God's word to the wicked Ninevites. But long before Jonah's mission, the city was a religious centre for the goddess Ishtar. Hazo pulled out the pictures from the cave, studied the woman who'd been depicted on the wall. Had she been a living being? Or might this be a tribute to the Assyrio-Babylonian goddess Ishtar, as Karsaz had suggested?

An eight-pointed star was Ishtar's mythological symbol, and the woman depicted on the cave wall wore a wristband bearing an eight-petalled rosette. Close. But close enough? He tried to remember if Ishtar was ever portrayed carrying a radiating object in her hands. Nothing came to mind.

Like most Iraqis, he could recall bits and pieces of the goddess's lore: how the cunning seductress would cruelly annihilate her countless lovers; how after failing to bed the Babylonian hero Gilgamesh, she'd persuaded the supreme god Anu to release the Great Bull of Heaven to deliver apocalyptic vengeance upon the Babylonians; how the Queen of the Underworld, Ereshkigal, had been so infuriated by Ishtar's antics that she'd imprisoned the harlot and inflicted sixty diseases upon her.

Could this really be Ishtar? he thought

Nineveh faded in the distance and the chopper began tracing a white pipeline that ran north towards the Tawke oil fields. Crude was once again flowing out from Iraq, and making Hazo think that it wasn't only Ishtar who'd been a prostitute.

Back to the pictures, he flipped to an image that showed a warrior presenting the female's disembodied head to an elder. He couldn't recall anything about Ishtar being executed so cruelly. Too many inconsistencies. Though if this wasn't Ishtar, then who could she be?

The fact that these images came from inside a cave raised even more questions. It was assumed that beneath every earthen mound in Iraq lay remnants of a civilization come and gone. To find such evidence tucked away beneath a mountain, however, seemed highly unusual. Ancient cults *were* known to practise secret rituals in caves, so maybe the cave was linked to those who worshipped Ishtar.

The chopper dipped and began its descent.

Ahead Hazo spotted Mount Maqloub jutting skywards along the fringe of the Nineveh plain. Only as the chopper closed in over the craggy sandstone mountain did the angular lines of the multi-storey Mar Mattai monastery seem to materialize from the cliff face. Its only architecturally significant features were an Arabian-style loggia running along its top level and an onion dome marking the main entrance. Nestled behind the modern façade, however, was one of the world's oldest Christian chapels, founded in AD 363.

The Chaldean monks who resided within the monastery's walls proclaimed to be direct descendants of the Babylonians. They were the earliest Arab Christian converts; the preservers of Aramaic, 'Christ's language'. Here they safeguarded the world's most impressive collection of Syriac Christian manuscripts and ancient codices chronicling Mesopotamia's lesser-known past.

None knew ancient Iraq better.

And like the Kurds, the Chaldeans had suffered their share of persecution in northern Iraq. The Chaldean community was still reeling from the execution of Archbishop Paulos Faraj Rahho, who'd vehemently dissented against the proposed inclusion of Islamic law into the Iraqi constitution. On February 29, 2008, he'd been kidnapped at gunpoint by Islamic militants. The body turned up two weeks later in a shallow grave outside Mosul.

The pilot manoeuvred over the empty visitors' parking lot and expertly set the Blackhawk down.

Hazo removed his flight helmet, unbuckled his harness, and hopped out from the fuselage. The copilot, already outside, motioned for him to stay low while scrambling under the slowing rotor blades.

Climbing the monastery's precipitous front steps, Hazo pulled the olive wood crucifix out from beneath his galabiya to display it prominently on his chest. Beneath the onion dome he tried opening the main door, but it was locked.

Before he could knock on the door, a bespectacled young monk with a long black beard and opaline eyes appeared on the other side of the glass and turned the deadbolt. The monk was wearing a traditional black robe with white priest collar, an elaborate Inuit hood and *msone* ceremonial sandals.

'*Shlama illakh,*' the monk said, peering over at the unorthodox sight of the Blackhawk plunked down in the parking lot. He turned and glanced at Hazo's crucifix. Switching to English, he said, 'How may I help you, brother?'

Hazo introduced himself, apologized for his late arrival. Then he explained, 'I was hoping that one of your brothers might help me. You see, I have these pictures . . .' He held out the photos.

The monk kept his hands folded behind his back as he examined only the top photo.

'And I've been asked to determine what these images mean . . . who this female might be, here,' he said, pointing.

'And this is of interest to them?' He motioned to the Blackhawk.

'That's right.'

The monk hesitated, weighing the facts. His lips drew tight. 'You must talk to Monsignor Ibrahim about these things. I will bring you to him. Please, come,' he said, and set off in a steady shuffle.

The monk remained silent as he led Hazo through the modern corridors of the main building and out a rear door that fed into a spacious courtyard boxed in by two storeys of arcades.

The humble stone building they entered next was much, much older. They passed through a barrel vaulted corridor, redolent with incense and age, into an ancient stone nave with Arabian design elements – pointed archways, spiral columns, mosaic tile work.

The original monastery.

Hazo noticed that the inscriptions glazed into its intricate friezes and mosaics were not Arabic; they were from a language that the world outside these walls considered dead – Aramaic. There were plenty of carved rosettes adorning the archways too.

The monk ducked beneath a low archway and continued to a staircase that cut deep beneath the nave. Here Hazo noticed that the stone blocks had given way to hewn, chisel-marred stone worn smooth by passing centuries. To one side, electrical conduit had been installed along the wall to run power to sconces that lit the passage. The subterranean atmosphere was disorienting. It seemed as if the monk was leading him into the mountain itself.

Hazo's anxiety eased when up ahead he saw bright light coming out from a formidable glass doorway fitted with steel bars.

The monk stopped at the door and entered a code on the handle's integrated keypad. A lock snapped open. He turned the handle, pushed the door inward, and held it as Hazo stepped into a small empty foyer. The air immediately became warmer, dryer. Hazo could hear a filtration system humming overhead.

Without a word the monk shut the first door and made his way to a second door that was nothing but metal and rivets. Another code was entered and he led Hazo into a vast, window-less space divided into neat aisles by sturdy floor-to-ceiling cabinets. The air was sterile and dry. Trailing the monk past the long study tables that lined the room's centre, he glimpsed countless spines of the ancient manuscripts lined neatly behind glass panels.

Deep in the library, they found the elderly monsignor. Wearing a black robe and hood, he was stooped over a drafting table equipped with a gooseneck LED lamp, sweeping a saucer-sized magnifying loupe horizontally across the open pages of a thick codex.

Well before they reached him, the monk turned to Hazo and motioned for him to go no further. 'A moment, please.'

'Of course,' Hazo replied.

The monk quietly circled the table and bent to whisper in the monsignor's ear. The monsignor inclined his head so that his suspicious eyes shifted over his bifocals to appraise Hazo. He dismissed the monk with a curt nod. Then he summoned Hazo with a hand gesture.

Hands crossed behind his back, Hazo approached the table and bowed slightly. 'Thank you, Monsignor Ibrahim. I was asked to—'

'Let me see your pictures,' the dour monk demanded. He held out his hand, the severely arthritic fingers quivering.

Clearly the man disliked formalities, thought Hazo, as he handed Monsignor Ibrahim the photos.

The moment the monsignor laid eyes on the first picture, Hazo noticed the creases in his brow deepen.

The monsignor cleared his throat then said, 'Where did you find these?'

'A cave . . . to the east, in the Zagros Mountains. Those images were carved into a wall. There was writing too and—'

The monsignor's hand went up to stop him. 'I suppose you want to know who this is?' he said, almost as an accusation. 'Yes?'

'Well, yes.'

The monsignor stood from the table. He eyed Hazo's crucifix again. 'As you wish. Come. I will show you.' He rounded the table and set off down the aisle.

19
BOSTON

The Concorde's frigid engine turned over with a grinding cough. The interior was so cold that Thomas Flaherty's breath crystallized the instant it came into contact with the windshield. He clicked on the defrosters, blew into his hands a couple times, then grabbed his trusty scraper off the floor.

Hopping out, he cursed the Boston winter a few more times while he swept snow and wet ice off the windows. It took him another three gruelling minutes to chip away at the stubborn ice encrusted on the windshield's wiper blades. Back inside, the artic freeze had barely budged, so he gave the accelerator a few pumps to warm up the engine and speed things along. He blew in his hands again before burying them in his armpits for a long minute.

Once his fingers had thawed to an itchy tingle, he took out his BlackBerry and started thumbing his preliminary findings into a secure e-mail message addressed to his boss, with a CC to Jason Yaeger.

Jason Yaeger. They'd met during orientation at Global Security Corporation only two years ago. That high school valedictorian from Alpine, New Jersey, was meant to teach some arcane history course at an Ivy League university or find a cure for cancer – not scour the Middle East for terrorists. But Jason Yaeger was out for vengeance. In his eyes, that hard determination glimmered like a razor's edge. To lose a brother the way he had . . .

Composing the e-mail helped Flaherty formalize his initial assessments: Professor Brooke Thompson had been forthright in answering questions about her involvement in an excavation that had taken place in northern Iraq in 2003; though Ms Thompson was unwilling to breach her confidentiality agreement about the findings in aforementioned project, the nature of her involvement seemed consistent with her expertise in deciphering ancient languages; and though her back-story would require verification, he would not consider her a flight risk should further inquiries be warranted. Flaherty did, however, emphasize that the excavation's implied covert coordination by the US military merited further investigation.

He fixed a couple typos, then sent the report off into space.

A more comprehensive summary would be required. That would happen tonight, on his laptop, at Doyle's Café over a pint of Guinness and an order of steak tips, with the Celtics hoopin' it up on the big screen. And all the snow in the world wasn't going to put the kibosh on that.

He pocketed the BlackBerry and put the car in drive. The mounting snow constricted the street, making a U-turn impractical. So he continued straight on Museum Road and made a right at the T intersection. As he started along The Fenway, a splash of happy pastel colours set against the dreary grey museum edifice caught his eye. He glanced over to the steps leading up to the columned portico overhanging the building's north entrance. Immediately he recognized the puffy sky-blue ski jacket, pink wool cap and rainbow-striped scarf that had been hanging on the back of Brooke Thompson's chair.

Oh yeah, she's definitely from Florida, he smiled.

The sidewalks had yet to be shovelled and she was having a tough time getting the wheels of her rolling attaché case to spin. The snow won, and she settled for dragging the case over the fresh powder. En route to her car, he guessed.

Luckily, she didn't spot him cruising by, because he certainly didn't want to come off as a stalker.

As Flaherty continued slowly along the slippery roadway, he noticed the north door open a second time. Out came another familiar face: the nosy guy with the Dumbo ears from the café. The guy's beady eyes immediately went to Brooke Thompson, scanned the area, then snapped back to Brooke Thompson. They were the leering eyes of a *real* stalker.

Bundled warmly and revelling in the beauty of the fresh snowfall that blanketed the Fens, Brooke Thompson plodded through the snow while towing her attaché case like a dog pulling a dogsled.

To her right, she noticed that the reflecting pools had frozen over and the snow now reached up to the nose of Antonio López García's monumental bronze doll's head, crowned with a dollop of pristine snow. If there was artful expression in plopping a huge head on to the museum's lawn, the message was lost on her. Seeing it today did manage, nonetheless, to evoke a deep response – it jogged memories about the etchings Brooke had studied in that Iraqi cave, which included a graphic retelling of a woman's beheading. Those images, though masterfully crafted, were not intended to illicit artistic appreciation. They were meant to convey a warning.

Maybe if Brooke had been allowed to decipher the entirety of the story chronicled on those walls, she'd know it completely. And she was certain that it was there, deeper in the cave's recesses. During the excavation she'd been told that other writings and images had been discovered in the protected areas for which she lacked proper clearance. Perhaps if she hadn't been able to crack the language using only the writings found in the cave's entry tunnel, they'd have let her examine those other finds.

She had figured out enough of the story to know that whoever the beheaded woman had been, the devastation that followed her into that ancient Mesopotamian settlement was of a grand scale. And those ancient storytellers had attributed all of it to her.

During the dig, one of the commissioned archaeologists had come outside the cave entrance to get a clear satellite signal for a phone call. She'd overheard his conversation concerning some carbon-dating results. Though he'd not specified the types of organic specimens that had been dated, she'd guessed at some traces of food, flowers, or maybe bone. Certainly plausible since the famous Shanidar cave, also in Iraq's Zagros Mountains, had yielded ten Neanderthal skeletons, as well as decayed flowers used during their ritual burial.

The archaeologist had specifically mentioned 'a tight confidence interval around 4004 BC'. In the context of Iraq, this date was impossible for Brooke to forget since a seventeenth-century Irish archbishop named James Ussher had meticulously reconstructed the chronology of biblical events to come up with a very precise date for Creation: Sunday, October 23, 4004 BC. And like most theologian scholars, Ussher placed Eden's locale in ancient Iraq, land of the four rivers mentioned in Genesis 2 – the Tigris and Euphrates, plus the long-ago dried-up Pishon and Gihon.

What could they have found inside the cave that could be so important . . . and so ancient?

The secrecy of the excavation never sat well with her, particularly since nothing she'd witnessed there had ever surfaced in academic journals. And being that that cave was easily the most important archaeological discovery of the last hundred years, such a withholding seemed downright criminal. Who was really behind the dig? And why had the operation been conducted by the US military so soon after the invasion of Iraq?

It wasn't all that uncommon for benefactors sponsoring excavations to remain aloof. But recalling the extensive background check she'd gone through with the facilitator known only as 'Frank', now she couldn't help but think she might have taken part in something nefarious. And this Agent Flaherty who'd just bought her tea and quizzed her on stuff *he* should already know? Why hadn't he been apprised of what had taken place at the dig?

She continued past the museum and clambered over a dirty snow berm that lined the kerb along Forsyth Way. Across the street, the only car that remained was her Gumby-green Toyota Corolla. Thanks to a snow plough the car had practically been buried beneath ice and snow.

'Great,' she mumbled, making her way across the slushy street. Luckily, by now she'd learned to keep a shovel in her trunk for just such occasions.

Pulling out her car keys, she went to the rear of the car and tried working the key into the frozen trunk lock. But since she'd refused to take off her mittens, she fumbled the keys and they plopped into the snow. When she dipped down to fish them out, she heard a small popping sound. Something whisked overhead an instant before the lamppost behind her let out a resounding clang.

Startled, she spun to look at the post. She remained in a low crouch. 'What the hell . . .?'

Another small pop sounded and something thwacked into the Corolla's rear quarter panel, hit the inside of the trunk, and dimpled the sheet metal outward right in front of her face. She screamed and tumbled back into the snow.

That was when she realized that somebody was shooting at her.

20
IRAQ

The marine colonel stood at the base of the slope next to Big Mama – the boulder slightly taller than she was and streaked with some of the MRAP's camouflage paint. He was glaring up at the partially reopened cave where Jason's men were helping the marines clear more debris. The larger stones were being manhandled out and tossed down the slope. The smaller debris was being ferried out in buckets along a human chain. With the sun dropping fast over the horizon, they were working double-time against the imminent nightfall.

'Once the sun's down, we'll need to keep any lighting to a minimum,' Crawford told Jason. His eyes combed the surrounding mountains. 'No need to draw more attention to ourselves. Plus we're light on batteries and I wasn't planning for a sleepover.'

'Should be clear skies tonight,' Jason said. 'We'll have plenty of moonlight. The guys probably won't even need their NVGs. The only place we'll need some lighting is in the tunnels.'

Crawford circled his gaze to the two snipers posted outside the cave entrance. 'If it was up to me, I'd skip the formalities and firebomb the fuckers. Yup . . .' Crawford exhaled. 'Al-Zahrani or not, I'd vote for Arab barbecue. These slick bastards have nine lives. If they're on the grill, I say light the fire.'

Jason knew the colonel was only half sincere. 'Washington wants him alive. Intel says he's plotting to—'

'Don't preach the rhetoric to me, Yaeger. I know the score. This war's gotten too goddamn civil for my taste, is all I'm saying. You saw what that prick did to those cathedrals last month. Killed almost 500 civs in one day. In less than a year he's racked up another thousand or so by sending his martyrs into subways, bus stations and malls strapped with C-4. No warning. No conscience. Just wants to put fear into every human being that doesn't bow down to Allah. And this psycho's just getting warmed up. Wants to make a nice impression on his boss. That way when Bin Laden's diseased kidneys finally give out, he can take Al-Qaeda to the next level. If we still had some balls in Washington maybe we'd get this done the old-fashioned way.' With arms crossed tight over his chest he gave Jason a sideward glance.

Avoiding a political debate, Jason pointed his chin up at the cave. 'Think we should gas them out?'

'Not sure how effective that'll be if we don't first get in there and see how deep those tunnels go. Wouldn't be smart sending men in there.'

Jason agreed. 'You fellas bring a SUG-V?'

The Small Unmanned Ground Vehicle, or SUG-V, was a thirty-pound compact radio-controlled reconnaissance robot equipped with a single articulating arm, cameras and dual rotary tracks for climbing stairs and rolling over rubble – invaluable for infiltrating terrorist hideouts and diffusing roadside bombs.

'I was getting to that, Yaeger. Don't be a smart ass. We've got a shiny new PackBot in the truck. Not sure how she'll respond in a cave – transmissions might get sketchy.'

'We'll use a fibre-optic line,' Jason tactfully replied.

'Worth a try, I suppose.' Then Crawford added, 'Let's just try and skip the heroic stuff this time, *capeesh*? You remember where that got you guys last time.'

'Duly noted, sir,' Jason appeasingly replied.

Though friendly fire and civilian casualties were common-place in any war, there seemed to be zero tolerance when the error could be attributed to an outside contractor. Despite the fact that Jason's unit had maintained a flawless record here in Iraq, another of Global Security Corporation's deep-cover teams working Fallujah had bombed a purported weapons-manufacturing facility that instead wound up being a car parts machine shop. Fifteen Iraqi civilians died in the explosion. The mistake had been a black eye for both the firm and the US Defense Department. And lifers like Crawford, who no doubt felt undermined by the presence of freelancers, were more than happy to keep a scorecard.

'Tell me, Yaeger: where's your Kurd sidekick? Why's he not back here yet?'

'Had to go north of Mosul. Shouldn't be much longer.'

'You said he needed to look into something. That was two hours ago. What exactly is he doing?'

'He's following up on a very important lead.'

Here's where relations with Crawford might get sketchy, thought Jason. When Hazo had called earlier, he'd indicated that his restaurateur cousin had positively identified the American scientist, who'd apparently been chaperoned by a number of military types. Only minutes ago he'd also received an e-mail from Thomas Flaherty, which summarized an initial briefing of the archaeologist in Boston – facts that perfectly corroborated Hazo's story. Until it was clear what the military's role had been in all this, Jason would need to sacrifice diplomacy. The bigger question was: did Crawford already know something about the excavation that had taken place here in 2003?

'Hazo's got lots of contacts in the area,' Jason half explained. 'Influential people who know things.'

'Don't diddle my pie hole, Yaeger. Exactly what kind of "things" are we talking about?'

Jason squared off with the colonel and said, 'The kind of things that lead us to trapping Fahim Al-Zahrani in a cave when every branch of the military thinks he's in Afghanistan. So I tend not to bust his balls too hard for staying out too late on a fact-finding mission. *Capeesh?*'

Crawford's sharp jaw jutted out. 'Stand down, Yaeger. I'm warning you – don't fuck with me. If I find out there's something you're not telling me . . .' For maximum effect, he let the threat linger.

But Jason wasn't backing down. Guys like this had tried to intimidate him during his short career with the Corps, and were precisely why he'd left it all behind for the private sector. Bullying was a poor supplement for stunted intellect. 'Info sharing is a two-way street, Colonel. We're both fighting the same enemy, both on the same side.'

Crawford's jaw eased back. 'If my scouts find something and that chopper's not here to back them up, I'm gonna be mighty pissed.'

'Yes, sir.'

'All right, then,' Crawford said. 'I'll have the men prep the bot.'

21

BOSTON

During her life, many unexpected things had happened to Brooke Thompson with most surprises having fortunately been good ones. The instant realization that someone was trying to kill her, however, certainly ranked first on the undesirable surprises list. The adrenaline shooting through her was like nothing she'd ever sensed – a fight-or-flight response that pushed all her senses to the max and had her heart and lungs pumping triple-time.

Without hesitation, she responded the way her mom had drilled into her head since childhood: 'Help!' she screamed. '*HELP!*'

With the snow storm having driven everyone home early, there was no one close by to hear her plea. The nearest pedestrian was almost a block away, strolling blissfully unawares along Huntington Avenue. A big guy in a hooded fleece. She tried again, even louder this time: '*Heeeelp!*'

The guy kept moving.

Both shots seemed to have come from the same trajectory – 10.30 on a clock face. That meant the shooter was somewhere along the path she'd walked from the museum. On all fours and keeping low, she scrambled along the kerb to keep the Corolla between her and the shooter.

A hasty visual survey to the rear and sides was discouraging. Nothing in the vicinity qualified as adequate cover. Even the scant, leafless trees lining the street seemed too skinny. Staying behind the car, however, was a losing proposition.

If she could just see the gunman, orient better . . .

Brooke pulled off her bright pink cap, then popped her head up over the four inches of snow that covered the Corolla's hood. Closer than anticipated, the shooter was easy to spot: a thin man wearing a grey overcoat and a black snowcap. She fully expected the face to belong to Agent Thomas Flaherty, but the big ears and aquiline features weren't his. Across the street, the gunman bounded over the snow berm where her attaché case and boots had left a clear trail. He swung a handgun directly at her head and the muzzle flashed white with barely any sound.

As she ducked, the shot glanced the snow on the Corolla's hood and zipped out perilously close to her scalp.

'Heeeeeeeelp!'

In less than five seconds, she guessed, he'd be circling the car to close in for the kill. And there was nothing she could do about it.

When Flaherty saw Dumbo-ears step up his pace and pull out a Glock, he pushed down hard on the Chrysler Concorde's accelerator. The car fishtailed in the snow before finding traction on a patch of rock salt and shooting forward. The slight delay allowed the agile gunman to corner the museum and fire off two shots that kept the archaeologist pinned down behind her car.

Christ, did he hit her? was all Flaherty could think. Then the guy dashed out in the roadway on Forsyth Avenue and managed a third shot.

'No, no, no!'

Sliding a wide right on to Forsyth Avenue, Flaherty fought the steering wheel to straighten the car on the slick road. He leaned on the horn and depressed the accelerator again. Now he had Dumbo's attention. The guy planted himself in the centre of the street at twenty metres, levelled the Glock at the Concorde's windshield.

Dipping below the dashboard, Flaherty jammed down on the brakes while cutting the wheel hard to the left. The round thwunked into the passenger-side doorframe. The Concorde swung into a sideways skid, but the forward momentum kept it along a direct line for the shooter.

Still low, Flaherty reached for his underarm holster and unsnapped his Beretta.

There was a thump that continued over the car's rear window, then trunk, that was certainly the gunman. Flaherty immediately popped up and saw the Corolla directly ahead. He braced himself for the impact. The huge Concorde's bumper clipped the side of the Corolla and the car spun another ninety degrees so that he was now looking at the erratic tyre tracks he'd left in the snow.

The downed gunman was already making a move for his fumbled Glock, his right leg hobbling from the car-jumping stunt.

Flaherty threw open the driver's-side door, thrust the gun between the V opening and pulled the trigger. The shot wasn't well aimed, but it forced Dumbo to abandon the Glock and go scrambling for cover behind a concrete construction barricade that cordoned off the sidewalk beside the museum's new American Wing.

While keeping his eyes on the barricade, Flaherty reached across to the passenger door, pulled the handle, and pushed it open.

'Brooke, it's me, Agent Flaherty! Get in the car!'

There was a sickening pause that had him wondering whether Dumbo's third shot had found its intended target.

'Brooke! Let's go!'

Finally, he heard feet crunching through snow. She bounded into the seat beside him then pulled the door shut.

'Stay down,' he told her.

After confirming in the rearview mirror that the street behind him was empty, Flaherty pulled his door shut, shifted the car into reverse, and pushed down on the accelerator, spinning the tyres. As soon as the car got moving, he flipped the gun to his left hand, powered down his window, and hung his arm out.

Sure enough, Dumbo jumped out over the barricade and began running at the car. Like every tenacious assassin, he was gripping a backup pistol. Flaherty immediately shot at him. His left-handed aim was lousy, and the assassin sensed it – didn't break stride or deviate to either side, just kept coming.

'Damn, he's fast,' Flaherty grumbled. He fired again and saw the round spit snow close to the assassin's feet. He pushed harder on the accelerator, trying like hell to keep the car on a straight line. Another quick glance in the rearview showed that the inter-section was directly behind. No time for a three-point turn. Blindly racing into traffic wouldn't be smart, either. That meant another fancy manoeuvre.

'Keep down,' he told Brooke.

Flaherty pulled his left arm in and jerked the wheel all the way to the left while at the same time easing off the gas. With the tyres grabbing nothing but ice and powder, the car initiated a wicked spin. At the ninety-degree mark, he cranked the wheel in the opposite direction and pushed down on the accelerator again. The timing was good, but the result was far from perfect. The car slid more than the 180 degrees he intended, caught the kerb and the snow heaped along it. Luckily, it wasn't enough to stop the car from moving forward. Anticipating the assassin's next move, Flaherty ducked low, pulled the wheel slightly to the right and gave it more gas.

The rear window clacked three times in quick succession – one round cutting into the top of the dashboard, one drilling into the aftermarket Bose stereo, and one pounding into the steering wheel an inch above Flaherty's hand.

Flaherty punched the gas and held the wheel straight. When he poked his head up over the dash, he realized that blind steering had put the car on a collision course with a three-car commuter train plodding along the above-ground median railway – the Green Line. And he realized that if he jammed on the brakes, he'd either sideswipe the train, or be crushed by a huge municipal dump-truck-turned-plough that was heading right for his door with its air horn blaring.

'Hold on!' he yelled to Brooke.

He hit the gas harder and cut the wheel sharp left. The car cleared the plough and skidded sideways into the train's path. The conductor had apparently anticipated what was happening, and brought the train to an abrupt stop, just as the Concorde thudded over the rails and continued a sideways slide into a snow bank.

With no time to think, Flaherty got the car moving again and didn't look back.

22
IRAQ

Despite his years, the elderly monsignor wove deftly through the aisles of the subterranean library. Hazo trailed closely behind him, scanning the amazing collection of manuscripts in the sealed bookcases. There were no windows in sight, making him wonder how deep beneath the mountain they were.

'I've been told that your collection contains some of the world's oldest books and scrolls,' he said to make polite conversation.

The monsignor shook his head and swatted his hand at the idea as if it were a fly.

Though Hazo didn't appreciate the old man's crotchety disposition, he knew the monk had good reason to avoid the topic. Back in the fourteenth century the monastery's entire collection had to be clandestinely relocated to avoid destruction by Timur's invading Mongol army. The monastery itself could not escape partial destruction and remained abandoned until 1795. With a similar threat now brewing outside these walls, Hazo guessed the monks were rightfully concerned about opportunistic looters sacking the library.

'Here.' The monsignor stopped at a bookcase. He slid open the glass door, pulled out a leather-bound codex. He eyed Hazo's crucifix. 'First, let me ask you: as a Christian you are familiar with the stories of the Bible . . . the book of Genesis?'

'I am.'

'Then I presume you know the Creation story? How the world began?'

Hazo nodded.

The monsignor's lips twisted into a wry smile. 'Is that so? Please, tell me what you know.'

Unsure of how this exercise could possibly relate to his query, Hazo conveyed what he could recall: how in six days God created Heaven and Earth then made light to separate day and night across the formless waters . . . then land and sea, vegetation . . . then sun, moon and stars . . . then creatures from the waters and the birds to fly above the earth . . . then he ordered the land to be covered with living creatures dwelling upon it. And finally he created Adam then Eve. When he'd finished, the monk seemed impressed.

'Not bad,' the monsignor said. 'Like most Christians, however, you have made a critical omission, though I will not fault you for it. It is a very minute detail that is easily overlooked. We'll get to that shortly. Come, there is a table over here.' He motioned for Hazo to follow.

Entering a study niche, the monsignor brought Hazo to a work table and set the codex on a bookstand. Using a flat-tipped stylus, he began gingerly leafing through the ancient pages.

Looking on, Hazo admired the book's wonderful text and drawings complete with gilding and vibrant colours. The pages were deeply stained along the corners by countless fingerprints – oils and contaminants left behind in the vellum, he guessed.

'The problem with books and scrolls,' the monsignor explained while turning the pages, 'is their fragile nature. Time is cruel to them. You can see these discolorations in the black lettering.' He indicated where complete passages had faded from crisp black to a greenish brown. 'In the old days metals, like copper and lead, were mixed into the ink. Naturally, metals oxidize over time. If there hadn't been men dedicated to preserving and transcribing these ancient works, they'd have been lost long, long ago. We've begun to digitize the collections . . . to *permanently* preserve them.' He kept flipping pages. 'Did you know that 7,000 monks once lived on this mountain?'

'I did not,' Hazo admitted. With the monk hunched over the book, Hazo now realized just how stooped the man's shoulders were; partly from age, Hazo was sure, but partly from the decades-long repetition of this very act.

'Yes, it is true. Seven thousand monks. And many of those men dedicated their lives to the task of preserving our history. Without them . . .' He shook his head gravely while keeping his eyes buried in the pages. 'Though some criticize the accuracy of transcriptions through the ages, there come times when source material – the very origin of a story – is discovered, and it vindicates the written legacy. What you found in that cave is a fantastic example. Ah, yes. See here,' he said, stopping on a page and tapping the lollipop tip of the stylus on its central drawing. He straightened and took a step to the side. 'Look familiar?'

Hazo stepped closer and leaned in to examine the drawing, which replicated images in his photos. 'Oh my,' he said. The detail was incredibly accurate. So accurate that he could only believe that the artist must have seen the cave itself. 'It is the same.'

'A perfect match, I would say.'

'And the words?' Judging by the characters that matched the inscriptions he'd seen in the church, they appeared to be Aramaic. 'What do they say?'

Strangely, the monk didn't need to read the text to answer Hazo.

'The words speak of the beginning of recorded history. A time when God cleansed the earth with water to begin anew. When the first woman created by God had returned to paradise to seek retribution.'

'This has to do with Eve?' Hazo said, now completely perplexed.

The old man shook his head and smiled knowingly. 'This is the mistake you made earlier. Not *Eve*.' He whispered conspiratorially: 'Lilith.'

23

'Lilith?' Hazo scrutinized the ancient drawing. 'I don't understand.'

'Eve was *not* the first woman created by God,' the monsignor explained. 'The Bible is full of contradictions. And the scriptures' opening pages are no exception.'

From a nearby bookshelf, he retrieved a bible; opened the front cover and turned to the first page.

'If one carefully reads Genesis 1 and Genesis 2, one will discover two separate accounts of God's creation of humans. In Genesis 1, man and woman are created simultaneously. Listen.' He traced the lines of the Bible with the stylus then read, '"So God created man in his own image, in the image of God he created them; male and female he created them."' His eyes shifted up from the page. 'Just like He created every living creature in duality to facilitate procreation, you see.'

'Simultaneously,' Hazo said in a low voice. How could it be? he thought.

'That is right. Yet it is the second account told in Genesis 2 that most remember. When a lonely Adam wanders the garden paradise, and God, in afterthought, decides that man needs a spiritual companion.'

'When God takes Adam's rib to make Eve.'

The old man smiled. 'Not literally a rib. A better translation would refer to "his side",' he corrected, before continuing: 'Eve was Adam's *second* partner, his consummated wife, who the Bible tells us was destined by God to be dominated by her husband. Lilith, the *first* woman created by God, was much the opposite. She had a voracious sexual appetite, always demanding to be, how shall we say . . . on top of Adam. She was anything but subservient.'

'But it doesn't say those things in the Bible, does it?'

The monk smiled. 'That, too, is true. Any references to Lilith's name were long ago removed from Genesis by the patriarchal Catholic Church, which didn't like the idea of such a dominant female figure. However, if you wait here a moment, I can show you another picture that will help you understand this. You are like me, a visual learner, am I right?'

Hazo smiled. 'I suppose I am.'

'This is good, because pictures hold many truths, many secrets. I'll just be a moment.'

The monk disappeared behind the stacks, and in under a minute he returned with a modern coffee table book titled *Masterpieces of the Vatican Museums*. He opened it and laid it flat on the table.

'In 1509, Michelangelo painted Lilith's picture on the ceiling of the Sistine Chapel – the fresco called *The Temptation of Adam and Eve*.'

In the index, he found the correct page and flipped to it. Then he turned the book to Hazo so he could better see the photo.

'Michelangelo based this narrative painting on an apocryphal text called *The Treaty of the Left Emanation*, which told that after God had banished Lilith from Eden, she'd vengefully returned in the form of a serpent to coax her replacement, Eve, into eating the forbidden fruit.'

Hazo studied the image that combined two scenes: the half-woman, half-serpent, entwined around the tree, reaching out to Adam and Eve, and beside it, the angel expelling the couple from the paradise.

'This is the pivotal event in Christianity that speaks to Original Sin and the downfall of humankind. All attributed, of course, to the sin of a woman.'

'Amazing,' Hazo said.

'There is one obscure reference to Lilith in the Old Testament as well. When Isaiah speaks of God's vengeance on the land of Edom, warning them that the lush paradise will be rendered infertile and pestilence will bring desolation.' Going back to the Bible, the monsignor turned to Isaiah 34. 'Now listen to this: "The wild beasts of the desert shall also meet with the wild beasts of the island, and the satyr shall cry to his fellow; the screech owl also shall rest there, and find for herself a resting place. There shall the great owl make her nest, and lay, and hatch, and gather under her shadow." A bit cryptic, yes. Unless one reads the original text from which it was transcribed.' He then read from the page's right-hand side: Hebrew text panelled alongside the English translation. 'The literal words are: "yelpers meet howlers; hairy-ones cry to fellow. Lilith reposes, acquires resting place".'

'So she *is* specifically mentioned in the Bible,' Hazo said.

'Indeed. Lilith is also mentioned throughout Jewish apocrypha, the Dead Sea Scrolls, the Talmud, the Kabbalah, the Book of Zohar, and the medieval Alphabet of Ben Sira. All portray her as a demonic seductress who tortured men and made them impotent; a jealous vixen who killed babies out of spite. As such, her earliest depictions – statues, amulets and figurines – morph her voluptuous beauty with beastly features, like wings and talons. But Lilith's story goes back much, much further than this, you see.'

The monk explained that when the Babylonians destroyed Jerusalem in 586 BC, King Nebuchadnezzar II exiled the Jewish priests to Babylon. Having lost the Jerusalem temple and its sacred texts, the priests recreated a written account of their heritage and ancestry, borrowing heavily from the Mesopotamian mythology learned from the Babylonians. Many of those stories had been traced to the third millennium BC, to Akkadian cuneiform texts that spoke of the *Lilitu* – demons of the night; bearers of pestilence who wandered desolate places to wreak havoc on humankind. Centuries of oral tradition preceded even those writings.

'The legend of Lilith may be the most ancient tale ever told,' the monsignor said. 'How old, no one really knows. But most would agree that Lilith is the progenitor of all female demons that later emerge in Mesopotamian, Greek and Roman mythology.'

The monk removed his glasses and his expression turned severe.

'Perhaps now you know too much, my son. Because these photos of yours . . . these are very ancient images of the story of God's creation of the first woman. The story of paradise lost. And though it may sound crazy, if not impossible, it appears to me that you've stumbled upon a most legendary place.'

'Please, tell me,' Hazo beseeched.

The monk pointed to the last photo image showing men busily preparing a headless body for burial. 'Lilith's tomb.'

24

BOSTON

'What the hell was that all about?!' Brooke fumed, as she tried again to buckle her seatbelt with tremulous fingers. 'Who was that guy?'

'Damned if I know,' Flaherty said, checking the rearview again.

'Slow down, will you,' she insisted in an agitated tone.

Feeling like his nerves were supercharged with electricity, Flaherty let up on the gas and settled in behind a bus that crept down Huntington Avenue.

'Who do you work for again? CIA?'

He shook his head. 'Global Security Corporation. Just like it says on my business card. We're a US defence contractor, among other things.'

'Other things?'

Hesitant, he sighed, then told her, 'GSC provides the staffing services every civilized country needs lots of nowadays: mercenaries, spies, bodyguards, counter-terrorist agents, cyber defence techs. Those kinds of "things".' He glanced over at her to gauge her response.

'Not to insult your work, especially since you just saved my life . . . but GSC sounds like a glorified temp agency,' she cynically replied.

'Temp agency sounds a lot better than what some senators call us. They have really affectionate names like "The Death Broker" or "Assassins Incorporated".'

She managed a smile.

'You all right? Doesn't look like you're bleeding or—'

'How do I know that guy with the gun wasn't one of your men?'

'Definitely not one of ours,' he assured her. 'Our assassins are a helluva lot better than that rookie. You'd have been dead, probably from a car bomb. Or at least a *discreet* sniper shot,' he said after giving the logistics momentary consideration.

'Thanks. That's comforting.'

'Hey, if you didn't notice, those bullets were coming in my direction too,' he reminded her. He pointed to his trashed stereo. 'Could've been my head instead of my CD player.'

'I suppose,' she relented. 'You know, you weren't exactly a marksman back there, either.'

He couldn't help but grin. This woman was definitely feisty. 'For the record, that's the first time I've ever had to fire a gun at something other than a range target. And in my defence, shooting with my *left* hand while speeding in reverse *on snow* wasn't in my training repertoire.'

She curled her fingers to her lip and fought back the horrible thought of what the alternative outcome might have been had he not shown up. 'Thanks, I guess. I don't know what I'd have done if . . .'

'You're welcome,' he replied humbly. 'Just glad the timing worked out.'

A pause.

'So what exactly *is* your repertoire?' The words had bite, but she couldn't help it.

'I'm an information guy. Intelligence. Glorified desk jockey. I interrogate witnesses and suspects . . . that sort of thing.'

'Sounds like you're a paid conversationalist.'

'Or a bullshit detector.' He smiled.

She tried to suppress a laugh, but failed. The adrenaline buzz was abating and her muscles were starting to go limp again. 'God, that was scary.'

'Amen, sister. That was wicked crazy back there.'

With Agent Flaherty's defences down, she noticed a much more pronounced Boston accent. Running her fingers through her wet hair, she blew out a long breath. 'So now what? Are you supposed to protect me or something?'

'I'll have to see what the manual says . . .'

'There's a manual?' she scoffed.

He shook his head and grinned.

She groaned in frustration.

'Our local office is next to the Federal Building downtown, near Faneuil Hall. We'll head there, figure out what to do.'

Brooke crossed her arms tight over her chest and stared out the frosty window.

'Look. Here's the deal. A colleague asked me to find you. He's a deep-cover operative in Iraq. He's the one who found your ID badge. I know that if he suspected you were in danger, he'd have told me.'

'How do I know he didn't call that guy too?'

'Not a chance,' he said.

'Well, someone wants me dead. And the timing can't be a coincidence. It's got to be someone in the military, right?' she insisted.

Flaherty said nothing, because on that point, he'd have to concur. It had him wondering who else besides Jason could possibly have known about Brooke's involvement in Iraq *and* could also be capable of coordinating a kill order so quickly. Why now – *right* now – had she suddenly become a threat?

'I remember reading the small print in my confidentiality agreement. I don't recall any mention of assassination as a means of recourse—'

'We need to find this Frank guy you were talking about. I need that e-mail address. I can run its profile, the host server . . . find his IP address and trace him.' Flaherty dipped into his pocket, pulled out his BlackBerry. He keyed in his security code, tapped on the web browser and held it out for her. 'You said his address was on your computer, right?'

Staring at the device with narrow, incredulous eyes, she asked, 'Why didn't you just give this to me earlier if you needed his e-mail address?'

'Basic psychology. I ask you for information, and your future response, your compliance or lack thereof, indicates your propensity to cooperate.'

'Or maybe you just wanted to give me your card so I'd call you. I have a bullshit detector too.' She took the BlackBerry and began finger-pecking the URL for Yahoo!.

He smiled. 'You always so shy?' But he saw that she'd suddenly become preoccupied with the BlackBerry.

'Huh. That's weird.'

'What?'

She tried logging into her e-mail account again. 'Says my username and password are invalid. Like my account is gone. That's impossible.'

Flaherty sighed. 'No, actually it's not.'

'What do you mean?'

He nodded. 'NSA. That's my guess.' He knew that telling her this wasn't smart, but he'd done it anyway.

'But they can't do that! I mean, *who* can do that?' she protested. She felt violated.

'Thirty thousand computer scientists and cryptographers under one roof in Fort Meade, dedicated to cracking data and voice communications can do just about anything when they have your number. Remember those geeks in high school, the computer hackers, videogame junkies, Dungeons and Dragons types? Imagine a building – a city – full of 'em.'

'God,' she groaned. 'I like videogames too,' she confessed. 'But I'm not snooping around people's private information.'

'You've got to have something else from this guy, right? A business card, a paycheque . . .?'

She shook her head. 'No card. And the money was wire-transferred to my account.' Then she thought back to eavesdropping on the archaeologist who'd performed the carbon studies. 'Wait. There was this archaeologist who was at the cave when I was there. He was outside the cave, making a cell phone call. Something about test results on samples he'd sent out. I overheard him mention an AMS lab where he'd sent samples for testing.'

'AMS lab?'

'Accelerator Mass Spectrometer. The machine used for carbon-dating studies.'

'Remember the name of the place?'

She tried to recall, but couldn't. 'No. Damn.' Then she remembered something else. 'But there were other tests results he'd mentioned. Biological cultures or something. He was reading from a report that had an official seal on its cover. Some kind of insignia, I think. But it was weird, because I remember it had a symbol representing a DNA helix, or chromosomes. And it had a long acronym that began with USA . . .'

Flaherty tightened up, fearing he knew what she meant. 'Did the insignia have a five-pointed star to the right of the helix and a circular symbol beneath it?' He tried tracing the layout in the air with his index finger to help her picture it.

She fished her memory. 'Not sure.'

He checked the mirror to ensure no one was shadowing him then pointed with his chin at the BlackBerry and said, 'Type in this web address.' He had to repeat the tricky URL three times before she got it right.

Once Brooke brought up the home page, she immediately recognized the insignia. 'Yeah, that's it! That's the insignia!' She held the BlackBerry out for him and pointed to it on the mini LCD screen.

For Flaherty, this was anything but good news. 'Great,' he grumbled.

There was a long acronym beside the insignia: USAMRIID. 'I remember the two "I's" in the name too,' she said. 'Reminded me of Roman numerals. Says here "United States Army Medical Research Institute for Infectious Diseases".'

'Exactly,' Flaherty said. He let out another sigh. This assignment was fast snowballing into something much bigger. 'Among other things, that's America's bio-weapons division.'

25
IRAQ

'What do you mean she got away?' Crawford snapped through the sat-com's microphone in a loud whisper. He practically bit the filter off the Marlboro that dangled between his lips.

'There was someone else there already. A detective, I think,' the caller replied.

'*So?*' He circled around the MRAP to avoid be overheard by the marines milling around the camp.

'I had her pinned down. Was moving in to finish her. The guy came out of nowhere. Took me down with his car, started shooting. He managed to take her away.'

The inept assassin's recap of what had transpired at the museum pushed Crawford's rage to the boiling point. 'Isn't that Jim-fucking-dandy,' Crawford spat. 'You listen to me, you incompetent scumbag . . . You find her, you kill her. Or I'll have your head, you hear me?'

'I'm already tracking them. I'll take care of it.'

'You better be calling me real soon with good news.' He terminated the call. He pulled a long drag on the cigarette, then flicked it at a scorpion scurrying through the sand. Deliberating on how to inform Stokes about the mishap, he finally settled on sending a text message – short and sweet. The he shut the phone and slid it into the pocket of his flak jacket.

Who was this detective that beat them to the archaeologist? Only someone on the inside could have sent him. Maybe Stokes had something up his sleeve. Seemed unlikely, because, even though Stokes wasn't exactly the lucid soldier he'd known for so many years on the battlefield, he was no idiot. In fact, Stokes seemed hell-bent on covering his tracks, as evidenced by the way he'd commenced countermeasures the moment the cave was infiltrated by the militants. Considering the fact that the woman's ID badge had been sitting next to Yaeger's computer left little doubt as to the true culprit.

Crawford bounded over to the command tent where Sergeant Jason Yaeger and his linebacker-sized tech were helping the marines prepare the recon robot. They were loading gas canisters into the rotary magazine of what resembled an oversized tommy gun mounted on the robot. Crawford stood back a minute, reined in his fury, and considered how to approach Yaeger. Unfortunately, this clever kid was no automaton – wouldn't be doing this kind of work if he was. Any guy who passed the psych profile to go deep cover wouldn't be the type to back down or conform to protocol. If Yaeger had an agenda, he certainly wasn't going to divulge it. Autonomy was poisonous, thought Crawford. Especially on the battlefield.

'Yaeger,' Crawford finally called out.

The mercenary looked up. 'Yeah.'

'Need a moment with you, son.'

Jason handed the last gas canister to Meat, then went over to the colonel.

'Walk with me,' Crawford said, pacing away from the tent.

Jason kept step beside him.

'I need to know if you've spoken to anyone about what's happening here.'

Jason's response was forthright: 'You, air command . . .'

'Don't be coy with me, Sergeant,' Crawford warned. He needed to be direct, without raising undue suspicion. 'Someone on the *outside*. Did you communicate with non-military, civilians perhaps?'

Jason was a master of reading between the lines. Best to answer him with a question. 'Why would I do that?' He could tell Crawford was unsure how to push the issue.

Crawford turned and tried to decipher Yaeger's gaze, but read nothing. 'Until we confirm exactly who's holed up in that cave, I want all communication running through me. I know you want this guy in there to be Al-Zahrani. But until we're absolutely certain, this operation has to be airtight. Let me have your sat-com.' He held out his hand.

Jason merely stared at the hand. 'You know I can't do that, Colonel.' He waited for the hand to go down, then looked deep into Crawford's hard eyes. 'No one is more sensitive to secrecy than me. Same with my men. We *survive* on trust. From what I see, none of your boys have surrendered equipment and it's far more probable that a leak or mole might exist in your platoon. Don't make me remind you that I'm accountable to a different authority. So if you have a concern, best for you to voice it. I don't like playing games. Especially not when the stakes are so high.'

Jason knew he struck a chord, because Crawford's jaw was jutting out again.

Folding his arms tight across his chest, Crawford shook his head like a disappointed parent. 'Yeah, the stakes *are* high. Ten million high for you, isn't that right? Free agents like you don't get it, Yaeger,' he said with venom. 'True soldiers aren't motivated by a 401(k) plan and bonuses. And don't cry to me about your story, 'cause I've already heard it: how your brother died in the Towers and, instead of grieving, you dropped out of Dartmouth and did your time with the marines. This little vendetta of yours' – he twirled a finger up and down at Yaeger's outfit – 'seems too personal. One might say it compromises your objectivity.'

Jason kept his cool, and his distance. 'Since you've done your homework, you should know that my psych examination suggests otherwise,' he replied levelly. 'My profile shows that I approach my work quite clearly and without bias. Don't forget that I have people too. And I'm starting to feel that I need to check *your* background.' He saw Crawford's jaw extend to the max. 'I called for backup. I didn't call for a dick-measuring contest. Unless you'd like for me to file a formal complaint with the brigadier general, I suggest you start helping me. Stop talking to me like I'm your bitch.'

Crawford let out an exasperated sigh, flashed a sardonic grin. 'Until we know what and whom we're dealing with up there' – but Stokes had already provided concise details – 'I'd appreciate it if you could not stir the hornets' nest, is all I'm saying.'

While staring into the colonel's shifty eyes, Jason counted to five to decompress. 'The bot's prepped and ready,' he replied calmly. 'I've got work to do.' He didn't wait to be dismissed – just sidestepped Crawford and strode to the tent.

26

LAS VEGAS

Randall Stokes stared at the computer screen wondering when Frank Roselli's elusive e-mail would make an appearance in his inbox.

'If you have something to say, Frank, let's get on with it,' he said to no one.

This morning's clean-up had Stokes's lower left eyelid twitching and his neck muscles quaking in spasm – his body's most recurrent stress valves. Even the skin on his hands was breaking out in an itchy rash. No doubt that was due to the message that *had* turned up in his inbox: Crawford's blunt update concerning the botched kill order on the Boston mark. Normally, this wouldn't overly concern Stokes. Except this time the mysterious white knight who'd thwarted the assassin had been overheard asking the mark probing questions about Iraq. That the guy had a gun and managed to escape with the mark posed some serious questions concerning his motive and his employer.

Three kill confirmations had already arrived: an archaeologist in Geneva, a biocontainment engineer in Munich, a micro-biologist in Moscow. No complications or interference. No interloper. Therefore, the archaeologist was an isolated problem that, in all probability, linked directly to the ID card the deep-cover unit found near the cave. That would soon be remedied too. But for now, Stokes mothballed his concerns.

Turning his attention back to the business at hand, Stokes brought up a new window and entered three pass keys in the software's prompt boxes. A chequerboard of live video feeds came on line, each shot glowing in eerie green monochrome. In all, sixteen closed-circuit cameras equipped with audio and infrared transmitted interior shots of the labyrinth via an encrypted digital signal bouncing through military satellites.

Fourteen cameras showed no movement – only still shots of winding passageways walled by jagged rock glowing in emerald night vision. The scene on the cameras numbered '01-E' and '11-G', however, were far from static.

Stokes double-clicked the grid box for '11-G' and the video window enlarged on the screen. The live shot showed the five heavily armed Arabs funnelling single file through the tunnel, moving deeper into the mountain, still frantically searching for an alternative exit.

No such luck.

No one knew better than Stokes that the cave had only one accessible opening. Precisely the reason the ancient Mesopotamians and Stokes himself had chosen the site. After all, the lair's primary purpose was to contain evil, both then and now.

'Sorry, boys. One way in, one way out.'

The lead man had enabled the flashlight tool on his cell phone – the device's only useful feature so deep beneath the earth – and was holding it out to illuminate the ominous path that lay ahead. The fellow looked extremely distressed, and rightfully so, thought Stokes. What could possibly be going through his mind right now? Could he know that he was a caged animal being led to the slaughter?

Stokes grinned widely. 'Hello, gentlemen. Welcome to Armageddon. So glad you could make it. Those weapons aren't going to help you now. Nothing can help you now.' He put both elbows on the desk and cradled his chin on folded hands, beaming.

When the tall man in the middle came close to the camera, Stokes paused the feed and minutely studied the infamous, iconic face. How Crawford could plant reason for doubt was impressive. Fahim Al-Zahrani. The odds were incredible, on the outer fringe of impossible. Yet the picture didn't lie. The Lord had brought the Dark Prince into the lion's den for ultimate judgement. How poetic, thought Stokes.

Stokes estimated that it wouldn't be long until they reached the main chamber.

He switched the camera back to the entry tunnel. Though it was nearly eleven a.m. in Las Vegas, nightfall had already descended over Iraq's northern mountains. It wasn't sunlight that now filled the passage – it was floodlights. And at the opening, he could just make out two marine snipers lying prostrate on the incline. Crawford had indicated that a SUG-V would soon be sent into the tunnels.

Then just outside the window, Stokes heard a pecking sound. He turned to see a white dove perched outside his window. An untrained observer would easily consider this a miracle since doves weren't native to the Mojave Desert. However, it wasn't uncommon for local hotels to release flights of doves during wedding ceremonies. But surely this lone messenger had been sent for Stokes.

135

He has given me a sign that the time has come. 'Thank you, Lord. I am your servant. I am your avenger.' With renewed vigour, he turned back to the computer and input the encryption keys that brought up the Remote Systems Interface. Using this simple command module, Stokes could manage virtually the critical systems installed in the cave's deepest, most protected chamber. He stared at the main panel where seven indicator icons blinked 'SEALED'. He moved the mouse pointer over the first icon and let his index finger hover over the mouse button.

'Is it time, Lord? Give me a sign.'

The sign he received was not what he expected: a new message alert chimed over the computer speakers. His heartbeat quickened.

Stokes immediately switched program windows to check his e-mail inbox. An absurd thought came to him: might God be so bold as to communicate through e-mail?

But the message was not from Heaven. It was from Iraq. Crawford's simple message read: 'NEED MORE TIME.'

Disappointed, Stokes clamped his jaw tight.

When he turned to the window, the dove was no longer there. The rash on his hands suddenly flared and he scratched at it incessantly with a letter opener, with little relief. Then he dipped into his pocket for his pillbox.

27

BOSTON

Studying the USAMRIID insignia on the BlackBerry's display, Brooke positively recognized the three icons central to its design: a chromosome helix, a Petri culture dish and a five-pointed star. Such a unique image was easy to remember, and she was certain that this was the exact insignia embossed on the scientist's report cover. 'I don't understand. How could the Infectious Disease guys have anything to do with the cave?'

Flaherty shook his head. 'We've had bioweapons teams in Iraq since we first stepped foot there. Remember, Iraq supposedly had a huge cache of WMDs?'

She vividly remembered the Department of Defense's elaborate slideshow on national television that included ominous, yet hazy, satellite images of Iraqi weapons facilities ready to churn out biological agents. In the context of it all, the mission statement listed on USAMRIID's website made perfect sense: 'To conduct basic and applied research on biological threats resulting in medical solutions to protect the warfighter.'

'Maybe they found something in the cave, like a chemical weapons stash,' he guessed.

'I don't remember anything like that.' She keyed the agency name into *Wikipedia* and scrolled the entry. 'Says here the agency began in the fifties at Fort Detrick, Maryland . . . biomedical defence . . . opened a state-of-the-art biocontainment facility in 1971 . . .'

'The Crozier Building. That's where they test and stockpile weaponized Ebola, anthrax and smallpox, among other things. You know, Cold War goodies.'

'Nice.' She kept reading. 'What's a BSL facility?'

'Biosafety containment lab. I toured a BSL-4 mobile unit at one of our security conventions. Picture a tractor trailer with a state-of-the-art safe lab, a built-in airlock and Hazmat gear. I remember the guide saying they used them during the Gulf War.' He considered this for a moment, then said, 'Hey, any chance you saw something like that at the cave? Any guys wearing bio-suits?'

It didn't take much thought before she replied, 'No.'

The more Brooke read, the more the military's biodefence division sounded like a biological bakery that specialized in the most unsavoury recipes. She wasn't sure whether to praise or fear its existence. 'Who runs this place?'

He pronounced the acronym USAMRIID phonetically: 'You-sam-rid. It answers to the US Army Medical Research and Materiel Command. An army colonel oversees the operation.'

'Not a scientist?'

'Nope.'

'Isn't that a conflict of interest?'

He chuckled. 'Most would argue that bioweapons are a matter of national security. But you go ahead and write your senator, Brooke.'

'So why would an archaeologist have been talking to these people?'

'Probably wasn't an archaeologist, is my guess.'

'Wait. If samples had been sent to this agency for testing, there'd be a record of it, right?'

'Maybe.'

'Can you call one of your people to check it out . . . to see if tests were performed on samples from Iraq during that time? Maybe we can figure out who ordered them and why.'

'That's a good idea,' he said. 'But first, I need to call my guy in Iraq . . . let him know what happened back at the museum.'

In the side mirror, Flaherty eyed the illuminated headlights of a Ford Explorer that had turned in behind him three blocks earlier. The SUV trailed at a comfortable distance, occasionally falling back two or three car lengths. Nothing to worry about . . . yet.

Flaherty pulled out his sat-com and put a call out to Jason.

28

'Hey, Jason,' Flaherty said loudly into the sat-com's microphone. The dense storm clouds over Boston made the satellite signal sputter like crazy. 'It's Tommy. Can you hear me?'

'Yeah. What's up, Southie. You're a bit choppy . . . but . . . hang on a sec . . .'

Flaherty heard crinkling static and squawking, as if Jason had stuck the phone in his pocket. In the slow lane, he continued cruising steadily along Huntington Avenue towards downtown. The snow had slowed to a sprinkle, but the roads were coated in briny slush, bringing traffic to a crawl.

A few seconds went by before Jason came back on the line.

'Sorry, buddy. Have to be super careful with these calls. I've got a real ball buster commanding the marine platoon that came to back us up. Doesn't want me talking to anyone. Gotta keep everything on the down low.'

'Understood.'

'What do you have for me?'

'Found your scientist in Boston.'

'She as cute as her picture?' Jason asked.

Having overheard the comment, Brooke looked expectantly at Flaherty with raised eyebrows.

'Eh,' Flaherty said in a minimalist tone.

She hit him in the arm and he smiled to let her know he was teasing.

'Actually, she's in the car with me,' he explained.

'Oh,' Jason said in a confused tone. 'Okay . . .'

'So let me put you on speaker. That work for you?'

'Sure.'

Once the introductions were over with, Flaherty said, 'Like I said in my text message, Brooke was there in 2003. Part of an excavation team that studied that cave you uncovered. She deciphered an ancient language . . . some writings found on a wall.'

'There were also picture engravings,' Brooke added.

'I've seen the writing,' Jason confirmed. 'The pictures, too . . . carved into the left wall of the entry tunnel.'

'That's them,' she said. 'Beautiful, aren't they?'

'Um. What does it all mean?'

'It's a bit complicated. But it's the earliest recorded specimen of ancient Mesopotamian mythology . . . a story about a woman who came from another land.' At this point, having almost been murdered, she was comfortable with throwing her confidentiality agreement to the wind.

'The woman who was decapitated?' Jason asked.

'That's the one.'

'Why did they kill her?' Jason asked.

'The story implies that many people died shortly after her arrival. Similar to a colonial witch hunt, I suppose,' Brooke guessed. 'She was different, came from a faraway place. They didn't understand her.'

'And they blamed her for the deaths,' Jason said.

'Absolutely.'

There was another pause, and Brooke knew that Jason was trying to understand the military's interest in this archaeological discovery. He was incredibly intuitive in sifting for the devil in the details.

'What was her name?'

'Actually, it wasn't specified in the writings I studied.' Evil didn't really need a name, she thought.

Flaherty jumped in, anxious to get to the juicy facts. 'Hey, Jason, you're not going to believe who brought Brooke and the other scientists over there, all expenses paid . . .'

Brooke gave him a thumbs-up.

Flaherty recapped Brooke's story. He explained her role in the excavation sponsored by none other than the US military – the tight security protocols; the mysterious facilitator known only as 'Frank'. Jason had plenty of probing questions, most of which Flaherty fielded, with Brooke occasionally chiming in for clarification. Jason focused mostly on Brooke's recollection of the cave's layout.

'Brooke, you only saw the first leg of the tunnel?' Jason clarified.

'That's right.'

Flaherty felt a tug on his sleeve. When he looked over, Brooke held up the BlackBerry and tapped on the USAMRIID logo. Then she pointed to the phone and mouthed, 'Tell him.'

'I'm afraid it gets even stranger,' Flaherty warned. 'It wasn't just the military that watched over the excavation. Seems the guys at USAMRIID were involved too.'

'What? You mean the biochem guys?'

'Yeah.'

A pause.

'Any idea what the connection might be?' Jason finally asked.

'No,' Brooke said. 'Sorry.'

'Brooke didn't see anyone suited up in Hazmat gear,' Flaherty added. 'So I don't think there is any hazardous material in there.'

'All right,' Jason said. 'We're prepping a recon bot to send into the cave. I've got enough surprises to worry about.'

Flaherty wanted to ask Jason if the quarry was still trapped in the cave, but ruled against it. Jason sending a bot into the cave did, after all, provide indirect confirmation that the hunt was still under way. 'I'm afraid there's something else. Something you should definitely be concerned about.'

'Great,' he said. 'Hit me.'

'Right after I spoke to Brooke, some guy with a gun came after her. Tried to kill her.'

'Christ,' he groaned in frustration.

'Yeah, we barely got out of there alive,' Flaherty said. He painted a quick picture of the incident that took place outside the museum.

'That's too much of a coincidence for my taste,' Jason said.

'Not sure who the gunman was . . . or who might have sent him,' Flaherty said. 'But Brooke offered a good suggestion. Seems USAMRIID sent out some samples for processing. If our guys can dig through USAMRIID's records, we might find out what they were studying . . . and who ordered the tests.'

'Smart thinking. Look, Tommy, you two need to keep safe until we figure out what's going on here.'

'I know. I'm taking Brooke to the office now,' Flaherty said. 'You watch over your shoulder too.'

'Will do,' Jason said. 'You're in good hands, Brooke. Nice talking with you.'

'Thanks,' she said.

'Gotta go,' Jason said. 'I'll be in touch shortly.'

The line went dead.

Flaherty pocketed the phone.

'Sounds like a clever fellow,' Brooke said.

'If only you knew,' Flaherty said. In the rearview mirror, the angular headlights swooped in from behind – the vehicle a mere shadow through the rear window's crackled glass. Checking the side mirror, he saw a Hyundai sedan was putt-putting along in the fast lane, about three car lengths back. Then the vehicle tailing him made another abrupt manoeuvre and eclipsed the Hyundai. The silver Ford Explorer had returned, and for the first time, Flaherty glimpsed the driver's silhouette. When he finally discerned the driver's narrow face and big ears, his heart jumped into his throat.

29

'Red light!' Brooke yelled, throwing both hands on to the dashboard. Instead of slowing, Agent Flaherty stomped on the accelerator and blew through the intersection. He nearly clipped a green and white taxi that was cutting along Belvidere Street. The taxi slid to a stop in the busy crosswalk outside Prudential Center's south exit.

'Just hold tight,' he said. In the mirror, he saw the Ford Explorer weave erratically around the taxi and shoot forward in pursuit.

'Are you crazy! What are you—!'

'That's him in the Explorer . . . behind us.'

She turned to get a look. 'Oh my God. . .' she gasped. 'Does this thing have airbags?' she nervously asked, staying low in the seat.

He didn't reply, and focused on the traffic up ahead. A meandering canary-yellow duck boat chugged along the centre lane, splitting between a bus in the slow lane and a car easing to queue for a left turn where signboards pointed to Prudential Center's underground parking lot.

Flaherty's anxiety spiked. 'Come on . . . *come on!*' he yelled at the half boat, half truck.

'You can't stop!'

'I know . . .'

He considered an evasive U-turn along the wide avenue, but the traffic coming in the opposite direction was too thick and allowed no adequate opening.

Any hope of making a right on to Garrison was instantly dashed as the bus eased to a stop with its right blinker on, waiting for pedestrians to cross the side street. The Chrysler Concorde's front bumper practically kissed the duck boat's rear as Flaherty angled around the bus. The rowdy tourists on board the modified WWII amphibious troop carrier began quacking loudly, just like they'd been told by the driver at the tour's inception. Having been cheated of a full tour, thanks to the frozen Charles River, their pent-up energy was now fully directed at Flaherty's Concorde. Under better circumstances, Flaherty might have thought the scene comical.

An aggressively driven taxi slipped in behind him, one step ahead of the Explorer. Flaherty expected the Explorer to move in behind the taxi, but it didn't. His eyes darted back to the road. The next opportunity to make a turn would come on Harcourt Street, just ahead on the right. However, he could see that that walkway was also clogged with pedestrians.

'Shit,' he growled. Staying the course towards the bottleneck at Copley Square was a losing proposition.

'Look out!' Brooke yelled, pointing out his side window.

Flaherty turned just as the Explorer swerved into the centre lane and forced the duck boat to fall back with a dissenting blow of its air horn. The Explorer's passenger window was already down and Flaherty glimpsed the assassin steadying the gun for a clear shot.

'Down!' Flaherty yelled. He ducked low and jammed on the accelerator just as the assassin fired a triple shot. The rounds blew Flaherty's window into a thousand pieces. Luckily, Brooke had already squirmed down on to the floor, because the slugs that would have cut through her neck instead pounded through the door handle on the passenger-side door.

Flaherty popped up again.

The assassin nearly slammed into a bus that stopped abruptly in the centre lane, but made a hard turn that put the Explorer directly behind the Concorde, in the same spot the alarmed taxi driver had abandoned a split second earlier.

As Flaherty was about to pass under the enclosed pedestrian bridge that connected Prudential Center to the Copley Place shopping mall he saw nothing but taillights flashing red all the way to the split for Stuart Street. Worse yet, the bus had boxed him in on the left. Even steering up on to the crowded sidewalk and mowing a path through pedestrians would only get him so far.

If the assassin did manage to push him into the gridlock, things would get very ugly very fast. That left only one possibility – to outrun the Explorer; the worst possible scenario.

'Here we go,' he grimly warned Brooke.

Crouched low, Brooke saw the narrow pedestrian bridge sweep overhead, just before Flaherty cut a hard right that threw her up against his legs hard enough to make her see stars.

The Concorde careened through a line of garbage-can-sized orange construction barricades, giving the Explorer the split second needed to close the gap. The assassin drove full speed into the Concorde's rear, shattering plastic and snarling metal. The trajectory of the impact nearly sent the Explorer into a spin, but did little to stymie the Concorde's forward advance.

The assassin righted the wheel and got the Explorer back on track.

The roadway fed into a wide tunnel with tiled walls and began a sharp descent beneath Copley Place. The Concorde's tyres squealed as Flaherty steered into the bend.

Brooke was disoriented by what little she could see: ceiling tiles and lights. 'You turned into a garage? What—?'

'Not a garage. I'm taking a shortcut to the Mass Pike.'

'Shortcut?' That's when she realized what he meant. 'You're going down into the tunnel?'

He nodded.

She'd driven this ramp many times – a main exit for Interstate 90, which the ambitious Big Dig had diverted through massive tunnels snaked deep below the city centre. Problem being that she knew the traffic flow only went *up*. 'This tunnel is a one-way exit! You're going the wrong—'

'I know! I know . . .' He checked the mirror and could see the Explorer's headlights skimming the curved wall behind him. 'The ramp's closed for construction. It's okay.'

But up ahead, where the ramp merged at a Y, he spotted a contradiction to what he'd just told her – a hulking utility truck mounted with bright lights and workers in hardhats repairing tiles in the tunnel ceiling.

Not okay, he thought.

The truck was at a standstill in the centre of the roadway with barely any room to spare to its right. But there was no stopping now, thought Flaherty.

He punched the accelerator and leaned on the horn.

Seeing the headlights racing towards them, the befuddled workmen barely had time to react. They hit the deck and grabbed hold of the safety rail that looped around the truck's platform, fully anticipating a violent collision. One brave worker vaulted the rail and dropped clumsily to the roadway before scurrying out of view.

Flaherty gripped the wheel at ten to two, pulled slightly to the right to aim for the narrow opening. He winced on the approach and clenched his teeth.

The wide-bodied Concorde slipped cleanly through the gap with inches to spare on either side. But not fifteen metres ahead, a second truck blocked his lane. Flaherty corrected the wheel hard to the left and slalomed around the truck, so close that the passenger-side rearview mirror sheared off with a loud clack.

His heart was in overdrive and adrenaline had all his senses buzzing. And knowing that the most dangerous leg of this obstacle course still lay ahead only added to his anxiety.

In his remaining side mirror he saw the Explorer bob and weave to avoid the second truck. But the assassin's slight miscalculation ground the Explorer's metal side panels along the tunnel wall with a showering plume of orange sparks. It cost the assassin precious seconds, but he quickly resumed the chase.

'Son of a bitch. Can't shake him,' Flaherty grumbled.

He focused again on the tunnel, which now began arcing downward like the curl of a question mark. He braked lightly along the sharp bend that gradually semicircled until yielding to a long and empty straightaway. He hit the gas hard again and the surreal sensation of rocketing through the tunnel's tight confines made him feel like a bullet being shot through the barrel of a gun – the lights whipping by.

Knowing the worst was yet to come, he clamped his hands tighter around the wheel.

The straightaway angled slightly and Flaherty spotted construction barriers topped with flashing amber lights shaped like lollipops. Immediately beyond the cordon, the ramp tunnel yawned open where it joined the wide interstate tunnel at an extremely tight Y. However, with Flaherty coming the wrong way down the ramp the turn would be treacherous. He could see the headlights of vehicles zipping through the tunnel at highway speed, as well as the formidable cement barricades that lined the tunnel median.

He drew breath, held it, stomped on the brake pedal. The car bowled through the barriers, flinging them up and out. He pulled the wheel all the way to the right and the car commenced a runaway spin into the oncoming traffic.

The next second was a blur of screeching tyres and blaring horns.

The Concorde dragged heavily across the roadway, managed to avoid hitting a sedan cruising along the slow lane, but careened sideways into a yellow moving truck that was speeding in the fast lane. Flaherty felt the Concorde's front end crumple and snap. The collision was bone crunching, but prevented the Concorde from striking the cement median, even managed to pull the car straight with forward momentum. Disbelieving that he was still alive and that the truck's driver had enough where-withal to not lose control, Flaherty immediately hit the accelerator and cranked at the wheel to tug free from the truck. The manoeuvre blew out the truck's front tyre, forcing it to roll to a stop.

'Sorry, buddy,' Flaherty muttered.

Flaherty's heart nearly gave out when he heard a bellowing air horn that could only belong to a very large truck. All his muscles went tight as his eyes snapped to his side mirror. He saw the Explorer cut blindly into the roadway – a grave miscalculation that put the assassin directly into the path of a hulking semi. The big-rig locked its brakes . . . the cab jostling madly from side to side . . . the tractor swinging wide with its locked tyres churning grey smoke.

But still the Explorer couldn't accelerate fast enough to skirt the semi, which struck with brute force. The Explorer seemed to explode into a thousand pieces – glass and metal shooting out in all directions.

Flaherty barely glimpsed the assassin's body as it was cata-pulted out through the Explorer's windshield, over the median, and into the windshield of another big eighteen-wheeler bar-relling through the Pike's westbound tube.

In the side mirror, he stole a final glimpse of the jackknifed tractor trailer and the mangled Explorer. Then he sped off through the tunnel.

30

IRAQ

The Blackhawk bounced to a rest in a grassy field just beyond the perimeter of the encampment. Hazo gazed out the fuselage window to the jagged cliff face. Surprisingly, during the three hours he'd been away, the debris that blocked the cave had been thoroughly cleared and muted light glowed within the passage. Mammoth boulders strewn at the base of the cliff had raked deep lines into the hillside.

There was a lot of activity at the site – marines moving up and down the slope, snipers posted along a tight perimeter. He spotted Jason to the side of the opening, consulting a trio of techs huddled around a small tactical robot. They were preparing to infiltrate the cave, he surmised. Not just any cave, though, Hazo reminded himself. Lilith's tomb.

The photo of Michelangelo's ceiling fresco scrolled through his mind's eye again – the half serpent, half woman entwined around Eden's forbidden tree. He still grappled with the notion that the opening page of the Bible loosely chronicled an ancient story linked to this very place.

Not one to succumb to superstition, Hazo felt vulnerable to

sudden dread. What if the enigmatic Lilith *did* exist long before written history? What if she *had* been some demoness who'd brought mass death to this place? Could her spiteful spirit still haunt this cave?

They are only legends, he reminded himself.

A marine crab-walked beneath the chopper's slowing blades and slid open Hazo's door. Hazo pulled off his flight helmet, unbuckled himself, and hopped out. By the time he was clear of the rotorwash, Jason had come down the slope to meet him.

'Glad you're back,' Jason said.

Before Jason said anything else, he hooked Hazo by the arm and led him past a dozen marines gathered nearby in a loose circle.

In passing, Hazo curiously observed the marines. Some sat cross-legged, dutifully cleaning their weapons. Other sat on their helmets scooping rehydrated ravioli rations from foil packs. Four of the unit members were women, though he could tell they took great pains in downplaying their femininity when consorting with the men. A short male marine with close-set eyes – who looked more boy than man – seemed to be recounting an epic bar brawl.

'After you left, Crawford sent them over the mountain,' Jason told him, motioning to the group. 'They came back just after sundown. Didn't find anything.' Once he had led Hazo safely out of earshot, he asked, 'How did you make out?' Glancing back to the command tent, he saw Crawford standing stiffly with arms crossed, leering over at him.

'I discovered many things. Many disturbing things,' Hazo clarified. 'As I told you earlier, my cousin recognized the woman whose picture was on the ID badge.' He expounded on the information he'd given Jason shortly after his meeting with Karsaz –

the woman's presence in 2003 and her apparent close association with US military personnel.

'Not long after you left, my guy in the States found this woman. Had a talk with her. It all agrees with what your cousin told you.'

'Oh,' Hazo said, somewhat disappointed.

'How about your visit to the monastery? Were the monks able to help you with the pictures from the cave?'

'Oh yes,' Hazo said. 'Very much so.' He told Jason about the shocking conversation he'd had with Monsignor Ibrahim – the incredible story of Creation and a wicked woman named Lilith. 'Jason, the monsignor told me that this place . . . this cave . . . The legends say that it is Lilith's tomb.'

'Tomb?' Brooke Thompson hadn't mentioned this.

'That is right. These monks . . . they are very smart men. They know many secrets, many hidden truths.' He gazed warily at the cave opening. 'The monsignor told me that she is buried beneath the mountain. The head . . . the body,' he said in a whisper. 'This place is evil, Jason. Cursed.'

Hazo looked genuinely spooked and Jason had to struggle not to smirk. 'Buddy, don't let the monk's stories scare you,' he said, cupping a hand on the Kurd's shoulder. 'Last I checked, ancient tombs don't have steel security doors. And the only evil inside that mountain is still alive and kicking and armed with a rocket launcher. All right?'

Hazo nodded.

'You did great,' Jason said, giving him a gracious pat on the shoulder. 'But right now, we've got a much bigger problem to deal with.' But he could tell by Hazo's downcast expression that he didn't agree.

'I understand,' Hazo said. 'The terrorists—'

'Not just the terrorists, I'm afraid,' Jason corrected. 'I'm more concerned about this guy Crawford. He hasn't said one word about the military having been in that cave.'

'But *would* he know about it?' Hazo said.

'I'm thinking yes, he does. And I'll tell you why.' He detailed the call he'd received from Thomas Flaherty – the thwarted assassination attempt on Brooke Thompson.

Hazo was deeply disturbed by this new information. 'Crawford sent an assassin to find her?'

'The timing is too convenient for me to think otherwise.' He glanced back to the command tent. Now Crawford had his back to them, talking furtively into his satellite phone again. 'And he's been on that phone an awful lot. I'd love to know who's bending his ear.' Jason shook his head. 'We've got to tread very lightly . . . watch our backs on this one. Whatever's going on here, I don't want our men being dragged into it.' He saw Hazo's preoccupied gaze slink back up to the cave.

Suddenly something caught Jason's eye too – a dark form sweeping in and out of the moonlight high up near the mountain's crest. Keeping his head still, he honed his gaze on the spot. He detected more subversive shifting along the ridge. A watcher was skulking in the darkness. 'We've got company.'

Hazo's eyes shifted up to the mountaintop and panned slowly back and forth. He squinted when he thought he'd found the nearly indiscernible anomaly. 'Yes. I see him.'

'I don't like this one bit,' Jason said. 'Let's walk over here.' With Hazo keeping pace beside him, Jason headed for the terrorists' four abandoned pickup trucks, which the marines had parked in a neat row beside the road. When they'd reached the vehicles, Jason looked back to make sure no one was watching.

He reached into his pants pocket and pulled out a long, tubular object.

'I am sorry. I do not smoke,' Hazo meekly replied.

Jason chuckled. 'It's not a cigar, Hazo. It's a paint pen . . . a marker. Compliments of Israeli Intelligence.' He uncapped it and began drawing a circle on the hood of the first Toyota.

Not seeing any ink coming out from the marker's tip, Hazo was confused. 'I don't understand. It doesn't do anything. I don't see anything.'

'Exactly. That's the point. The ink is invisible to the naked eye,' Jason explained. 'But not to military satellites.'

'Ah,' Hazo said. 'Very clever.'

'Makes it very easy to track vehicle movements from the sky.' He casually moved to the next pickup and scrawled an invisible star on its hood. 'I've already got the serial numbers for all the military vehicles in Crawford's platoon. Those can be tracked in-house by our agency using GPS, no problem. If, however, one of these trucks goes missing, they fall off the grid. Unless they're marked.' Another glance to the camp, and Jason stepped up to the third pickup. This time, he traced out a square. On the hood of the fourth pickup, he drew an invisible triangle. Capping the marker, he slipped it back inside his pocket. Then he pointed to each pickup in turn, saying, 'Circle . . . star . . . square . . . triangle.' He committed each pickup to memory – paint, model, distinguishing marks (like the blown-out windshield and blood-smeared cab of the pickup that had been the convoy's lead vehicle).

'Very good,' Hazo said, impressed.

'And since we're on the topic of satellites . . .' Jason pulled out his binoculars, activated the infrared, and discreetly spied Crawford's position in the tent. The colonel was still on his call, pacing in small circles. 'Who *are* you talking to, Crawford?' Jason muttered to himself. He used the laser to calculate Crawford's GPS grid. Then he flipped open his sat-com and put out a call of his own – one which Crawford certainly would not approve.

31

'Mack, it's Yaeger. I need a big favour,' Jason said. Thanks to the cloudless Iraqi sky, the sat-com's reception was flawless. On the other end of the call, he could easily hear GSC's star Communications and Remote Weapons Specialist crunching away on some potato chips.

'Another favour?' Mack ribbed him. 'You're very needy lately. Dare I say clingy?'

More crunching.

'You sound like an angry girlfriend.'

'You wish you were so lucky.'

Now some slurping.

'You're not my type, big fella.'

'Yeah, I suppose. Too much back hair and you like 'em smooth. I get it. Anyway . . . what can I do you for you this time? Fire some missiles up some Taliban's asshole? Or do you need a Predator to deliver a care package to a Hezbollah Tupperware party? Name it. I'm yours.'

Scary thing was, Jason thought, the guy was willing and capable of either act. 'Nothing that dramatic.'

'Darn.'

'Just wanted to test your IQ on satellite phone communications. Put your NSA skills to the test.'

As with most of the firm's intellectual assets, Macgregor Evan Driscoll – MIT Summa Cum Laude graduate and part-time hacker – had been recruited from the Department of Defense's most obscure branches known only by obscenely long acronyms. In 2002, he'd been instrumental in helping the NSA design a covert listening station inside AT&T's San Francisco international telecommunications hub. The programme's focus had been to monitor phone chatter and e-mails originating from Al-Qaeda safe houses in places like Riyadh and Yemen. But a whistleblower outed the programme for spying on domestic communications as well, exposing a myriad constitutional violations. This chapter of the Bush Administration's unwarranted wiretapping programme promptly folded and its developers, including Mack, became victims of the political fallout. But Mack was quickly scooped up by GSC – a firm that used a much different playbook and embraced the frustrated, cavalier brainiacs who'd been disenfranchised by the tight monetary and operational constraints of government agencies.

'What've you got for me?' Mack asked.

'I've got a guy here in Iraq who's been making lots of calls, with the intent of undermining our mission. If I give you his coordinates, can you see if you can listen in on him?'

'I'll give it a go.'

Jason twice repeated the GPS data for Crawford's current position. Then he heard Mack tapping away on a keyboard. He'd gone through this exercise many times in the past, so he knew Mack was linking in to the commercial satellite network to triangulate the signal.

'Hum. Got the signal . . .' More tapping. 'Oh yeah, that's gonna be a problem. Your caller's not using a voice channel . . . and he's transmitting in digital, not analogue. *And* it's all bouncing through military satellites. Nice if you would just say that you want me to eavesdrop on the marines.'

'Sorry about that,' Jason said. 'Can you crack the encryption?'

'Four-thousand-ninety-six-bit RSA secure-key encryption?' Mack cackled. 'Don't think so. That shit was invented *because* of guys like me. The number of possible key combinations borders on infinity. Would take decades for the world's fastest super-computers to crack that kind of encryption.'

'All right,' Jason said. There had to be another way. 'So the caller and the person being called each have a key cipher, right?'

'That's right. Both phones use the same key encryption software to swap permissions.'

Jason thought it through. Two keys. Two sources. Encoded data packets being fed back and forth between two points with an ultra-tight digital handshake. Maybe he was approaching the problem from the wrong angle. 'How about this: can you locate the second key?'

'Yeah, sure,' Mack replied matter-of-factly. 'May not do you any good if the person on the other end is mobile. 'Cause once this call's over, it's a whole new ball game. New keys, new session—'

'Humour me, Mack.'

'All right.'

Jason listened to fifteen seconds of click-clacking accompanied by Mack's heavy breathing.

'Well *hell-o-o-o-o* . . .' Mack sang in pleased revelation. 'You just got very lucky, Yaeger.'

'How's that?'

160

'This call's being routed through a ground station in San Francisco. Jeez, it's going through AT&T at Folsom Street. Same place I used to work . . .That's fuckin' rich . . .' he said with some resentment. 'Anyway, the satellite feed is routing through the Backbone network.'

'So whoever he's talking to is not using a mobile phone?'

'Tell you in a second.' Mack did some more tracing. 'Nope. Definitely a landline. Still can't tell you what they're talking about. But I can tell you exactly where the other caller's phone is plugged into a wall jack.'

'That would be great.'

Now Mack was humming the *Jeopardy!* theme song to the rhythmic keyboard clicks. 'And . . . got it.' A pause. 'Huh. I think your guy might be calling his bookie.'

'Come again?'

'Yeah, your marine is talking to someone in Vegas.'

'*Las Vegas?* You sure about that?'

'Yup. And it gets even weirder. Seems his bookie is an evangelist.'

32

BOSTON

Only minutes ago, Agent Thomas Flaherty and Professor Brooke Thompson had arrived at the branch office of Global Security Corporation. Sipping tea from a Styrofoam cup, Brooke sat alone in Flaherty's spartan cubicle, peering out the east-facing window that provided a spectacular tenth-floor view of downtown Boston. Directly below was Quincy Market, where the city's historic colonial centrepiece, Faneuil Hall, sat dwarfed beneath the sleek skyscrapers of the financial district – a sharp juxtaposition of America's past and present. Her gaze panned out beyond the Christopher Columbus waterfront park and the Long Wharf promenade to settle on Boston's Inner Harbor. Shafts of sunlight lanced the grey clouds and joined in a sparkling circle atop the icy dark water. Maybe, she hoped, the bright spot portended more than just a passing storm.

The past half-hour had been a whirlwind. Following the harrowing escape in the tunnel, Flaherty had exited the Mass Pike and continued on to downtown. His wrecked car was ignored by the police cruisers, which sped past in response to the fatal collision blocking the interstate tunnel deep beneath Copley Place.

At this moment, she thought, another Big Dig was currently under way.

She was still struggling to reconcile how Flaherty had so brazenly put their lives on the line, though he had done an adequate job of explaining to her that assassins were incredibly driven to finish their work. 'Those guys are hardwired to do whatever it takes to eliminate their targets,' Flaherty had told her. 'Failure to do so means the end of an assassin's career, and possibly his own life. Gives them a pretty powerful incentive to win.'

Flaherty had also told her that he'd been trained to avoid at all costs getting into a shooting match with hired guns, since most were former marine snipers and Special Ops commandos. So the prudent course of action was simple: flee. And, miraculously, Flaherty had managed to do just that.

The assassin's failed attempt would take time to disseminate back to the unknown client, Flaherty had told her. And that precious time 'off the grid' provided them a fleeting tactical advantage.

It was no wonder that he'd headed directly here, she thought, turning her attention back to where she was. This seemingly innocent office was a veritable fortress that would be near impossible for an outsider to infiltrate. At the entrance to the building's parking garage, Flaherty had been required to present his encrypted security badge to a trio of heavily armed, burly security guards wearing crisp navy coveralls with red arm bands and GSC shoulder patches (the agency's patriotic emblem purposely designed to convey a symbiotic relationship to the US military). The head guard had quizzed Flaherty about the Concorde's alarming condition, while one of his minions performed a cursory search of the car's interior and trunk.

Meanwhile, the third guard had requested for Brooke to step out from the vehicle so he could wave a security wand over her limbs and torso. Then he'd brought her to a computer terminal and vetted her while running a check on her driver's licence. Satisfied that she harboured no propensity for espionage, he had escorted her back to the Concorde and held open her door in polite valet fashion.

After the head guard had let down the retracting thick metal posts that blocked the garage's entrance ramp, Flaherty had driven on to his reserved ground-level parking spot. He'd used the same ID as a keycard to access a dedicated elevator that had no control panel, only an emergency stop button and panic phone, and a security camera. The elevator had let them out directly into an elegant entry foyer, furnished with plush leather armchairs, oak-panelled walls, flat-screen televisions tuned to MSNBC, CNN and Fox, and a receptionist seated behind a sliding glass window. At first, Brooke had felt like she'd stepped into her dentist's office. But the main entryway, situated at the end of a short corridor leading off the reception area, was fitted with a formidable security door. With two more armed guards flanking the door, it was anything but welcoming.

The facility itself took up the building's entire tenth floor, with a 'team-based' open-plan office that provided clear views to windows on all four sides. When Brooke had commented to Flaherty on the irony of all this security for an office surrounded by glass, Flaherty had explained that the windows were blast-proof, tinted to keep out prying eyes both day and night, even dampered against vibration to prevent hi-tech spies from tracing conversations with parabolic microphones. 'This ain't no fish-bowl,' he'd conspiratorially confided.

No matter what work was performed here (or at the firm's

twenty-six similar offices Flaherty had said were located around the globe to ensure maximum redundancy and logistical advantages), the layered security protocols seemed excessive. She figured the firm was a living testimonial to its products and services.

But even this hi-tech nerve centre had no knowledge of why Brooke Thompson had been secreted into Iraq in 2003, and why now someone wanted her dead because of it.

God, how can this be happening?

33

'Brooke,' a voice suddenly squawked over the intercom on the desk phone.

'Yes?' Brooke spoke quietly into the phone.

'It's me. Flaherty. Stand up.'

'What?'

'Just do it.'

She did.

'Look to your left. See me over here?'

Directing her gaze left, she saw a hand waving to her. Flaherty's head popped up over the cubicles. She waved back at him.

'Come on over here,' he said, before disconnecting.

Noting his position, Brooke set off through the partitions.

Angling her way through a maze of office cubicles, Brooke snuck glances at Global Security Corporation's resident employees – mostly attractive twenty-something males and females wearing business casual attire and slim headsets. Each techie monitored not one, but three to five flat screens packed with streaming data.

Nearer where Flaherty stood at the centre of the floor, the hi-tech workstations were laid out along a wide semicircle. Here the computer displays were dominated by tactical maps and schematic blueprints.

'Come on over, Brooke,' he said, waving her closer. 'There's someone I'd like you to meet.'

The person to whom Flaherty was referring stood from her chair. Barely reaching the agent's shoulder, the petite woman had bobbed grey hair and wore a tasteful flannel pants suit.

'Annie is our resident expert on satellite surveillance. Our eye in the sky.'

'Hi, Brooke. A pleasure to meet you,' Annie said.

Brooke immediately pegged Annie's refined New England accent, heard so many times at university charity events and museum fundraisers. It sang of old money. Annie proffered a dainty, manicured hand that hosted a jaw-dropping emerald-cut diamond ring that validated Brooke's assessment.

'Thanks. Nice to meet you too,' Brooke replied warmly.

'Tommy's told me you've had quite a crazy day.'

Brooke rolled her eyes and sighed. 'It's like a bad movie.'

'You poor dear,' Annie said, smiling sympathetically.

'Brooke, I want you to take a look at this,' Flaherty said, pointing to the images on the display that they'd been reviewing. 'Have a seat.'

Easing into the chair, Brooke stared at the monitor, which showed an incredibly detailed aerial shot of a highly diverse terrain. The software interface looked like the next generation of Google Earth. There were mountains to the top and right of the screen, green flatlands in the middle and to the left, and brownish tans blending in at the bottom. Roadways appeared as thin lines, and webbed throughout the land to connect a disparate matrix of dense cities. Though for Brooke, the rivers snaking through the plains were the region's true fingerprint.

'Just want you to confirm something for us,' Flaherty said. 'We're looking at—'

'Northern Iraq,' she said.

Annie smiled. 'Right.'

Brooke anticipated Flaherty's request. 'The cave was right here, in the mountains.' She pointed to the exact spot. 'There.' She looked up at Flaherty. 'Did I pass the test?'

He smiled. 'Yup.'

Annie leaned in to get a closer look. 'That's it,' she confirmed.

'With the eight-hour time difference, it's nighttime there right now,' Flaherty said. 'So this isn't a live shot. It was taken earlier today. But you'll get the idea.'

Annie pulled up a chair, sat beside Brooke, and used the mouse to steadily zoom in on the Zagros Mountains. As the eye in the sky homed in on the military encampment set at the bottom of a hill, Brooke felt like she'd been transported back in time. Goosebumps prickled her arms.

Bending over Brooke's shoulder, Flaherty used a pen as a pointer. 'A few hours ago, our deep-cover field agents ambushed four trucks on the roadway here,' he said, pointing to the winding gravel ribbon running along the bottom of the screen.

Brooke could see bodies littering the ground around what looked like four pickup trucks left askew in the roadway. 'God,' she gasped. 'Are those men dead?'

'Oh yeah,' he said. 'But trust me, they deserved it.'

'Wait. Is that . . .' She pressed her face close to the monitor and tried to make out another form heaped in the roadway. 'A camel?'

'Uh . . . yeah.' Flaherty paused. 'But that's a story for another day. Annie, let's get in closer.'

Annie tightened the zoom using the monitor's touch-screen controls.

'Anyway,' Flaherty continued, 'some of the militants escaped . . . went up this slope.' Using the pen, he traced the approximate path. 'Our guys pinned them down behind some rocks . . . here and here.' He pointed to a structure that still stood, then to a blackened crater. He went on to explain how Jason had called in an air strike and that one missile had obliterated one of the rock piles, while a second had inadvertently blasted away the steel door that concealed the cave entrance. Then he told her that five of the militants had ducked into the cave opening. He wasn't yet prepared to tell her that Fahim Al-Zahrani was among the survivors.

'Wow,' Brooke said, staring at the mini war zone. 'It's hard to imagine that this area was once a lush paradise.'

'Really?' Annie said.

'Back in 4000 BC there was a huge village here,' Brooke explained to her. With her finger she indicated the wide open plain to the west of the foothills. 'A trading outpost inhabited by industrious, vibrant people. The major trade routes for ancient Persia ran through the mountain passes.' She indicated the deep valleys connecting Iran and Iraq in the screen's extreme upper right. 'That's how they brought in stone, timber and copper.'

'Just terrorists moving through there now,' Flaherty mumbled sarcastically.

'So what happened to the people that lived there?' Annie asked Brooke, genuinely intrigued.

'Well, the simple explanation points to climate shift. Massive floods silted the soil, destroyed practically everything . . . made

169

northern Mesopotamia unsuitable for crops. The survivors were forced to migrate east and west across Eurasia, and to the south as far as Egypt. In fact, starting around 4000 BC, the archaeological remains of human occupation completely disappear for nearly a thousand years in this entire region. It's often referred to as the Dark Millennium.'

'So how do you explain that the cave seems to have been occupied during that time?' Flaherty asked.

'According to the inscriptions on the cave wall, the floods were just beginning. Floods of epic proportion.'

'You're saying the world was flooded for forty days?' Flaherty jested.

'Not the whole world. But certainly the world these Mesopotamians knew. The oral tradition would have been passed on from generation to generation for over a thousand years before any written account was created. And like any fish story . . .' She shrugged.

'The minnow becomes a whale,' Flaherty said.

'Exactly.'

'Flaherty!' a stern female voice called from somewhere beyond the cubicles.

Instantly, Flaherty's expression soured. He rolled his eyes.

'Show time,' Annie said, trying not to laugh. She patted his shoulder. 'Time to talk to Mama.'

'Fabulous,' he groaned. 'Just fabulous.' Tonight's Celtics game was slipping further and further from the realm of possibility.

The voice called for him again at the same time as his cell phone rang. The caller ID came up blank. He flipped open his phone. 'Flaherty here.'

'Tommy, it's Jason.'

'Hey. Hang on a just a sec.'

'Flaherty! I see you!' said the faraway voice.

Flaherty turned and spotted his boss, Operations Chief Lillian Chen. The petite 45-year-old Korean, dressed in a severe pants suit, threw up both her hands and made a summoning gesture.

'Be right there,' Flaherty said, holding up his hand, then pointing to his phone. Clearly short on patience, Chen shook her head, executed a crisp about-face, and disappeared around a wall.

'Looks like someone's in trouble,' Annie said. Brooke grinned.

'Sorry, Jason,' Flaherty said into the phone. 'What's up?'

Flaherty listened intently as Jason got right to the point and told him about encrypted calls Colonel Crawford had been exchanging with someone inside an evangelical church in Las Vegas. The background check Mack had run through the NSA database indicated that the church's leader, Randall Stokes, was a former Force Recon Special Ops commando who'd served time with Crawford in Beirut, Kuwait, Afghanistan and Iraq.

Jason said, 'I'm guessing he's somehow involved in what's happening over here in Iraq. Stokes might even have something to do with the hit order on Brooke Thompson. I already spoke to Lillian, explained the situation.'

'I can see that.'

'She told me you wrecked your car and caused quite a commotion on the Mass Pike. That right?'

Flaherty sighed. 'Affirmative. It was bit messy. I did manage to lose the assassin, though – permanently.'

'Nice work,' Jason said, impressed. 'One other thing . . . I asked Lillian to check out that USAMRIID lead. She's got people at Fort Detrick sifting the archives for anything sent in from Iraq back in 2003. If any biological tests were performed, we should have confirmation within a couple hours. In the meantime, I need you to talk to Stokes . . . in person. Lillian's already made arrangements to get you to Vegas.'

No wonder the Chief was anxious to chat. A wrecked car, a major pile-up on the interstate, a thwarted assassination attempt *and* a last-minute jaunt to Vegas? That was a lot to take in one day. 'Vegas? When?'

Brooke's ears perked up. 'Vegas?' she muttered.

'You'll be leaving immediately. Lillian's preparing a file for you with everything we know about Stokes. Plenty of juicy reading. So get to Logan ASAP and you can study up on him on your way out there. I don't think I need to tell you that there's a lot riding on this, Tommy.'

'You can count on me.'

'I knew I could. I'll be in touch,' Jason said, then ended the call.

34
IRAQ

'For Christ's sake, I could have invaded North Korea by now,' Crawford said, glowering. 'Are you ready yet?' His eyes traced the fibre-optic cable from the PackBot's rear to a large spool, which in turn patched into a suitcase-sized remote command unit, painted in desert camouflage. The unit's unhinged hard-shell cover was inset with a seventeen-inch LCD viewing screen; its base hosted a computer hard drive, keyboard and toggle controls. This space-age gadgetry was lost on Crawford. Results were the only thing he controlled. And it was high time to see some progress.

'Almost there, sir,' replied the bot's technician – an attractive 28-year-old female with the sharp edges of a pageboy haircut sticking out below her helmet. Being a combat engineer, she was an expert with explosives, and was accustomed to using the bot to disarm or detonate roadside bombs and mines. But this was the first time she'd employed the gas-canister-firing appara-tus, and she didn't like the fact that Crawford was rushing things. 'Just running the final diagnostics on the software utilities . . .' She worked the keyboard and controls until the display synched with the bot's onboard cameras. The live images panelled onscreen. She held her breath as the interface for the rotary firing mechanism came online. When no errors came back, she exhaled.

Below the mountain, Crawford surveyed the tight perimeter his marines had formed around the encampment. Everyone was on high alert after Sergeant Yaeger purported to spot an Arab watcher lurking in the high ground. Inside the MRAP, he had a pair of marines monitoring the surrounding hillsides and mountains with infrared scanners. For good measure, the airwaves were also being closely monitored for enemy chatter. An ambush could turn this whole operation into an even bigger quagmire, thought Crawford. Plus, if there were an enemy in wait, the darkness would prove a huge tactical advantage for them.

Crawford's gaze shifted to Yaeger and his motley unit members, who were huddled around the bot's technician watching the viewing screen. Cleverly dressed like nomadic desert dwellers, they had certainly fooled the enemy. But the fact that they had no affinity to a 'uniform' was deeply unsettling for Crawford. Damn chameleons, he swore inwardly.

Crawford's appraising eyes settled for a long moment on the Kurd. Yaeger had yet to fully disclose what his sidekick had discovered during his earlier fact-finding mission. But the copilot who'd escorted the Kurd had plenty to say. He'd told Crawford about the brief visit to a restaurant in As Sulaymaniyah, which led to a second excursion to a mountaintop monastery near Iraq's northeastern border. This confirmed for Crawford that Yaeger knew much more than he was letting on. And the implications were highly unnerving.

Where did Yaeger's true allegiances lie? Crawford wondered. Undeniably, Global Security Corporation, Yaeger's employer, was a huge ally for US counter-terrorism forces. The face of war was changing too quickly for federal defence agencies to adapt. Increasingly, outside firms were needed to fill the huge deficiency gaps in manpower and technology. GSC was nimble, amenable to risk, and heavily capitalized by the world's wealthiest investors and industrialized economies (both of whom had the most to lose if terrorism ran amuck). Ironically, even Saudi and Kuwaiti oil money fed its coffers. As with any outside contractor, however, accountability was an issue, particularly when profit was the driving force.

Was Jason Yaeger an opportunist? If it came down to it, could he be bought? Or would his stubborn moral code simply get in the way and require Crawford to apply a more potent remedy to temper his growing disobedience?

Huffing impatiently, Crawford bent at the waist to inspect the bot's rotary firing assembly loaded with miniature gas canister projectiles that contained a mixture of eye irritant and sedative. He always thought that fanciful talk of warfare without soldiers was hogwash – on a par with paperless offices, everlasting gobstoppers and wives who didn't nag. Yet this thirty-pound motorized robot was about to perform a most perilous task that not long ago would have resulted in multiple human casualties. With remote drones patrolling the skies and unmanned fighter planes already in production, a new age of warfare was dawning.

All this technology, thought Crawford.

Yet as long as weak-minded politicians controlled the 'utilities' of the war machine, the terrorists would still thrive in the long run. Just like cockroaches, thought Crawford. The fact remained that war was never meant to be civil. Since the first humans attacked one another with stones, the goal of conflict had not changed. *Survival* was the objective. And history proved time and time again that diplomacy served only to blur the lines between the 'victors' and the 'vanquished'.

The bot came online with a sudden jerk of its articulating arm, and Crawford gave a start.

'Okay. We're good to go,' the combat engineer reported.

Crawford stepped back from the bot and stood next to Jason. 'All right, Yaeger. It's show time.'

Crawford and Jason knelt to either side of the combat engineer, intently watching the live transmissions coming back from the bot. On the command unit's viewing screen, the tunnel branched off in both directions at a near perfect T.

'Right or left?' the engineer asked, bringing the bot to a stop at the end of the cave's entry passage.

'Go right,' Crawford immediately blurted, before Jason could give it a thought.

Jason's muscles went rigid, but he managed to hold back his tongue. He exchanged glances with Camel and Jam, who stood close by to feed fibre-optic cable from the spool. Camel's jaw was grinding tobacco and his eyes were locked to Crawford's skull. Jam was silently mouthing a string of obscenities. Hazo shared the sentiment, but chose to smile and shrug. And Meat was clenching and unclenching his fists, like a guy ready to brawl.

'We don't have time to take a vote,' Crawford barked at the engineer.

Jason rolled his eyes and nodded to the engineer.

'Okay,' she replied hesitantly, sensing the tension. Pressing forward on the joystick control, she advanced the bot forward into the junction. Then she toggled right and the onscreen image rotated until the camera was directed down the tunnel branch. It was evident that this winding, craggy passage, approximately two metres wide according to the laser measurements coming back from the bot, had not been altered from its natural state. 'Here we go.'

As the bot advanced beyond the dimly lit entry passage, rising and falling over the undulating ground, the light quickly melted away and the camera's night vision automatically compensated for the darkness. On the command unit's viewing screen, the live feeds transformed to green-tinted monochrome. The glowing airborne dust swirling in the camera made it seem like the bot was trapped inside a snow globe.

'It's quiet in there,' the engineer said. She adjusted the volume slide control upwards. The only sounds coming over the audio feed were the bot's low-humming gears and the crunching of gravel beneath its rotary tracks.

'Too quiet,' Crawford added.

'God, that looks creepy,' Jam muttered, craning his head to get a better view.

While Crawford was preoccupied with the screen, Jason glanced down at the cell phone clipped to the colonel's belt. Why was he talking with Randall Stokes? For moral support and spiritual guidance? Highly unlikely, thought Jason. Maybe Crawford was soliciting tactical advice. Whatever the case, he was anxious for Flaherty to report back on Stokes's shady involvement.

'The air quality in there is surprisingly good,' the engineer reported, after glancing at the data readings coming back from the bot's onboard sensors. 'Plenty of oxygen for—'

'Wait,' Jason interrupted. 'Back it up a bit.'

The engineer did.

Eyes narrowed to slits, Jason attempted to discern something in the image. 'Can you shine some light in there?'

'Hey, hey,' Crawford protested, throwing up his hands. 'What about the element of surprise, Yaeger? If they see the light—'

'It's important, Colonel,' Jason insisted firmly.

Crawford's jaw jutted out. Circling his eyes at those assembled around him, he realized that his opinion was vastly outnumbered. He relented by throwing up a hand. 'Fine. Give it some light.'

The engineer pressed a button that shut off the infrared. The screen went black for a split second before the bot's floodlight snapped on. The refreshed image showed crisply the tunnel's raw features.

'There,' Jason said, pointing to an unnatural form partially hidden along the ceiling. 'Can you get a better shot of that?'

'Sure.' The engineer worked the controls to angle the camera up and zoomed in on the compact object fitting snugly into a hole in the rocky ceiling. It had an angular body and a circular eye.

There was no doubt as to what they were now looking at. 'A camera?' Jason gasped. 'What the hell is that doing in there?'

Staring dumbfounded at the image, Crawford was speechless.

'What . . . like a surveillance camera?' Meat said, coming over for a better look.

'Yeah,' Jason said.

Meat stated the obvious: 'That's not good.'

Clearing his throat, Crawford finally spoke up. 'First the metal door. Now this? It has to be a bunker.'

'Could be.' Jason studied him. For the first time, Crawford's unwavering confidence showed signs of cracking. Oddly, Crawford seemed to be feigning surprise. Why?

'Let's kill the light and keep moving,' Crawford suggested.

Jason concurred.

The engineer adjusted the camera and flipped back to night vision. Before she got the bot moving again, she warned, 'We're about thirty-five metres in, and we only have a fifty-metre cable.'

For another five minutes, they all watched in silence as the robot wound through the mountain's stark bowels. Twice, the engineer needed to swivel the camera sideways to study openings in the wall. But both times, the floodlight revealed dead ends. Along the way, they'd spotted two more surveillance cameras.

Deeper the bot went, until the fibre-optic cable spool nearly emptied.

Then the passage's repetitive structure changed abruptly. The jagged walls, glowing emerald in night vision, widened before falling away. Only the ground was discernible at the bottom of the screen.

'What do we have here?' Jason said, squaring his shoulders.

'Looks like . . . a cave?' The engineer paused the bot and its audio feed went eerily silent. Pushing another button, she said, 'Let's try sonar.'

Crawford was locked in constipated silence.

A small panel popped up in the monitor's lower right corner. Within seconds, the sonar data-capture was complete and a three-dimensional image representing the interior space flashed on the screen.

'Wow. It's pretty big,' the engineer said, interpreting the data.

To Jason, the sonar image resembled a translucent blob. 'How big?'

It took her a second to put it to scale. 'Like the inside of a movie theatre.' She studied the sonar image five seconds longer. 'It's not picking up any exit tunnels. Looks like a dead end. Nothing throwing off a heat signature in there either.'

'So no one's in there?'

'Nothing living.' Her eyes narrowed as she studied the image more. 'There's some strange formations along the outer edges of the cave. See here?' She pointed to the anomalies for Crawford and Jason and they each had a long look at them.

'Probably just stones,' Crawford said dismissively.

'No,' Jason disagreed. Atop the strange mounds structured like beaver dams, he could make out plenty of orb-like shapes. 'Those aren't stones,' he gloomily replied. 'If no one is in there, let's turn on some lights.'

This time, Crawford was hard pressed to protest. He reluctantly nodded. 'Fine. Do it.'

The engineer clicked off the infrared, turned on the floodlight.

Onscreen, the immense space came to life.

'My God . . .' she gasped.

Jason cringed. The space was indeed a cavernous hollow deep within the mountain. And heaped like firewood all along its perimeter were countless human skeletons.

35

LAS VEGAS

Stokes noted the time again and felt his adrenaline bubble up. Over an hour ago, the assassin Crawford had dispatched to Boston was supposed to have provided a kill confirmation on Professor Brooke Thompson. Twenty minutes earlier, he'd tried to take matters into his own hands by calling the assassin directly. The call had immediately gone to voicemail. That meant the pesky professor could still be alive – a *very* sloppy loose end.

Looking over at the photo wall, Stokes glared at a framed shot of himself and Crawford, barely men, dressed in full combat gear. Their hands were clasped in a victory handshake. We were so glad to be alive, he thought. The photo was taken the same day US peacekeeping forces had withdrawn from Beirut following the 1982 Lebanon War – one in a long line of Arab–Israeli turf wars.

It was in Beirut that he and Crawford had engaged in their first covert operation together. The CIA had planted them in Lebanon at the onset of hostilities, long before the peacekeeping operation had formally begun. They'd assisted Israeli Mossad agents to take down unsuspecting senior members of the Palestinian Liberation Organization. He'd learned immeasurably from the Mossad agents – men unparalleled in their drive and focus, with a centuries-old bloodlust imprinted in their DNA. They were the most cunning killing machines Stokes had ever met.

This same snapshot, however, also reminded Stokes of Osama bin Laden's 2004 videotape, in which the coward specifically mentioned Beirut as his inspiration for bringing down the World Trade Center. Another example of how winning the battle did little to win the war. That got his adrenaline pumping even harder. Fucking terrorist scum, Stokes thought. I've got inspiration too, you Muslim freak. You wait and see. I'm gonna make your little jihad look like child's play. You'll all pay. Every single one of you.

He scratched nervously at his raw palms again before turning his attention to the computer monitor, where the cave's camera feeds were showing plenty of activity. As Crawford had indicated during their last phone conversation, the PackBot was being sent into the cave to explore the passages and pinpoint the Arabs' location.

To buy some time, Crawford had cleverly diverted the robot down the passage leading away from the Arabs. Stokes had watched the machine rove through the winding tunnels, on three occasions pointing its robotic eye up at the cave's surveillance cameras. But Stokes wasn't concerned, because not one component of the security system could be traced back to him.

The bot was now parked in the cave's voluminous burial chamber, panning its camera left to right. For those viewing the bot's video transmission, the macabre sight would be nothing less than terrifying – like glimpsing Hell itself.

All those skeletons, he thought.

He remembered the first time he'd seen the massive bone piles. He'd tried to imagine how gruesome it must have been when the festering bodies had first been interred in that cave, so many millennia ago. Pools of rancid blood. The stench of decaying flesh. Insects and vermin feasting on the rotting corpses.

He vividly recalled the skin-crawling sensation he'd felt upon entering that chamber – an unsettling energy which could only come from another realm where the souls didn't rest. It was the first time he'd come to terms with the idea that true evil – a malevolent force – had been trapped beneath that mountain.

Not just evil: *a weapon.*

This subterranean mass grave was even more shocking than the excavated pits unearthed in Iraq's southern deserts. Stokes had no doubt that the marines, and particularly the Kurdish interpreter who Crawford had said was assisting the mercenaries, would attribute the atrocity to Saddam's secret police. But they'd be sadly mistaken.

On another panel, Stokes honed in on the distraught Arabs, slowly making their way deeper into the tunnel and still determined to find a way out. He shook his head in amusement.

The Arabs were very close to the cave's most secret chamber now. Too close. And Stokes was concerned that if they were to stumble upon the installation that was the heart of the operation, they might try to destroy his precious handiwork.

'It is time,' a voice suddenly called out to him.

Startled, Stokes sat bolt upright and scanned the room.

'Let loose the fury,' the voice calmly commanded.

'Yes . . .' Stokes said, still hoping the Lord would reveal His countenance. The voice was all around him. It even seemed to permeate his skull. How would God eventually manifest Himself? 'I understand.'

Composing himself, Stokes brought up a new window on his monitor to access the cave's command interface module.

'Let loose the fury,' he said to himself.

He stared at the seven icons blinking 'SEALED'. It was time to slay the Hydra. Time to eliminate the Middle East threat. For too long, humankind had interfered with the natural order of things. The balance God intended needed to be restored – the checks and balances that truly determined history's winners and losers.

With trembling fingers, he clicked each icon in turn, and the flashing indicators flipped from red to green; 'SEALED' now changed to read 'OPEN'. When the password box came up to confirm the changes, he paused.

Finally the appointed hour had arrived. The culmination of years of research and sweat. After taking a few seconds to savour the moment, he whispered, 'When the lamb had opened the first of the seven seals, I heard the first of the four beasts say with a thundering voice, Come and see. And I beheld, and lo a white horse; and he that sat on him had a bow: and there was given unto him a crown, and he departed as conqueror and to conquest.'

Pastor Randall Stokes slowly typed in the password – A-R-M-A-G-E-D-D-O-N – then entered it again to authorize the command.

36

BOSTON

The black GMC Yukon zipped through the Callahan Tunnel, making Brooke Thompson's pulse accelerate. Her mind was flashing a fireworks display of images from the earlier car chase. Tunnels had never bothered her before. But they did now. She imagined the SUV careering into the tight walls – envisioned a ceiling collapse that brought the harbour flooding in around her. Crossing her arms over her stomach and squeezing tight, she glanced over at Flaherty, seated to her left in the rear passenger seat. He was staring through the SUV's bulletproof glass, entranced by the streaming lights high up on the tunnel wall.

Agent Flaherty had enough on his mind to ignore irrational fears, Brooke thought. In fact, it had to be *rational* fears that plagued his thoughts. Prior to leaving the office, he'd spent twenty minutes in a closed-door session with his firecracker of a boss. He'd been highly contemplative ever since.

Feeling her anxiety ballooning into panic, Brooke couldn't help but reach over and grab his right hand. He turned, unsure of her intention, but quickly realized by her clammy complexion that she needed some consoling. 'Sorry, but I'm kind of freaking out,' she said, her fingers clamping tight around his palm.

'It's all right,' he said with a reassuring smile. 'I'm feeling it too. Don't know if I'll ever look at a tunnel the same way again either.' He placed his other hand on top of hers.

She nodded and released a long breath to calm her nerves. Focusing on the back of the driver's huge, shaved head somehow calmed her. The guy was like a caricature – a mountain of muscle. Even his ears seemed pumped up. The handgun strapped under the man's arm, however, implied that his duties involved more than simply playing chauffeur.

'I still don't think you should be coming with me,' Flaherty said. 'I can't guarantee your safety. I don't want to be responsible for—'

'Tommy, if you have a waiver form, I'll sign it,' Brooke said. 'Otherwise, let it go. You need me and you know it. And your boss seems to be okay with it too.'

Lillian had indeed given him the green light to bring Brooke along. Logically, it made sense, since Brooke was the only person who'd actually met the conspirators face to face, and her visual confirmation could certainly expedite matters. 'With the high stakes involved, we need to be certain about this, Tommy. Any slip-ups could cost us dearly,' Lillian had said.

'Are you always this stubborn?'

Brooke thought about it for a moment. 'Pretty much.' She leaned to the middle, looked forward out the windshield. 'Could this tunnel be any longer?' she pleaded, squeezing Flaherty's hand even tighter.

Flaherty chuckled.

They sat there holding hands for a few seconds until Flaherty asked, 'You ever been to Vegas?'

'Once . . . two years ago. The Archaeological Institute of America had its convention at Caesar's Palace. Hard to forget, because they didn't realize that there was a swingers' convention going on in the adjacent ballroom.'

'So you got to kill two birds with one stone?'

'Very funny,' she said, scrunching her face. 'I'm not that kind of girl. How about you? Are you a Las Vegas guy? "What happens in Vegas, stays in Vegas", and all that?'

'Nah,' he said, with no elaboration, and shifted his eyes to the floor.

She gave him an incredulous look. 'I'm not buying it. Remember, I've seen the way you drive. You're a guy who likes to take chances.'

He sighed. 'Not to be a downer, but my dad's a wicked gambler. When I was a kid, he lost a year's salary in one night at a poker table. Caused a lot of heartache for my ma. Didn't stop with him, either. My oldest brother Jimmy lives by the ponies. And Chris, the middle child . . . he'd wager the weather if he could. Seems the Flahertys are genetically predisposed to bad bets. Seen enough to know that I shouldn't even buy a lottery ticket.'

'Then you should be happy I'm coming with you,' she replied delicately. 'I'll keep you away from the casinos.'

He smiled. 'I doubt there'll be any slot machines where we're going.'

Up ahead Brooke spotted an emerging circle of dull daylight at the end of the tunnel. She relinquished her grip on Tommy and pulled her hand back. Their destination returned to the forefront of her thoughts. 'What kind of evangelical preacher builds a humongous church in Las Vegas, anyway?'

Flaherty shrugged. 'Actually, it's a pretty smart idea. In Sin City there are plenty of misguided sheep to herd.'

'I still can't believe a preacher is involved in all this. It's so absurd.'

'Don't let the righteous-holy-man stuff fool you. From what my office dug up on this guy Stokes, he's in deep. Lillian told me Stokes is under investigation for untraceable offshore funds running through his not-for-profit corporations. He's got some powerful, highly influential friends too. You ever see him on television?'

She shook her head.

Flaherty took out the folder Lillian had prepared for him, flipped to a picture of Stokes.

'Recognize him?'

Studying the photo, she couldn't quite place the handsome face. He looked like he belonged on a daytime soap opera. 'Don't think so.'

'He's got this weekly show that's huge in the south. He's got a band, celebrity guests, the works. Big production with big aspirations. Not so big here in the northeast, though.'

'Too many liberal thinkers,' Brooke said.

'I suppose. Around here, Pastor Stokes broadcasts on some obscure Christian cable channel. I forget the station. Anyway, he's managed to build quite a following. With everything going on in the world these days, people are looking for answers. And his message seems to resonate.'

'Exactly what is his message?'

Tommy shrugged. 'I've only seen his show once. From what I remember, he's pretty positive. Focuses on finding inner peace, Jesus as a personal saviour . . . Mixes in some apocalyptic material to keep folks honest. Really animated guy . . . super charismatic, smooth talker. Could charm the stripes off a zebra. Like a New Age version of Billy Graham. He's got a good line of patter.'

'Sounds to me like you're a fan.'

'Nah. I just find it fascinating.'

The Yukon emerged from the tunnel and curved along McClellan Highway towards Logan Airport. Overhead, a wide-body jet was roaring in for a landing.

'Jason says Stokes has been talking to that platoon colonel in Iraq?' she asked.

'That's right. And he wants me to find out why. There are a few more things you'll need to know about the preacher.'

Flaherty didn't need to go to the folder to relay what Lillian had told him. He explained that in a previous life, Stokes was a Special Ops commando who'd served loyally in some of the most hostile regions on the planet, alongside Bryce Crawford. Then he told her how in 2003 Stokes had been discharged from service after losing half his right leg to a soccer ball packed with explosive.

By the time he'd finished, the Yukon had turned off Logan Airport Service Drive and was angling between the massive aeroplane hangars bordering the airstrip.

'Aren't you going to tell him that he missed the terminal?' Brooke whispered to Flaherty, motioning to the driver.

'We're not going to the main terminal,' Flaherty said. 'We don't have time for that. Especially with all the flight delays from the storm. Lillian made other arrangements for us. She's fond of Jason. Pretty much gives him whatever he wants.' He pointed through the window to a sleek Cessna Citation X jet idling on the tarmac. It was brilliant white with no markings. Not even an N-number on its tail fin. 'We'll be getting express service at 700 miles per hour.'

37

LAS VEGAS

Like those of a fiendish voyeur, Randall Stokes's prying eyes glimmered with immense pleasure as he watched how his unwitting Arab detainees reacted to the eerie noises emanating deep within the mountain's belly. In the background, mechanical sounds echoed through the passage – gears engaging, pistons whining, a droning whoosh. The Arabs were mistaking the noises for guns, or artillery. A man with a patchy beard was trying to hush the others, but to little avail. Adjusting the audio level, Stokes listened to them yammering on in their native tongue. During his extensive tours in the Middle East, Stokes had picked up enough Arabic to get the gist of the animated exchange. The Arabs spoke of infidels, Allah's divine plan and retribution in the name of the Great Prophet. All the while, they were readying their weapons.

And while the four underlings, huddled around the dim cell phone light, attempted to hash out a hasty defence strategy, Al-Zahrani was surprisingly cool; resolute beyond what the situation warranted. Though he stood away from the light, the infrared clearly showed him studying the exchange – assessing behaviour; mentally separating the strong from the weak. Clearly he wasn't pleased with what he was hearing.

There was an unmoving solemnity and drive about Al-Zahrani that commanded respect – qualities typical of a general. The fact that this revolutionary was a star Oxford University graduate and hailed from a wealthy Saudi oil family was most intriguing. Most men could only dream to gain the luxurious life that Al-Zahrani had staunchly abandoned. Such indifference to material things required incredible inner strength, yet, to Stokes, underscored the potency of the new enemy that threatened the modern world. Tainted ideology was a most fearsome force.

In videotapes Stokes had heard Al-Zahrani repeatedly mention that Allah spoke directly to him and protected him like an avenging sentinel. If that claim once seemed farfetched to Stokes, Al-Zahrani's current actions dispelled any doubt that the man believed his own story. The dire circumstances Al-Zahrani was facing would ruin even the best of men. Clearly, however, this cave bore little threat for him.

'Who *are* you?' Stokes said, glaring at the notorious terrorist.

In Al-Zahrani, Stokes couldn't help but see his own reflection, for he too claimed to speak directly to God and proclaimed to know the path to Heaven. And just as Al-Zahrani had been tutored by Islam's most prestigious imam, Stokes, too, had been enlightened by a prodigious mentor. For an iota, Stokes entertained the possibility that God might be pitting him and Al-Zahrani against one another.

Lord, show me the righteous way, he thought.

Suddenly, Al-Zahrani silenced his four underlings in a punishing tone. Stokes watched as the fearless leader pointed towards the noises and scorned the men for their faulty appraisal. 'What you hear is not soldiers,' he seemed to be saying. Stokes pieced together his next words: 'The soldiers are behind us . . . back there.' Al-Zahrani pointed in the opposite direction. 'If there is an enemy in our midst, it is not human. Yet we must confront it. We cannot turn back now.'

Goosebumps ran up Stokes's spine; he was amazed by Al-Zahrani's remarkable precognition.

Next, Al-Zahrani commanded the men to move forward – *towards* the commotion.

Stokes eased back in his chair and pressed his fist to his chin, wondering how this might play out. He hadn't expected them to press on. A retreat was the expected outcome – the *sane* choice. Either Al-Zahrani had profound faith . . . or a death wish. Harbouring concern that the Arabs might critically impact Operation Genesis, Stokes quickly dismissed the notion that these five men could materially affect what was now under way. The numbers were heavily weighted against them.

Concern quickly gave way to intrigue. Stokes squared his shoulders and leaned forward with renewed intensity.

The Arabs disappeared from camera view for a three-count before the next camera picked up their trail. Now the passage was tightening, allowing just enough room for single-file procession.

The ringleader, a man with a patchy beard, was at the front, cell phone light extended out in his left hand, AK-47 clutched tight in the crook of his right arm. The other three men trailed in his wake, weapons at the ready, and Al-Zahrani pulled up the rear, swinging a handgun at his side. They'd stopped talking and their trepidation was rising to a fever pitch. Now even Al-Zahrani was visibly tense, because the metal-on-metal sounds they'd been hearing had given way to something much different.

Ahead in the darkness, something was moving.

Writhing.

'Best to turn around, my friends,' Stokes muttered, his left eyebrow tipping up.

The audio crisply picked up scratching and clicking.

The procession halted abruptly as the ringleader made the first visual confirmation.

When he spotted the horror that lay ahead, he screamed out in terror and wheeled around so fiercely that he barrelled into the two men behind him. He stumbled and the cell phone fumbled out of his grasp, clattered along the rocky ground.

Then the panic infected the others.

'Go back! Go back!' the ringleader was pleading as he regained his footing. He shoved at the others, trying to speed them along. Spinning, he attempted to retrieve the cell phone, but it disappeared beneath the slithering mass that crashed into him like a violent wave. He recoiled, levelled the AK-47, and opened fire. The weapon's consecutive muzzle bursts flashed brilliant white in the infrared images on Stokes's monitor; the deafening retort squelched the computer's speakers.

'No . . .' Stokes grumbled.

Comfortably ahead of the others, Al-Zahrani was now back in the previous camera frame, blindly clawing his way through the darkness. But something scurried beneath his feet and caused him to trip and fall. He screamed out when something took a chunk of flesh out of his hand.

Then Stokes's eyes bounced back to the other frame where the gunman lost his footing and suddenly tumbled backwards, forcing the assault rifle to swing up over his head, spraying bullets along a wild arc. The lethal barrage strafed the two men trailing behind him about the face and chest, sending the pair crumpling to the ground.

An instant later, a ferocious explosion ripped through the passage and obliterated the camera.

38

'What in God's name—' the combat engineer gasped. 'What happened to those people?'

On the LCD panel, the bot's camera swept slowly side to side for the second time, panning over the ghastly bone pile forming an enormous ring ten feet high.

'Looks like a fucking mausoleum,' Crawford grumbled.

Jason looked up at Hazo, knowing that for him, the images would slice deep. It was a similar portrait of mass death that drove Hazo to become an ally to the Americans.

The Kurd stared emptily at the screen.

In 2006, US forces had used satellite imagery to scan the Ash Sham Desert for undulating mounds that hinted at the presence of mass graves. Over 200 sites had been identified for potential exhumations. One of the first confirmed graves contained three dozen male skeletons wearing Kurdish attire, all of which had been blindfolded and bound with arms tied behind the back. Every skull bore an executioner's bullet hole. Though most of the bodies could not be identified, Hazo's father – formerly an industrious carpet retailer – had been carrying business cards in his vest pocket. The name on the card, Zîrek Amedi, enabled forensic investigators to match dental records for the partial denture still affixed to the skeleton's jawbone. The positive identification brought bittersweet closure for the victim's surviving family members who'd already suffered tremendous loss at the hands of Saddam Hussein.

'You should take a break,' Jason said to Hazo in a low tone. 'Have something to eat with the guys.' He pointed to the cave entrance where Meat, Camel and Jam were blissfully spooning rehydrated beef stroganoff from foil packs.

Hazo sighed wearily and nodded. Then he went over to join the others.

'Looks to me like another hiding place for evidence of Saddam's genocide,' Crawford said.

'No,' Jason said. The only similarity he saw here was the sheer number of bones. 'Doesn't look anything like Saddam's handiwork.'

'How so?' Crawford challenged.

'First off, not one of the skulls we've seen on that screen shows signs of execution. No bullet holes, fractures—'

'Hey, smart guy, Sarin doesn't leave its mark on bones,' Crawford countered smartly.

Crawford was right. Sarin attacked the nervous system synapses. So once a victim's soft tissue decomposed, evidence of the toxin would be erased. 'There aren't any clothes on those bones. No jewellery, nothing. How do you explain that?'

'Maybe they burned the clothes, Yaeger,' Crawford said. 'Maybe they were a bunch of sick perverts who liked playing games with naked Kurds. Does it really matter? And we both know that soldiers have sticky fingers, would have confiscated any jewellery and valuables. For all we know, these bones might have been exhumed from another site and moved here for safe-keeping.'

Jason wasn't buying the colonel's argument, but held back a rebuttal. Crawford was clearly determined to see things his way.

'Wait . . .' the engineer interjected. 'Look at this,' she said.

Crawford and Jason turned their attention back to the screen.

'See this?' she said, pointing to something on the wall just to the right of where the bot had entered the cave. 'Looks similar to the pictures and writing on the wall of the entry tunnel.'

Jason examined the image. A section of the wall had been hewn flat, then covered in relief images and lines of wedge-shaped text.

'More pictures and scribble,' Crawford said. 'Let's cut the—'

But the colonel was cut short by a bellowing blast that echoed out from the cave and shook the ground.

39

MISSOURI

Professor Brooke Thompson stared out the jet's cabin window at the angular patchwork of docile farmland that blanketed the flat Midwest landscape in squares and circles hued in russet and ochre. The layout repeated itself as far as the eye could see, interrupted only by a random village or a grove of naked trees surrounding a rural home.

Even here, far from encroaching cities, humankind had dramatically altered the environment to suit its needs and ensure survival. Come spring, the fields would be sowed with plant seeds not native to this land. Over the centuries, America's hardy varieties of wheat, oats and various other grains had been imported from Europe. And long before those food staples had been transplanted in European soil and selectively bred over millennia, they'd been naturally thriving in the Middle East's Fertile Crescent – a veritable paradise for early humans.

Similarly, horses, cows, sheep, chickens and pigs – none of which had been native to the Americas – were brought in by early European settlers. But every one of these domesticated animals and beasts of burden originated from the Middle East.

The same pattern applied to humans themselves. Over 60,000 years ago, the first hunter-gatherer groups ventured out from North Africa and crossed the land bridge into the Middle East (an exodus across the Sinai long before Moses fled Egypt) to embark on their intercontinental migrations.

Though she marvelled at how this jet so smoothly cut the air to move her across a continent in mere hours, humans had been moving around the globe for millennia before planes existed – first by foot, then on the backs of animals, then by boats and ships and trains. Technology had quite literally sped things along. Technology had even permitted modern cities, like Las Vegas, to rise up in the heart of a desert.

All this moving around, she thought. All this trading of ideas and things.

This brief reflection on the pace of progress had her contemplating the fate of the ancient Mesopotamians who'd once inhabited Iraq's northern mountains. They too possessed sophisticated technology. But where had they gone after the floods had for ever changed the land? Did they go west into Europe? Or did they trek east to India or China? What happened to them?

The bigger mystery was that their incredibly sophisticated language hadn't made the journey from that cave. If it had, it would have spread like wild fire and set commerce and technology on a fast-track. The world as humans now knew it could be fundamentally different – possibly far more advanced.

Why hadn't they brought their language with them?

The cave etchings chronicled mass devastation. But could they *all* have died in the floods? Even the fastest rise in rivers, the most aggressive deluge, would have granted ample time for the Mesopotamians to flee the region. Then again, not all of them would have had the ability to write; only a handful of scribes would have been trained in the language. So it was plausible that the scribes who had stayed behind to complete their work in the cave subsequently drowned in the flood waters.

It amazed Brooke how such seemingly isolated events could ripple through human history.

'Here you go,' Flaherty interrupted.

Brooke turned as Flaherty set a plate and can of soda on the table in front of her.

'Turkey and provolone on wheat,' Flaherty said, pointing to the sandwich. 'The best I could do. I saw some chips and cashews in the galley too . . .' He thumbed towards the front of the plane.

'No, this is perfect, thanks,' she replied gratefully. 'I feel like I should be leaving you a tip.'

'Very funny.' Flaherty settled into the comfortable leather cabin chair opposite hers. 'Not too shabby, eh?' he said, raising his eyebrows and circling his gaze around the jet's spacious, sleek interior, aromatic with new-car smell. The rich furnishings included two mahogany tables inlaid with chequerboards of onyx and pearl, a fifty-two-inch LCD television, a fully stocked wet bar and leather divans.

'Sure beats flying coach,' she admitted. For Brooke, the jet further confirmed GSC's deep pockets and clout.

'I could sure get used to this. Wicked nice.' He cracked open his can and swilled some cola.

'I take it this is the first time you've been on this jet?'

'First time,' he confirmed. 'This treatment is usually reserved for VIPs, not the peons.'

'Well then I guess I should feel honoured.'

A phone suddenly rang and Flaherty had to look around

before spotting the portable handset mounted in the fuselage wall.

'I guess that's for us,' he said, getting up to retrieve the phone.

'The odds are in our favour,' she said.

'Agent Flaherty here,' he responded into the handset.

Pause.

'Wow, that was fast,' he said, turning to Brooke and giving a thumbs-up.

While eating her turkey sandwich, Brooke watched Thomas Flaherty for a solid three minutes as he kept the phone to his ear and jotted away on his mini notepad. She caught herself examining Flaherty's hands for a wedding ring.

Who were these people? she wondered. How could they simultaneously work for the government and outside of it? Justice certainly had many faces, and checks and balances were needed. Even the watchers needed watching, she decided.

Flaherty ended the call and returned the phone to its mount on the fuselage wall and came back grinning.

She spread her hands. 'So?'

'Good stuff,' he said, sitting. 'Remember back in 2008 when the FBI nailed that guy for mailing anthrax-tainted letters to a couple of senators right after 9/11?'

She nodded. On the coat-tails of the terror attack of September 11, 2001, it was hard to forget the frenzy resulting from the incident that killed five and infected seventeen others during September and October 2001. Letters containing refined anthrax had been mailed to Washington, New York and Boca Raton. She recalled that network news offices were among the targets, including ABC, CBS and NBC.

'Okay. Well, turns out the guy, Bruce Ivins, had been a senior biodefence researcher at USAMRIID. He was working on a vaccine for anthrax . . . and supposedly wanted to test it out in a real-life simulation. Bit of an eccentric . . . wound up dead before he was formally charged. Officially from suicide, unofficially murdered. Anyway, after those investigations implicated USAM-RIID, Fort Detrick set out to account for every vial in the Infectious Disease unit's inventory. Took them four months to complete it. By June 2009, over 70,000 samples had been catalogued . . . 9,000 of which had not been previously documented in the agency's database. Everything from Ebola to' – he paused to check his notes – 'stuff called "equine encephalitis virus". And among the overlooked samples were some very interesting specimens procured by one Colonel Frank Roselli.' He looked at her and smiled. 'Or, just plain "Frank".'

'Wait. Frank? *Our* Frank?'

He held up a hand, and said, 'Wait, it gets better.' He referred to his notes. 'In late 2003, Colonel Roselli was heading up the Infectious Disease lab at USAMRIID, but was asked to step down after it was discovered that he was overseeing unauthorized tests on live animals.'

'What kind of tests?'

'Didn't say. But the important part is this: the specimens Roselli brought into Fort Detrick's bio labs all originated from a cave excavation in northern Iraq.'

'No way.'

'Way. *And* . . .' Flaherty put his elbows on the table and leaned forward. 'When my office tried to contact him at home a little while ago, they were told by a babysitter that just this morning Frank Roselli wrapped his car around a telephone pole in Carver Park, Nevada. Only a few miles from Vegas.'

'My God . . .' she gasped. 'That's awful.'

But Flaherty had more to tell. 'So my office contacted the

coroner, who said that no official cause of death has been determined. Of course, they suspect he had a heart attack at the wheel. But I think we'd both agree that foul play shouldn't be dismissed.'

'Can't be coincidence,' she muttered. 'God, if they sent someone for him too . . . How high does this thing go?'

'Pretty high.'

'Exactly what samples did Frank send back from the cave? Had to be organic specimens, right?'

'Definitely. But not the kind USAMRIID normally collects. Seems Frank was studying bone samples. Lots and lots of bones.'

Brooke felt her blood curdle. 'Bones? From the cave?'

'Yup.'

'So what . . . like, animal bones?'

Flaherty shook his head, 'Human. And strangely enough, the samples were mostly molars. You know, teeth,' he explained pointing to his cheek. 'Almost a thousand of 'em. The inventory entry wasn't very detailed, but did indicate that every tooth had been drilled to perform genetic analysis.' He checked his notes again. 'Oh, and this was weird too: every tooth was from a male.'

Why teeth? she wondered. 'That's all the description said?'

'No. It also said that, like most of the 9,000 mystery samples not formerly sanctioned by the programme, Frank's tooth collection was incinerated.'

40
LAS VEGAS

Stokes stared at the computer monitor, befuddled by this most peculiar turn of events. The mysterious blast had knocked two of the tunnel's cameras offline. The heavy airborne dust was making it near impossible to see anything in the passage where Al-Zahrani had fled. What could have caused the explosion? Even a grenade couldn't cause this much damage. And he didn't recall seeing any of the Arabs holding one.

'Shit.' Stokes rubbed his knotted neck muscles. A sudden dread came over him. If Al-Zahrani was killed in the blast . . .Well that would prove most unfortunate. Could anyone have survived an explosion in such tight confines?

'Come on . . . show me where you are,' Stokes said, grabbing at both sides of the monitor with his hands and shaking it. 'Come on you son of a bitch. Show yourself.'

The desk phone suddenly beeped.

A cautious voice came over the intercom: 'Randall? Is everything okay in there?'

Stokes stared at the phone, sweat beading on his forehead. 'Everything's fine, Vanessa. Just fine, thanks.'

'Okay. By the way, your wife called again and was asking what time—'

He jabbed a finger at the disconnect button. His swollen hands felt like they'd been held over fire. He rubbed his raw palms on his legs, leaving blood smears on his trousers. For a brief spell, his vision became blurry with stars as a wave of nausea churned his stomach. He put his head in his hands and waited for equilibrium to return.

What's wrong with me?

Then his vision came back, crisp and focused.

Before he could give the bout of vertigo further consideration, he spotted movement on the monitor and his heart skipped a beat. Though hard to make out through the dust, a dark form was cutting swiftly through the passage. Then, as quickly as it had come, it was gone. Nerves ablaze, Stokes's eyes moved from frame to frame hunting for the runner. 'Come on . . . come on . . .'

The figure appeared two seconds later, slower now. It was one of the Arabs – *which* Arab was still unclear. On the periphery of the frame, the man stopped and pressed his back against the tunnel wall, panting. Stokes still couldn't make a positive identification since the man was using the tail of his headscarf to shield his mouth and nose from the dust. But with the air in this section much cleaner, he let his hand fall away and the scarf dropped to his shoulder. However, he immediately crouched and directed his eyes to the floor.

'Look up . . .' Stokes grumbled. 'Look at me, you son of a bitch.'

Then the Arab dropped to his knees and prostrated himself along the floor, hands pressed to the ground.

'What are you doing?'

Then the Arab began a familiar-looking ritual. Stokes immediately cranked up the audio level.

The chanting came through loud and clear: '*Allahu Akbar . . .*'

Praying? 'You've got to be kidding me,' Stokes said.

Only one way to get a fast answer. Stokes clicked on the control module window, resized it to long strip, and moved it to the bottom of the screen. Then he waved the mouse pointer over a square control button marked with a light-bulb icon.

'Smile,' he said. He clicked on the control button.

There was a slight delay as the command bounced through satellites. Then halfway around the world, the camera's bright floodlight activated and lit the praying Arab from above.

The effect amused Stokes. The astounded Arab screamed out in fright. He seemed to think that Allah was shining his brilliant countenance inside the cave. His head snapped up and the dark eyes squinted into the blinding light.

With the runner's face now in full view, Stokes smiled.

41
IRAQ

'For the love of God!' Crawford yelled. 'Someone tell me what the hell just happened in there!'

The combat engineer held up her hands. 'Everything's clear here,' she said, pointing to the PackBot's remote display.

'Damn it all,' Crawford growled, crouching to confirm her observation. Sure enough, the bot's feed remained unchanged. The cave was clear, the bone piles undisturbed.

'Sounded to me like it came from the other side of the tunnel,' Meat yelled over from the cave entrance.

Jason folded his arms and said nothing. He was tiring of Crawford's whipsaw moods.

'All right,' Crawford said. 'Let's back that lawnmower up and send it down the other passage.'

The engineer went back to the controls, spun the bot 180 degrees, and guided it out from the cave. It took less than three minutes for it to backtrack through the winding passage.

'Here she comes,' Meat called over. 'I can see the light.'

The engineer saw light spilling in on the screen's left side, indicating the spot where the entry tunnel joined the passage. She kept it moving straight.

'Yeah, there she is,' Meat said, peering to the end of the entry tunnel. The bot came in and out of view before disappearing to the left. He kept reeling in the slack fibre-optic cable.

'Keep in on night vision,' Crawford instructed the engineer.

'Yes, sir,' she said.

The bot roved through the tight, rocky walls that glowed dull green in night vision. There wasn't much to see, but then the audio began to detect activity.

'Wait,' Jason said. 'Hear that?'

The engineer brought the bot to a stop. The sounds became more pronounced.

They all listened intently. It was a voice.

'Someone's definitely in there,' she said, adjusting the audio level. 'Sounds like he's . . .' She tried to decipher the singsong chant.

'He's praying,' Hazo said to them. 'He's reciting the *Maghrib*. The Muslim prayer that follows sunset,' he specified.

'Well, it's a little late for that,' Crawford said. 'Let him pray all he wants. He's gonna need it.'

'Let's get visual confirmation,' Jason suggested. 'See what we've got. Use gas to root him out, if necessary.'

Crawford nodded. 'You heard the man, private,' he said to the engineer. 'Forward march.'

As the engineer advanced the bot again, a bright white light flashed from the bend in the passage.

Then came a startled scream, presumably from the same man who'd been praying.

'Now what?' Crawford grumbled. 'Where's that light coming from?'

'Don't know, sir,' she said.

By the time the bot rounded the bend, the mysterious light had gone away. And the audio had picked up the distinct echoing of fast footfalls.

'He's running,' the engineer said. 'Should we release some gas?'

'Not yet, keep moving. And for Christ's sake, speed it up.'

On the monitor, the bot accelerated. A few metres ahead, it began sharply rising and falling over heavy debris strewn about the tunnel floor. Dense dust began swirling around the camera lens.

'It's a real mess in there,' the engineer reported.

But Crawford was tuned into the audio feed – the footsteps. They were close now. Very close. 'Keep moving.'

Then the audio picked up the sound of the man again. He was coughing.

'Forget the gas . . . Seems the dust will do the job for us,' Crawford said, leaning closer to the screen.

'How's the air quality in there?' Jason asked.

The engineer peeked at the sensor readouts. 'Nothing toxic. But he's going to suffocate himself with all that dust.'

The footsteps abruptly stopped.

The coughing intensified.

Then the camera detected movement up ahead.

'I think we should stop there and shine some light,' Jason said. 'Let's see what we've got.'

Crawford told the engineer to do it.

When the floodlight went on, a figure sharpened onscreen, three metres from the camera. It was a man huddled in a fetal position beneath a pile of rubble that completely blocked the narrow passage from floor to ceiling. He was using his headscarf to shield his mouth and nose from the dust.

'Looks like he's not going anywhere,' Crawford said. 'Is he armed?'

The engineer zoomed in on the bloody hands, down along the body. 'Doesn't appear to be armed, sir.'

'Good.' Crawford stood and called over to a pair of marines posted near the cave entrance. 'Holt . . . Ramirez . . . Put your respirators on, get in there and pull him out!'

42

Tensions were high as everyone waited for Crawford's marines to emerge from the cave with the first captive.

Jason's anxiety was particularly acute. Five hostiles had gone into the cave. Only one was in the process of being extracted, the fate of the remaining four unknown.

The images staring back at him on the PackBot's viewing screen showed that the mysterious explosion had resulted in a complete collapse of the second tunnel branch. Was this an accident, or had the Arabs decided to buy more time by covering their tracks? Burying themselves in the cave seemed foolhardy. If there truly wasn't an alternative escape exit, the oxygen might not last very long.

'Miss me?' a voice interrupted.

Jason looked up. It was Camel. He was wearing a marine flak jacket and helmet so as not to be confused for a hostile. In his right hand, he gripped a night-vision monocular. 'Did you see anything up on the ridge?'

Camel spat tobacco on to the rocks and wiped some dribble from his lip. 'Nah. Walked the entire ridge. Nothin' there.

Couldn't really see much on the other side. Lots of rough terrain.'

'All right. Good work,' Jason said. Where could the watcher have gone?

'Was that an explosion I heard?'

'Yeah,' Jason sighed. 'Something went off in the tunnel. Take a look.' He pointed to the screen and Camel studied the image for a few seconds.

'Did they shoot off the RPG again?'

'Not sure,' Jason said. A commotion started up behind him. He looked back and saw the snipers shouldering their weapons.

'We have visual!' one of the snipers reported.

'What's going on?' Camel asked in a low voice. 'Visual on what?'

'One of the Arabs,' Jason replied.

'We caught one of them?'

Giving Camel a shushing gesture, Jason inched forward. He considered: five went in. One's coming out. A 20 per cent chance . . . He watched the snipers' weapons shift slowly upward as the target drew nearer.

'Looks like we're about to get some answers,' Jason said. He stood and crossed his arms.

'Let's give 'em some room!' Crawford barked at the snipers: 'You two . . . fall back!'

Forced to the sidelines, Jason felt like a paparazzo roped off from the red carpet.

'Should've been us going into that cave,' Camel grunted. 'This prick Crawford shouldn't be getting any glory.'

Then three figures emerged from the opening: two marines wearing respirators flanking a tall, bedraggled prisoner. One of the marines had a pistol pressed into the Arab's back.

At first, Jason couldn't make out the Arab's identity since the man had his bound, bloody hands raised up to shield his face.

Crawford quickly stepped in, pulled the man's hands down, and pointed a flashlight into his face.

Though the captive's face was smeared with blood and grime, Jason immediately recognized him. Confirmation brought both rage and relief.

'Holy fuck,' Camel said in astonishment. 'Is that . . .?'

'That's him,' Jason replied.

'Look who we have here. Fahim Al-Zahrani. Mr Jihad himself,' Crawford said, full of glee. He snapped off the light, put his hands on his hips, and stepped up to the Arab. '*As salaam alaikum*, asshole.'

The dour prisoner didn't reply, glaring defiantly at the colonel.

Confirmation of the prisoner's identity rippled through the ranks. The excited marines began gathering at the bottom of the slope, whooping.

'Another pussy ass terrorist pulled out from another hole,' Crawford said. 'Like a bunch of fucking gophers. Have the medic clean him up,' he told the marines. 'Make him look presentable. We've got to take some pictures to send back to Washington.'

From a neighbouring mountaintop to the south, the vigilant watcher – one of the dozen scouts sent to locate the besieged convoy – peered through a night-vision monocular and anxiously waited for the two marines who'd gone into the cave to reappear.

It had been almost seven hours since his lieutenant received the distress call from blessed brother Fahim Al-Zahrani's aide.

With all the gunfire in the background, the message had been difficult to understand. However, the critical points had been successfully conveyed by the aide: an ambush was under way, many had already been killed and urgent assistance was needed. As to the convoy's precise location, however, the aide had been far from clear. Perhaps Al-Zahrani's men had been disoriented with the redundant landmarks of this foreign country. Or maybe the local Al-Qaeda contact designated to navigate the convoy through the terrain had been killed at the onset of the firefight. Nonetheless, the aide had only been able to estimate that the attack had taken place four or five kilometres northwest of the intended rendezvous point.

The true locale was eleven kilometres to the northwest.

By the time the watcher had spotted the stranded trucks on the roadway, an American marine platoon had already arrived. The Americans were highly focused on clearing debris from a cave at the foot of the mountain that overlooked the roadway. Creeping in close to the encampment, the watcher had overheard them saying that five men remained trapped inside the cave. And he was hopeful that the intensity of the effort meant that Allah, in His bountiful grace, might have spared brother Al-Zahrani.

As the marines came out from the cave, the watcher's heart raced when he saw that they'd dragged a prisoner out with them. He tightened the monocular's zoom. Though the moon shone brightly from above, he strained to make out the prisoner's face. Then the platoon leader briefly shined a flashlight on the prisoner. The moment the captive's face came into view, the watcher's instant elation quickly gave way to terror. Our leader has been captured!

The watcher scrambled up over the ridge, his legs shaking coltishly beneath him, tears streaming down his cheeks.

Since the marines routinely monitored radio communication, he was forced to use a more discreet signal to alert the rescue team. In the pale moonlight, he could see the trucks parked in the valley below. He stood high up on the outcropping designated as the signal relay spot. Then he pulled a plastic glow stick out from under his tunic, cracked it, and continuously waved the luminescent green tube side to side in wide arcs.

43

Central to Crawford's encampment were two Compact All-weather Mobile Shelter Systems, or CAMSSs – barn-shaped, military-grade tents ten-and-a-half feet high at the eaves, twenty feet wide, thirty-two feet long, which four men could assemble in less than thirty minutes.

The first tent served the dual role of central command and billeting Crawford (not that he did much sleeping) and his staff sergeant.

Normally, the second tent stored boxed rations, and accommodated ten sleeping mats, used on rotation by the platoon detail. But Crawford had ordered the marines to clear out the sleeping area so that the space could be used for Fahim Al-Zahrani's temporary detainment.

The prisoner sat on an empty munitions crate, his hands bound tight with a nylon double-loop security strap. A second strap looped snugly around his ankles. Two marines with M-16s stood to either side of him.

The company medic, Lance Corporal Jeremy Levin – a scrawny 31-year-old bachelor, family practitioner, and reservist from Detroit who was five months into his third tour in Iraq – sat on a crate facing Al-Zahrani. He'd already flushed the wound on Al-Zahrani's hand with Betadine and cleaned the prisoner's face with sanitizing wipes. But he was concerned by Al-Zahrani's condition: clammy complexion, despondency and wheezing. So he immediately began a medical exam.

He inserted an otoscope in Al-Zahrani's left ear, which was perforated, then the right ear, which was leaking blood and clear fluid.

Crawford was watching over his shoulder. Jason and Hazo stood behind him.

'Hey asshole,' Crawford said loudly to Al-Zahrani. 'I know you speak English. Just want to let you know that I think the Geneva Convention is a load of camel shit. So don't expect me to respect your civil liberties.'

'The right ear shows severe tympanic perforation too,' the medic reported, peering through the otoscope.

'So both his eardrums are blown out?' Jason said.

'I'm afraid so. He must have been very close to the explosion.'

'Not close enough,' Crawford grunted.

'Unless he reads lips, Colonel, he won't understand a word you're saying,' Levin said. He cleaned the otoscope with a sanitizing wipe and put it back in the carrying case. Next he retrieved the opthalmoscope, flicked on its tiny light, and moved close to examine Al-Zahrani's unblinking, blank eyes. 'Pupils are responding just fine . . . no apparent neurological damage. Doesn't appear that he's in shock.'

'So he's just pretending to be mute?' Crawford asked.

'I'm sure he's a bit overwhelmed, Colonel,' the medic replied curtly as he went back to the case for an aural digital thermometer. He took the temperature in both ears and made a sour

216

face. 'Hmm. He seems to be running a high fever. That could explain the apathy.'

'You telling me he caught a cold?' Crawford said.

'More than a cold,' Levin replied coolly.

Apathy was an understatement, thought Jason. The world's premier terrorist seemed lifeless. His dark, emotionless gaze remained fixed on the ground. What could he be thinking? Was he humiliated or afraid? Jason wanted him to fight . . . wanted him to react. He wanted to choke the life out of him.

Levin swabbed some mucus out from Al-Zahrani's dripping nostril. 'Not sure if this is due to the dust he inhaled, or if it's something else. I'll test him for the flu, just in case.'

Crawford backed up a step. 'If this son of a bitch gets me sick . . .'

'I'm sure you'll be just fine,' the medic said, cracking open a plastic vial and sealing the swab stick in it.

'If Mexican pigs caused a problem, imagine what this one could be carrying,' Crawford said.

'Muslims aren't permitted to handle swine,' Levin reminded him. Next he wrapped a pressure cuff around Al-Zahrani's left arm, put the earbuds of a stethoscope in his own ears, and used the rubber bulb to inflate the cuff. Everyone remained silent as he assessed the patient's vitals. 'Given all the excitement, his blood pressure is awfully low.' He placed the stethoscope's chest-piece over Al-Zahrani's heart and listened intently. He moved it to the ribs and monitored the pulmonary functions. 'He's got a lot of obstruction in there. Lots of fluid. Probably inhaled a lot of dust.'

Not as much dust as the innocent civilians who'd been at Ground Zero, thought Jason, trying to reconcile how men like this were capable of evil on such a grand scale.

217

The medic removed the stethoscope, picked up Al-Zahrani's limp hand and studied the deep, ragged puncture wounds. Already, it seemed to appear worse than only minutes ago.

'What do you think happened to his hand?' Jason asked.

'Probably caught some shrapnel, or a ricochet. Could be a wound he already had. Not sure. But I don't like how the tissue looks – this discoloration and swelling.' He rolled up the sleeve of Al-Zahrani's tunic, turned the arm over, and traced his gloved finger along the protruding, dark veins in the wrist and forearm. 'Seems he's got a nasty infection. I'll give him some antibiotics . . . some ibuprofen for the fever.'

'Why don't you boil some tea for him while you're at it?' Crawford barked.

The medic's face twisted in a knot.

Jason spoke for the medic: 'If Washington wants to interrogate him, he won't be very useful if he's dead.'

'You mean he might not be worth ten million?' Crawford jabbed.

Jason was fast losing patience. 'The Department of Defense's bounty specifies "dead or alive",' he replied tartly. 'I don't have a preference. But for the sake of all parties, I'm sure we'd agree that "alive" would be preferred.'

'You and your boys get to keep that money, isn't that right, Yaeger?'

'That's right. It's part of our incentive plan. Keeps us all motivated. So yeah, the money will be ours to keep.'

'Must be a nice bonus,' Crawford huffed. 'You and your raghead buddies can retire to Thailand and have hookers suck your balls dry till the day you die. How about the Kurd?' he said, thumbing at Hazo, who stood close to the door. 'You gonna cut him in on this?'

'Absolutely. He's part of our team.'

'Two million apiece.' Crawford looked over to Hazo and whistled.

'Tax-free,' Jason said, to rub it in. The veins on Crawford's forehead instantly bulged, looked ready to pop.

'You're a disgrace, Yaeger.' The colonel's words seethed with loathing. 'Nothing but a sellout. And just remember that it was the US marines who pulled that cocksucker out from the cave. That's the story everyone here knows. So I wouldn't suggest spending your money just yet.'

'I've already sent plenty of video and pictures back to my office . . . make a nice documentary about the six-month manhunt that led us all here. Not to mention all the thrilling images of my unit's ambush, which feature this guy's ugly mug all over them,' he said, pointing to Al-Zahrani. 'Funny thing is, there aren't any marines in those shots. So don't you worry about us,' Jason said, grinning smugly.

And GSC's home office was equally keen to cash in on the bounty since its contract with the Department of Defense included a sliding scale of bonus payments for terrorism's most wanted targets. At the top of that list, Al-Zahrani fetched a 50-million-dollar kicker. There was even a chance that a few million more could still be had from the four militants yet to be extracted from the cave. After Lillian saw the pictures Jason had transmitted to her e-mail, she'd been fully behind Jason's requests – even commissioned a private jet to take Flaherty to Vegas. The almighty dollar was still a potent motivator. Though financial enticements didn't factor well into the military's strict moral code, they worked wonders in the enterprising private sector.

Levin pulled a blood-filled syringe out from a thick vein snaking up Al-Zahrani's forearm. 'We'll need to lay him down.'

Crawford took a few seconds to decompress before saying, 'Fine. Set up a cot for him. But you be sure to hang an American flag next to him. Remind him that he's ours now. When you're done, I want you to set up a video camera in here too.' He turned his attention back to Jason, who still wore a smug grin. 'All right, Yaeger. Time for you and your boys to earn your money. This cocksucker may not be able to hear us, but his hands are working just fine. So we'll do this with writing.' He pointed to Hazo and said, 'He stays with me, just in case Al-Zahrani decides to scribble some Arabic. You speak Arabic, isn't that right, Haji?'

Hazo nodded. 'I do, Colonel.'

'Of course you do. You're no millionaire yet, so go fetch a pen and paper. We've got work to do.'

Hazo paced to the other side of the tent and began rummaging.

'In the meantime, Yaeger, we've got another goddamn tunnel to unclog. Four more gophers to pull out . . . and God knows what else. And we still need to figure out what in hell blew up in that cave. Wrangle up your boys and get working on that. I'll have Staff Sergeant Richards help you.'

'I'd prefer to assist you in questioning the prisoner, sir.'

'Don't wet your panties, Yaeger. We both know he's not going to give us anything useful. If he does, your Kurd can fill you in later.'

Jason knew that Crawford was right on both points. 'Fine. But now that we've confirmed his identity' – he tilted his head to the prisoner – 'I need your assurance that backup is on the way. We can't risk losing him now.'

'Don't cry . . . You'll get your money—'

'I'm not worried about the *money*, Crawford!' Jason snapped. 'For Christ's sake! We've just captured Fahim Al-Zahrani! And up in those mountains, I saw someone who might well have already called for help to try to set him free. As far as I see it, the entire fucking battalion should be here!' He snatched the sat-com off the colonel's belt and held it up. 'Make the fucking call to General Ashford . . . or I *will*,' he threatened.

The two guards exchanged nervous glances. Even Al-Zahrani took interest.

Crawford's baleful eyes went wide. 'I don't take kindly to insubordination, soldier,' he hissed through clamped teeth.

Jason stepped closer, so that his nose practically touched the colonel's. 'I don't take kindly to incompetence,' he rebuffed confidently. 'Fuck this up and you'll be facing a shit storm in front of a military tribunal. Plenty of men here are witness to how you're handling this. I'm *hugely* interested in the success of this mission. Lots of innocent lives depend on it. Need I remind you, sir, *that* is why we're all here.'

Without breaking eye contact, Crawford plucked his phone from Jason's hand. He cocked his head sideways. 'That'll be all, Sergeant.'

'Make the call,' Jason repeated. He took two steps back and paused. Before he turned to leave, he added, 'And just so we're clear, Crawford: I'm not your soldier.'

44

Though Jason wasn't fond of Crawford's leadership style, he had to admit that the colonel's platoon was a well-oiled machine. In less than fifteen minutes after relaying Crawford's command to Staff Sergeant Nolan Richards, a human chain of twenty marines outfitted with respirators stretched through the cave's passages and began ferrying out the blast debris. Camel, Jam and Meat joined them. The remainder of Crawford's platoon went about securing the camp.

With Crawford focused on interrogating Al-Zahrani and the platoon set to work, Jason was intent on having a closer look at the cave's burial chamber. He grabbed a flashlight and filed past the marines lined up in the entry tunnel. At the T, he split right from the marines and moved swiftly through the winding passage.

Drawing lessons from the PackBot's earlier exploration, he tried to avoid the tunnel branches that led to dead ends. But the further he progressed into the mountain, nothing differentiated one passage from the next. Twice he forked off down passages terminating in solid rock and had to backtrack. Each time, he pulled out his knife and scraped an 'X' into the wall on either side of the passage.

Along the way, he managed to locate one of the surveillance cameras the bot had detected in the ceiling. Surprisingly, there was no visible wiring. Surrounded on all sides by rock, wireless signals would be near impossible. So where did the wiring run to? He didn't have time to investigate the matter. He had to keep moving before Richards came looking for him.

The subterranean atmosphere was completely disorienting; the air cool and loamy, thin on oxygen. It felt as if the earth had swallowed him whole. Imagining Al-Zahrani groping through the pitch black with no hope of escape gave Jason bitter satisfaction. It was hard to believe that after so many months chasing ghosts, the A-list madman was now their prisoner – bound like an animal.

Over the past months, the intelligence Jason's unit had pieced together through monitoring chatter and milking informants had pointed to a band of heavily armed operatives moving furtively from south to north, bouncing from one safe house to the next. Certainly cause for concern. But none of the intel even remotely suggested that Fahim Al-Zahrani might be among the group.

That was how the dirty business of counter-terrorism functioned: for every truth there were provocative rumours. Like the claim made by an informant in Baghdad which suggested that these phantom operatives had acquired two Soviet suitcase-sized nuclear weapons (over sixty of which were still unaccounted for after the fall of the Motherland) and were planning to erase Jerusalem and Washington DC from the map.

Accepting 'intelligence' at face value was anything but smart. 'Nothin' but a bunch of drama queens,' Meat had once said.

The tedious process of sifting good information from bad information had persistently put Jason's unit one step behind their quarry. Only when Jason moved on to more aggressive tactics did a clearer picture begin to take shape. Case in point: the tips extracted from a former Ba'ath Party lieutenant who'd sung like a canary after only one night of sleep-deprivation in a brightly lit windowless room with Britney Spears's 'Oops! I Did It Again' playing in a loop at blaring volume. Among other titbits, Britney got him to confess that he'd helped arrange transport for the quarry, from Mosul to Kirkuk, and that travelling with the group were senior Al-Qaeda members seeking safe passage to Iran. All true. Thanks, Britney.

From there, Hazo's contacts in Kirkuk pointed them to a local imam who'd been rumoured to have briefly hosted a number of unsavoury guests. Enter bright lights, Britney Spears and one sleepless night and the imam had provided detailed descriptions for the four-wheel-drive vehicles he'd procured for the operatives. Shortly after Jason requested aerial surveillance support from one of the Predator drones flying reconnaissance rounds over the northern plain, the caravan had been spotted heading east towards the Zagros Mountains. An hour later Jason's unit had staged a hasty ambush.

Now Jason was certain that the only contraband the Arabs aimed to smuggle over the mountains was far more ominous than plutonium: it had been Fahim Al-Zahrani himself. And Jason still feared that Al-Zahrani was plotting an escape. Crawford had better call for backup, he thought.

Finally, the passage widened and yielded to the cave.

At the opening, Jason paused and moved the light beam left to right. All along the walls the bone piles were stacked high – a circle of death.

What happened to these people? Jason wondered as he paced forward and shone the light on the skeletal remains. There had to be thousands of skeletons stashed unceremoniously in this cave. This was definitely not a modern mass grave, like Crawford wanted to believe. But it certainly was evidence of a large-scale burial. There was no telling if the bodies had been buried at the same time.

Working the cave counterclockwise, he walked the perimeter while using the light to scan the bones. Every few feet, something would catch his eye and he'd paused to examine the remains and hunt for clues. Even if these bones came from victims of an ancient war or genocide, there'd be signs of trauma – broken bones, cleaved limbs, gouges left behind by sharp blades. But there was nothing extraordinary about anything he was seeing.

Conversely, modern genocide wasn't about torture: its focus was annihilation – speed and efficiency. It wasn't uncommon for dozens or hundreds to be gunned down en masse by automatic weapons. Or if ammunition was slim, the modern executioner might opt to work his way along a line-up and deliver single-round headshots. Like Saddam's henchmen had done to Hazo's dad. There was no evidence of that here. Not one bullet hole. Even if shots had been delivered to the torso, once the flesh decomposed, the slugs would drop out from the bones.

Furthermore, the lack of clothing or personal effects strongly countermanded Crawford's chemical-weapons hypothesis. Not to mention that not a trace of flesh remained on these bones. That pointed to an event long, long ago. Well before Kurds were victimized by Saddam and his Ba'ath Party goons.

There definitely was a story to be found in these bones. But what could it be?

The bot sonar hadn't picked up any other exit tunnels branching out from this cave. Seeing how the bones were piled so high, however, Jason wondered if the sonar signal had been obstructed. Maybe there was something to be found *behind* the bones? There was only one way to determine if that was the case.

'They're only bones,' he told himself. 'Nothing but bones.'

Having witnessed plenty of battle zone carnage – from blown-off limbs to bullet-riddled and decapitated corpses – Jason wasn't squeamish when it came to blood and gore. But bones evoked a different, unsettling feeling.

To Jason, naked bones underscored the impersonal, undiscriminating finality of death – the living being stripped of flesh to its crude frame. Like a vandalized car stripped down to its chassis and left sitting atop cinderblocks.

The ancients revered bones as a vessel for resurrection or reincarnation. As such, they built pyramids and lavish tombs and even mummified themselves to preserve the body's sacred framework. This place, however, reflected a much deeper reality: death was cruel. Bones were nothing but remnants of a fleeting physical life. That's what Jason had to believe. Because for the sorriest souls, like his brother Matthew, who'd been incinerated by ignited jet fuel in the World Trade Center on a crystal-clear September morning, nothing physical remained. Jason needed to believe that, in the end, bones didn't determine one's ultimate salvation.

Cringing, Jason placed his free hand on a knobby femur to get a feel for it. 'Not so bad,' he tried to convince himself. 'Just like wood.'

Groaning, he tossed the light up on to the pile. Then he threw himself up on to the bones and began clambering his way to the top, using the skulls as steps.

'Sorry, fellas . . .'

Halfway to the top, the pile partially collapsed under his weight as hollow rib cages buried deep beneath him folded inward with a series of brittle snaps. As if he had just cracked ice on a pond, he spread his weight flat. Once the bones settled again, he cautiously continued his ascent. Near the top there was more cracking and popping. A dust cloud of decomposed flesh wafted into his nose and mouth. 'Aah!' He spat out the dust, but a foul taste lingered on his tongue. That's truly nasty, he thought.

He held the flashlight high and aimed the light into the shadowy gap behind the bone pile. Moving the light along the wall's arc, he was able to scan about a third of the cave's circumference. For good measure, he checked the ceiling too. Definitely no holes or openings.

He slid down the pile, sending a pair of skulls clattering across the ground. Then he continued slowly along the circle, shining the light on the skeletons. At the circle's midpoint, he grappled to the top of the pile again and checked the rear wall and ceiling. Nothing.

Again he slid to the floor, continued along the pile. Three-quarters of the way around the circle he climbed the pile for a final inspection.

'Okay. No way out,' he muttered.

As he came to the end of the circle, he noticed something peculiar: dozens of jawbones had been neatly stacked in a separate pile. Upon closer examination, he discovered that none of them had teeth.

That's odd, he mused.

Either these specimens were extreme examples of bad oral hygiene, or someone had extracted the teeth. But why would someone take them?

Then something on the ground glinted in the light. Jason bent down for a better look and at the foot of the pile saw a sharp silver edge covered in heavy dust. When he swept some of the dust away with his finger, he found something that was definitely *not* from long ago.

He picked up the object and held it under the light. It was a tool that resembled a hi-tech surgical instrument. Something a dentist might use to—

'Extract teeth.'

Had to have been left behind by one of the scientists brought in for the 2003 excavation. He pocketed the plier-like forceps.

There was one item left, and Jason remembered the bot had spotted it to the right of the exit. Shining the flashlight waist-high, Jason ran the light along the curve of the wall until he found the spot that had clearly been smoothed by tools for a very obvious purpose: to prepare the surface for etching. And the image etched into stone made his jaw drop open.

45

LAS VEGAS

As the Cessna's engines whined down for final descent into McCarran International Airport, Thomas Flaherty's BlackBerry chimed. He checked the display. 'It's from Jason,' he told Brooke Thompson. When he brought up the text message, he noted a handful of icons for picture attachments. 'Says: "Al-Zahrani in custody. Have Brooke review pix from inside cave. Is this Lilith?"'

Brooke sat bolt upright, not sure what to be most excited about. 'Wait. Is he saying that Al-Zahrani has been captured? Fahim Al-Zahrani?'

Realizing he just slipped up big-time, Flaherty's eyes went wide. Oops. 'Yeah. About that . . .' He cast his eyes to the BlackBerry, thinking how he could change the subject.

'Go on . . . you can tell me,' Brooke said. 'You know I'm really good at keeping secrets.'

He glanced up at her. 'I suppose.'

Flaherty briefly explained how Jason's team had been tracking Al-Qaeda operatives for the past few months leading up to the

229

ambush that forced Al-Zahrani and his surviving posse to take cover in the mountain.

'Wow. That is *huge*,' she said, mouth agape. 'That's like catching the Devil himself.'

Flaherty tried to wrap his brain around it too. 'It's ten million dollars huge,' he murmured.

'What?'

'Nothing.' He shook his head. 'Wow. I just hope he's okay.'

'Al-Zahrani?'

'No . . . Jason. See, Al-Zahrani is Bin Laden's new right-hand man. And, of course, Bin Laden was responsible for what happened at the World Trade Center. Jason's brother had been an insurance broker for Marsh USA. Went to work early that morning . . . to his office on the ninety-fifth floor of the North Tower. They never found the body. So indirectly, one could say that Al-Zahrani, or at least what he stands for, was also responsible for killing Jason's brother,' he explained.

She nodded.

'Jason must be freaking out.'

'I bet he is.'

'I hope he doesn't do something drastic.'

'What, like kill him?'

Flaherty nodded. 'Not that anyone would shed a tear for Al-Zahrani. But Jason could get himself in a lot of trouble.'

'I doubt he'd be anything but a hero,' she disagreed.

'I suppose. God, imagine when people find out about this. It's amazing.'

'So let's see those pictures,' she said, anxiously eyeing the BlackBerry.

'Sure, let's have a look.' Flaherty read aloud the name Jason had assigned the first attachment, 'Mass Grave'. He exchanged an uneasy glance with Brooke, then opened the file. When he saw it, he cringed. 'Yikes. Take a look at this.' He handed the BlackBerry to her.

The picture clearly showed a dense pile of human bones. Brooke wasn't sure how to react. 'This is what Frank's team had been studying?'

'Seems so. There are a few other pictures here,' he said, showing her how to open the remaining files.

There were two more shots of heaped bones showing wider angles that Jason obviously had taken to emphasize the magnitude of what he'd found. The continuous death pile seemed to circle the cave. In the images, Brooke could make out the rocky walls and ceiling.

'It's pretty spacious in there,' Flaherty noted as he looked on.

'And it's packed full of bones,' she muttered. 'God, look at all that . . . There's got to be hundreds, maybe thousands . . .'

'I'd go with thousands.'

The next picture Brooke brought up hit her like a sledgehammer. 'Look at this,' she said, turning the display to Flaherty.

He squinted to make out the details. 'What are those?'

'Mandibles.'

'Mandibles?'

'Jawbones,' she said, grabbing her own chin.

'I know what a mandible is. It's just that . . .' Still looking confused, his eyes went back to the picture. He pointed to his own mouth and said, 'There aren't any—'

'Teeth!' she exclaimed. 'Of course! *This* is where Frank got the teeth. From *these* bones.'

'All right, smarty. I would have figured that out. Still don't understand this bizarre fascination with teeth.'

'Me neither,' she admitted.

231

Three more pictures remained.

The next image took Brooke's breath away.

'What is that?' Flaherty said, tipping his head to see the image. It wasn't at all what he might have expected. 'Hubba hubba. Who's that?'

At first, Brooke didn't respond. She was absorbed in the image – a wall etching that depicted a voluptuous, naked woman in full-frontal. Flaring out from beneath her raised arms were bird-like wings and she wore an elaborate conical headdress. In her left hand, she held a serpent. Perched on her right hand was some kind of bird. And beneath her feet was a pile of human skeletons.

Flaherty tried to be more specific: 'This supposed to be the same woman whose head got lopped off?'

'Looks that way.'

'Why would they behead an angel?'

Without taking her troubled gaze off the image, Brooke sharply shook her head. 'No. Not an angel. Protective spirits . . . the *good* spirits,' she explained, 'are always shown with *upward*-pointing wings. See here how her wings are pointing down?'

'Okay. So what does that mean?'

Brooke took a deep breath and looked up at him. 'It implies that she is a demon.'

46

'A *demon*?' Flaherty said, smirking. Glancing at the naked woman portrayed in the picture on his BlackBerry, he felt like he was looking at the primitive equivalent to a centrefold model.

'That's right,' Brooke said.

'Hmm. Too bad,' he said in jest.

She rolled her eyes. 'I'm sure it's a real tragedy that such a nice pair of boobs went to waste,' she grumbled, grabbing the BlackBerry from him.

He held up his hands as if to declare his innocence. 'What?'

She held the picture close to her eyes and squinted.

'I can show you how to zoom in on it,' Flaherty offered. 'What are you trying to see?'

'Not her boobs,' Brooke said, to torture him a bit more. 'There's a symbol on her wrist . . .'

'Here, let me help you.' He wrapped his hand around hers and pulled the BlackBerry closer. Then he tapped on the display to enlarge the area she was interested in.

'See this rosette on her wrist?' Brooke said. 'It's an ancient symbol of divinity. This conical headdress she's wearing is also a symbol of godliness.'

'Okay. So she's a *divine* demon wearing a dunce cap.'

She panned across the image to the wide-eyed bird perched on the goddess's right hand. 'It's an owl.'

'Who-o-o?' Flaherty joked.

She ignored him. Zooming out to view the full image again, she shook her head and said, 'God, how did I not think of this? Jason's right. Of course this is Lilith. The serpent, the owl, the wings . . .'

'And who, pray tell, is Lilith?'

'In the pantheon of ancient Mesopotamian deities, she was the goddess of storms and pestilence. One of the demons the ancients called *Lilitu*.'

Just then, the jet hit a rough patch of air and jostled the cabin hard enough for Brooke to grip her armrests. Within seconds the turbulence smoothed away.

'Careful . . . Lilith hears you,' Flaherty whispered.

Brooke took a calming breath before continuing. 'Lilith was even said to be the first woman God created alongside Adam. But because she was seductive and mischievous, God banished her from paradise. In exile, she found a new lover to satisfy her carnal desires – one of God's fallen archangels named Samael. Better known as the Angel of Death or the Grim Reaper.'

'You don't say,' Flaherty said.

'By copulating with Samael, Lilith became immortal and acquired supernatural powers. Ancient apocryphal texts say that she morphed into a serpent and slithered back into Eden on a mission of vengeance against Adam and Eve. Using her powers of seduction, she persuaded the couple to disobey God so that they, too, lost favour with Him and were banished from Eden.

It's a common mythological theme,' she explained. 'Curiosity and forbidden knowledge leading to humankind's downfall. Usually at the hand of a woman.'

'Just like Pandora's Box.'

She grinned tightly. 'Funny you say that, because in the original Greek myth of Pandora, the vessel containing all the world's evils is described as a *pithos* – not a box, but a large clay jar, just like the one Lilith brought into that village.'

'So maybe Pandora was inspired by Lilith too,' Flaherty said.

'Maybe. And interestingly enough, Persian mythology separately developed Ishtar as the goddess of love, sex and war – the embodiment of vengeance. An image very similar to this winged figure here,' she said, 'is how Ishtar was depicted by the Babylonians. Anyway, I've given you an earful I . . .' she said apologetically. 'It's just that this is all so incredible.'

'You don't believe all that hocus-pocus stuff, do you? Demons?' he asked.

She shrugged. 'I believe evil has always been around and in the absence of science, ancient people attributed everything bad to the wrath of gods and demons. All mythology is crammed with superstition.'

'Let's have a look at the other pictures Jason sent,' he suggested, reaching out to help her open the remaining file. When it came up, he wasn't sure what he was looking at. 'Any idea what this is?' He turned the BlackBerry back to her.

Brooke's eyes went wide and she snatched the BlackBerry back from him. 'Writing,' she said, excited. 'The same kind of text I deciphered in the cave's entry tunnel.'

'I still don't see how *that* is writing?' The shadowy edges of the tightly packed, wedged-shaped symbols appeared more 'design' than text.

'The oldest writing ever recorded,' she reminded him. She noticed Lilith's feet and the bone pile images had been cut off along the top edge of the picture. 'Looks like Jason found this below the etching of Lilith.'

'What does it say?'

She shrugged. 'I'm sure I can decipher it . . . looks clear enough.' Luckily, Jason had used plenty of light to pull the shadows out from the characters. 'But I'll need to enlarge it.'

Flaherty glanced out the window and was surprised to see that the jet was already gliding in low over the runway at Las Vegas International. 'No problem. I'll transfer the file to my laptop,' he said, patting his carry-on bag. 'The screen is plenty big. You can read it in the car.'

'Awesome,' she said, beaming. 'Tommy, we might just get Lilith's story after all. Do you know what that means?'

She looked like a kid who'd just been told she'd have to wait to open her birthday presents. 'Not really, but I'm sure you'll tell me.'

47

IRAQ

Lance Corporal Jeremy Levin estimated that fifteen minutes had elapsed since Crawford's marines hung an American flag from the cross bar directly behind his patient's head. They'd also set up a tripod-mounted digital camcorder to record the colonel's systematic interrogation.

This was no ordinary patient.

As Colonel Crawford fired away his probing questions – mainly queries as to where the convoy had been heading and the rumour that Al-Zahrani was plotting to detonate a suitcase nuke in New York on the anniversary of 9/11 – the subdued Kurdish translator used a marker to scrawl the queries on to a notepad in both Arabic and English.

The patient was highly uncooperative; though not by choice, Levin was certain. He could tell by Al-Zahrani's withdrawn and hazy gaze – unresponsive when the Kurd held the notepad in direct view – that his condition was deteriorating at an alarming rate. Only five minutes ago, Al-Zahrani had begun coughing. Now that cough was persistent and accompanied by heaving lungs that wheezed and gurgled. Coupled with Al-Zahrani's

237

fever, malaise and runny nose, Levin suspected that the prisoner had come down with the flu. In a civilian setting where containment was a simple matter of bed rest, influenza wasn't critical, per se. But in the battlefield, the flu could be as deadly as a roadside bomb – which was why Levin had already used an influenza test kit to analyse the mucus sample swabbed from Al-Zahrani's nose. However, the test strip had shown a solid blue line that indicated with 99 per cent certainty that Al-Zahrani was 'negative' for both influenza A and B.

Not the flu? How could it *not* be the flu? Or perhaps, not the *common* flu, he'd thought dreadingly. That prompted him to unpack a second test kit recently made standard equipment for combat medics to simultaneously detect H5N1 avian flu and H1N1 swine flu. With a sterile swab stick pinched between the fingers of his right hand and a fresh test tube in his left hand, he slunk over to Al-Zahrani's bedside and inserted the swab's foam tip one inch into the patient's runny nose.

Crawford paused and cocked his head sideways disdainfully. 'Couldn't pick his nose right the first time, Corporal?'

'Just need to run another quick test.' He twirled the swab tip around Al-Zahrani's nostril, pulled it out, and dropped it into the reagent solution that filled the bottom of the glass test tube. 'There. All done.' He retreated quickly and Crawford huffed before continuing on with his questioning.

Sitting at his makeshift lab table, Levin twirled the swab stick in the solution and pulled it out. Then he slid the coated test strip that came with the kit into the solution. The results would take ten minutes, so he noted the current time on his wristwatch.

His left leg bouncing nervously up and down, Levin tried to focus on Crawford to alleviate his mounting anxiety. It seemed that Crawford was brushing away the concerns of everyone around him, including Jason Yaeger. After the tense exchange Levin had witnessed earlier, Crawford still hadn't called for the backup platoons Yaeger had sensibly demanded. If Yaeger hadn't been successful in breaking Crawford's blind stubbornness, Levin had little hope that the colonel would heed a request to have Al-Zahrani airlifted to the nearest hospital for proper treatment, which was what Levin's gut was telling him the situation might warrant.

He peeked down at the test strip, saw nothing. Checked his watch – five minutes left. He shifted his gaze back to Crawford.

Normally Crawford was cool and collected – a proven leader who performed best under pressure; a guy whose impressive career had placed him on every battlefront in the Middle East over the past two decades. Crawford's ostensibly prophetic insight into the mind of Islamic terrorists made him an indispensable asset in Iraq. But everything Levin had witnessed thus far today was completely out of synch with the colonel he'd thought he knew. Crawford's behaviour seemed borderline schizophrenic. Even now he seemed in denial as he persisted in interrogating a man who was barely coherent.

Levin passed his clinical eyes over Al-Zahrani again. Ethical concerns aside, he would prefer nothing more than to disregard Hippocrates' primary directive, 'above all, do no harm', and personally see to it that this most undesirable patient slowly choke to death on his own sputum.

Above all, however, Levin wanted to avoid at all costs Al-Zahrani unleashing a viral Trojan Horse on the platoon. The battlefield was a cesspool of bacteria. Even with decades of technological advances in trauma care, modern warfare was still plagued by more casualties associated with biological infection than friendly fire and hostile gunfire combined. Though troops lived in close quarters to promote comradeship, that thoughtful arrangement also provided a perfect breeding ground for communicable diseases. Particularly since the troops didn't enjoy the luxury of daily showers or clean toilets.

With a steady flow of US troops moving back and forth between the Middle East and domestic military bases, the Department of Defense had gotten very aggressive in containing even the smallest of outbreaks. Prophylactic treatments for contagions ranging from flu to anthrax were mandatory for all troops deploying to the Middle East – six inoculations over an eighteen-month period, followed by annual booster shots. Yet these measures were far from perfect, especially when it came to the highly virulent influenza microbe, which played an endless game of 'gene swap' with animals and humans. The recent swine flu pandemic was a potent reminder of how easily influenza could mutate and render vaccines obsolete.

Another glance at the test strip. Two more minutes to go.

Levin tried to block out the distressing thoughts of Al-Zahrani infecting the troops with some mutated flu strain. Worse yet, the terrorist might already have infected a number of Iraqis during his clandestine movement from city to city.

In Iraq, sparse terrain provided hardy, natural buffers that counteracted disease transmission. But one infected individual could easily ignite a lethal epidemic within one of the region's densely populated cities. A person infected in that city then travels to a virgin population in another city . . . and from there, the dominos would keep falling. It was a sobering reminder that most wars in history – from the Mongolian invasion of the Roman Empire, to Hernando de Soto's conquest of the Americas, to Napoleon's attempt at world domination – had been determined not by military might and superior weapons . . . but by germs.

Crawford was quick to label Levin a worry-wart. That was to be expected. Military types focused primarily on munitions and artillery, and needed constant reminding that the most potent threats of modern warfare were not armed militants with an eye on martyrdom. Crawford, in particular, was a diehard battlefield minimalist who believed that a marine could survive with only a Bowie knife. It took a lot of convincing that sensible preventive measures were not intended to soften Crawford's killing machine.

Even Crawford had learned the hard way that infectious disease should not be ignored. During a reconnaissance mission the previous summer, Crawford's platoon had been patrolling Iraq's southern desert, toting sixty to a hundred pounds of gear in scorching temperatures that reached 130° Fahrenheit. Short on water rations, thanks to chronic logistical problems with contractors deploying Water Buffalo supply trucks, the troops had been forced to drink from untreated local water supplies that were teeming with harmful microorganisms. That led to widespread bouts of dysentery that practically debilitated the entire platoon. Naturally, Crawford wasn't affected since he'd had plenty of bottled water for himself.

'Stop worrying,' Levin told himself. He wiped his clammy hands on his pants.

Suddenly Crawford's growing frustration with the patient's hopeless condition hit its crescendo. The colonel yelled bloody murder for a full minute, then kicked over a crate and stormed out from the tent.

'Lunatic,' Levin mumbled. 'That guy is a walking pressure cooker.' He made eye contact with the Kurd, who shrugged, set down the marker and notepad, then made his way outside. Levin looked down at his watch to see that it was now thirty seconds over the ten-minute mark.

He looked down at the test strip, fully expecting to see a pink stain that would indicate that Al-Zahrani tested positive for swine flu or avian flu. His anxiety kicked into overdrive when he saw a single blue strip.

Negative?

48

Reaching the top of the slope, Crawford caught his breath before summoning Staff Sergeant Richards from the cave entrance. 'How much longer till it's cleared?'

Richards pursed his lips. 'Maybe a couple hours,' he guessed. 'I'm pushing the men as hard as I can. It's too narrow in there to run a second line.'

'Push harder,' Crawford insisted. 'I want to find out exactly what they brought into that cave,' he reminded him.

'I understand.'

Crawford looked over to Jason Yaeger, who was hauling buckets from the last man on the chain team and dumping them down the slope.

Richards picked up on the colonel's preoccupation with Yaeger. 'He was on his phone again,' the staff sergeant told Crawford. 'Didn't seem to be talking to anyone . . . just fiddling around. And before that, I saw him go into the other tunnel. Disappeared for a good fifteen, twenty minutes.'

'Nothing but trouble,' Crawford said, shooting Yaeger a dirty look.

'I heard he got up in your face in the tent.'

'Certainly did. That boy has a problem with authority.'

With finesse, Richards asked, 'Not to disrespect you, sir, but shouldn't we be moving Al-Zahrani out of here? I mean, it's not exactly safe—'

Crawford's eyes drilled into him. 'Don't you worry, Richards. Everything is under control. I know you're scared of the dark, but the sun will up before you know it.'

'Yes, sir.'

Yaeger had jumped off the line and was making his way over. 'Just fucking dandy,' Crawford moaned.

Staff Sergeant Richards wisely left the scene as Jason squared up with Crawford.

'Hazo tells me you weren't able to get anything out of Al-Zahrani,' Jason said.

'That's right,' Crawford confirmed. 'Not that it's any surprise. Doesn't need to be deaf to keep his mouth shut.'

'I suppose.'

'Find anything interesting while you were poking around in there?'

'Plenty,' Jason replied with defiant eyes. 'But something tells me it wouldn't be news to you.'

'Is that so?'

'Call it instinct.'

Crawford stood his ground. 'I call it a loaded accusation, Yaeger. And one should be very careful jumping to rash conclusions. Could get one in a world of trouble.'

'I agree. Just like I've already concluded that you didn't call for backup. Isn't that right?' He crossed his arms over his chest.

Crawford grinned smugly. 'That's my call to make, not yours,' he reminded him. Except this time, he was sure to provide a plausible rationale: 'As soon as that tunnel is clear, shouldn't take long to pull those other ragheads out. Then we'll be on our way. I'm guessing it might take another hour or so. About the same time it would take for a support platoon to get here. Besides, my men have been monitoring the airwaves and haven't heard a peep.'

'An *hour*?' Jason repeated. 'We don't even know what's behind those rocks. So how can you be so sure it won't take a lot longer?'

'Call it instinct. And let's face it, Yaeger,' he said with forced diplomacy, 'if there were miles of tunnel behind that rubble, Al-Zahrani wouldn't have been heading for the front door. We're close to extracting these sons of bitches and you know it. You've done your part, now let me do mine.'

Jason studied Crawford for a few seconds. Something wasn't right. 'One hour,' he said.

Crawford nodded. 'If we're not done by then, you can make the call yourself. Call in the entire brigade for all I care.'

49

Frozen to the spot, Lance Corporal Jeremy Levin stared at the test strip for five seconds, then over to Fahim Al-Zahrani. If Al-Zahrani was infected by a biological contagion and it wasn't influenza, identifying it might prove beyond the scope of his capabilities in the field. Back home, he'd refer this patient to an infectious-disease specialist, or the emergency room at Sinai-Grace Hospital. Here neither alternative was an option.

Suddenly, Al-Zahrani vomited all over himself, the tent instantly filling with a putrid smell. The two marines standing guard close to him immediately backed away.

'Jesus, Doc,' the first marine said. 'What the hell's wrong with this guy? It's like he's dying or something.'

The second marine cringed while craning his head to get a better look at what came up from Al-Zahrani's stomach. 'Not sure what he ate last, but there's an awful lot of blood in there. That can't be good.'

Overwhelmed, Levin didn't respond. Could this really be happening?

'Doc? You all right?' the first marine asked.

'I . . . I'm okay.' But this was a complete lie. If such a high pro-file captive died under his watch, there'd be hell to pay.

'Aren't you going to give him some drugs or something?'

'I already did.' He hesitated. 'I'm just not quite sure what's wrong with him.'

'Crawford probably poisoned him,' the second marine said, deadly serious. 'Doesn't want those contractors to get paid.'

The second marine pointed his chin at the oozing wound on Al-Zahrani's hand. 'Hey, how about this: maybe he got bit by a snake? I've heard there're some really nasty vipers in these mountains. I think I might have seen one of them squirming around when we were clearing the rubble.'

Levin gave the comment serious consideration. Native to Iraq were six species of highly venomous snakes – five in the Viperidae family, or 'vipers', and one in the Elapidae family, or 'cobras' – most of which were common in the deserts and grass-lands. Iraq's northern mountains, if his recollection was correct, were home to the Kurdistan vipers and Persian Horned vipers, both highly poisonous. But since most troops took precautions to not antagonize snakes, and given the fact that vipers had a tough time biting through combat boots, he'd had no practical experience in diagnosing or treating snake bites.

He mentally recollected facts from the acclimation training he'd received prior to his first deployment to Iraq. Viper venom was a haemotoxin – primary target: blood cells. When bitten, a patient would develop severe pain and swelling around the bite. Left untreated, massive internal bleeding could occur.

So maybe a snake bite couldn't be ruled out. But the most obvious symptom would be the wound itself, thought Levin, and the infected gouge in Al-Zahrani's hand looked nothing like the twin punctures left behind from snake fangs. Unless, perhaps,

Al-Zahrani had ripped off the snake hard enough to tear away flesh. Even so, could venom act so quickly? Were Iraq's mountain vipers *that* poisonous?

'A snake bite,' Levin muttered. 'Maybe. The snake you saw . . . did it have two horns protruding out from above its eyes?'

The marine was quick to respond. 'Nope.'

'What did it look like?'

'Maybe a metre long. Its skin was yellowish with big brown spots . . . kind of like a giraffe.'

Kurdistan viper, thought Levin.

'Then there's something you can give him for that, right?' the first marine asked.

'Yes. Yes, there is.' Protocol dictated that snake-bite victims were to be stabilized in the field, then flown back to the nearest command base for treatment. Therefore, antivenoms for the region's snakes had become a standard provision, compliments of Israeli Intelligence.

Levin used his sleeve to wipe sweat from his forehead, then scrambled to open his medical case. After rummaging for fifteen seconds, he found the correct snake-bite kit. He quickly skimmed the directions, then used the kit's saline ampoules to reconstitute the freeze-dried antivenom powder. He filled a syringe and hurried over to Al-Zahrani. He gave it a second thought, but said, 'I guess it can't hurt, right?'

'Go for it, Doc,' the second marine encouragingly replied with a wink and a nod.

Levin injected the antivenom into a thick vein on Al-Zahrani's forearm. Panic set in the moment Levin stood back to reassess the situation. Had he acted too hastily? If Al-Zahrani hadn't been bitten by a viper, would the antivenom exacerbate his condition? 'I'm not sure if this will work,' he told the marines.

'We've got to get him to a hospital, immediately.' He addressed the first marine, saying, 'You need to convince Crawford to transport him. Tell him what's happening in here.'

'I'll see what I can do,' the marine replied noncommittally, then hurried out from the tent.

'Wouldn't that be a kick in the balls?' the second marine said. 'Finding this douchebag and having him die like this.'

'You're not helping matters. So please shut up,' Levin snapped. Frantic now, he was trying to figure out what else he could do. Whatever was making Al-Zahrani haemorrhage internally might be visible under a microscope, he reasoned. With the constant threat of weaponized biological agents turning up in Iraq, Levin's acclimation training had also included advanced microscopy. So if he could isolate and identify the culprit . . .

Collecting himself, Levin swiftly unpacked the battery-powered microscope, which resembled an espresso maker – a state-of-the-art tool developed exclusively for the US military in response to the growing need to assess bioterror threats in the field. Next, he turned on his laptop and connected the microscope's USB cable. Within seconds, the operating system identified the plug-in device and launched its associated software application.

With renewed vigour, Levin pulled on a fresh pair of Nitrile gloves and peeled open a lancet. Grabbing a glass specimen slide, he went over to Al-Zahrani, pricked his finger and squeezed a blood drop on to the slide.

Without warning, Al-Zahrani's wounded hand arced up and clamped down on Levin's wrist. Levin reeled, tried to pull free from the iron grip. Their eyes met and Levin noticed immediately the tiny veins webbing out from the prisoner's irises. There was raw terror in those dark eyes and for just that moment it so satisfied Levin that he couldn't help but grin.

The marine reached over and yanked Al-Zahrani's hand away. 'Looks like he's still got some fight in him.'

Levin hastened back to the table, placed a second glass slide over the first, and gently sandwiched the specimen into a dime-sized splotch. He centred the specimen over the microscope's diffusion screen. Then he used the software controls to adjust magnification. A darkfield condenser lit the specimen from the sides, so that bands of light fluoresced the blood's living components.

Since viper venom attacks blood cells, Levin expected to find visible proof in the specimen: sphero-echinocytes, or compromised red blood cells that had lost their definitive doughnut shape and sprouted short, blunt spicules. As he adjusted the resolution, he immediately spotted anomalies. And the damage wasn't limited to the red blood cells.

Many of the red cells were indeed misshapen and coagulated into clumps, plus many spiny platelets' and ovoid white cells' membranes had also been compromised and were lysing – proof that a foreign invader was aggressively killing the cells from the inside out.

'What in God's name. . .?'

He set the microscope to its maximum magnification. In micro-scale, an invading force – definitely not venom – was engaged in a fight to the death. But he'd need an electron microscope to effectively analyse the virions. Whatever it was, its primary objective was plainly evident: replication.

Dread poured over him. 'Jesus,' he gasped.

'Everything all right, Doc?' the guard nervously inquired.

A pause.

'No,' Levin replied grimly, his complexion ashen. Would the troops' inoculations protect against this elusive killer? If not, the repercussions were unimaginable. 'My God, we could all be infected.'

'Infected?' The marine shifted uneasily. 'Wh-what do you mean by that, Doc?'

But before the medic could respond, the sound of gunfire pierced the night.

50

LAS VEGAS

Agent Flaherty accelerated the rented silver Dodge Charger and smoothly manoeuvred around a tractor trailer that was moving sluggishly north up Interstate 515. He checked the display on the dashboard-mounted GPS unit the rental agency had provided. Only eight miles to go, he thought.

The GPS software still registered Our Savior in Christ Cathedral as an unknown parcel along North Hollywood Boulevard. So Flaherty chose a random street number that was in the same range as the cathedral. Plenty of signboards along the interstate pointed to another major landmark immediately north of the cathedral, which did show in the GPS's outdated database: Nellis Air Force Base. Isn't that convenient for Stokes, thought Flaherty.

In the passenger seat, Brooke held Flaherty's laptop and was studying an enlargement of one of the pictures transferred from his BlackBerry. Even when they'd driven past the opulent resorts and casinos along the Strip, her focus hadn't budged. He'd given her his pocket notepad and a pen to jot down her transcriptions. She'd already filled one page and was starting on a second.

'You're awfully quiet,' Flaherty said finally.

'Sorry,' she said, giving him a quick, apologetic glance.

'Anything useful in those pictures?'

'Oh yeah,' she said. 'Hang on just a minute . . . almost finished.'

'The suspense is killing me.'

She smiled. 'It should. This is really intense.'

He drove on in silence for a solid minute, and just after the GPS's bland female voice-command prompted him to 'exit on to Charleston Boulevard in point-five miles', Brooke exhaled, sat tall in her seat and folded the laptop shut. She rolled her neck.

'Done?' Flaherty said. He glanced over at her and saw concern in her eyes.

'All done,' she said. 'My God, Tommy.' Flipping to the first page, she shook her head in disbelief. 'You're not going to believe this.'

'Try me.' He hit the GPS's mute button.

'Probably best to just read this to you first,' she said. 'This is all a bit rushed, so this may not be 100 per cent . . .'

'Just let me hear it, will you.'

Brooke cleared her throat. 'It starts with this passage.' She began reading:

She came from the realm of the rising sun
She who holds dominion over beasts and men
She who is the Screech Owl, the Night Creature
She who sows vengeance and retribution on all men
Before the moon had twice come
Fathers and sons, all, were dead
Her hand touched them not
Bathed in blood they perished, destroyed from within

No mother or daughter did she punish
She commanded the rivers to consume the land
The demon who killed the many
The one sent by the great creator to end all

'Okayyyy,' Flaherty said. 'That is creepy.'

'Tommy, those skeletons Jason found in that cave were all the men in that village. And this is saying Lilith killed *all* of them,' Brooke emphasized.

'How?'

'If she didn't use physical force, then I'd assume she spread some kind of disease that made them bleed to death.'

'What kind of disease kills everyone in two days? And only males?' The car interior was silent for a moment as they contemplated what they'd just heard. 'Whoever wrote that must have been exaggerating,' he suggested. 'Maybe they all got food poisoning or something and just didn't know who to blame.'

'Food poisoning would have killed the women too,' she muttered, looking back at her notes.

'Well, at least it explains why all those teeth found at Fort Detrick all came from males. What good are the teeth, anyway?' But when he looked over, he saw that she was deep in thought. 'Brooke?'

Teeth. Pestilence. Males. 'Oh my God,' she said suddenly.

'What?'

'Just recently, in an archaeology journal I read about these excavations of mass graves in France and Germany where plague victims had been buried,' she explained. 'In ancient specimens, plague leaves an imprint in the pulp of victims' teeth. These archaeologists had found perfectly preserved *Yersinia pestis* DNA in the teeth.'

'Yur-what DNA?'

'*Yersinia pestis* is the bacterium that causes bubonic plague. It gets into your lymph nodes, replicates like crazy, and makes you slowly haemorrhage to death,' she explained.

'Pleasant.'

'During the sixth century, it was called the "Plague of Justinian", killed a quarter of the people in the eastern Mediterranean and stopped the Byzantine emperor, Justinian, from reuniting Eastern and Western Europe under the Holy Roman Empire. And remember from history class when in the fourteenth century the Black Death killed half the population of Europe?'

He nodded. 'Actually, I do.'

'That was bubonic plague too. It became a pandemic and killed over a hundred million people worldwide . . . at that time, almost a quarter of the world's population.'

'Jeez, and we're worried about the lousy flu,' he said. 'But the Black Death didn't just kill men,' he pointed out. 'And you're saying it might have killed half of them . . . not *all* of them.'

'True,' she admitted. 'And the Black Death took a lot longer than two days to spread. It took months.'

'So you think something like the Black Death killed these guys?'

'With such a high mortality rate, probably something worse. I'm no epidemiologist. I mean, humans have been fighting these kinds of diseases ever since they started living in sedentary set-tlements. Since Iraq was home to the earliest cities and gave birth to agriculture, Mesopotamians would have been among the first people to transmit infectious disease. They'd have picked up all sorts of germs from domesticated cows, sheep, chickens, you name it. So it makes sense. And these men that

Lilith killed belonged to a sizable, relatively isolated population. If they had no immunity to a disease brought in by an outsider, it would have spread like wildfire.'

Flaherty slowed to make a left on to North Hollywood Boulevard. 'All right, let's hold off on this for a little while, because we're almost there. We need to talk about how we're going to handle this Stokes character.'

'He may not even be here, Tommy.'

'He'll be here,' Flaherty replied confidently. 'Remember: he needs that encrypted phone line to talk with Crawford.'

Nestled at the foot of a desert mountain, the modern edifice of the megachurch glinted in the afternoon sun.

'Holy cow, will you look at that,' he said.

'Wow. It's *huge*.'

'Supposedly seats up to ten thousand.'

51
IRAQ

Jason was inside the tunnel entrance when he heard the *rat-tat-tat-tat-tat* of automatic gunfire. He dropped the rubble-filled bucket he'd just taken from the marine in front of him, ran to the opening, and squatted low. Then he cautiously poked his head out and scanned the camp. Behind him, four marines queued up.

'I heard it too,' one of the marines said. 'What's going on?'

Jason held up a fist to signal for them to remain quiet.

In the moonlight, he could see a marine crossing the roadway – presumably the shooter. On the other side of the road, the scout swiftly moved around a hillock with the stock of his M-16 raised up against his shoulder. The other marines stayed back and hunkered down to cover him.

Then the scout lowered his weapon and shook his head, pointing to something that lay on the ground behind the hillock. Jason couldn't hear clearly what the scout was saying, but saw five marines go out to have a look at what he'd shot. When the scout reached down and held up a limp, bloody fox by its tail, they all lowered their weapons and gave him a good ribbing.

Jason didn't like the fact that the scout was so quick to shoot a suspicious target. What if instead that had been some curious Iraqi kid who just wanted to see what was going on? He sighed and turned to the others. 'False alarm.'

Disappointed, they went back to their positions as Jason grabbed his bucket and lugged it outside.

As he dumped the stones down the slope, he was surprised to see that the carefree marines remained out on the open road, clustered together, heckling the shooter. Why wasn't Crawford or Richards reprimanding them?

'Not smart, fellas,' he grumbled to himself.

Jason scanned the area, but Crawford and his officers were nowhere to be found. Probably back in the tent grilling Al-Zahrani again, he guessed. Ten minutes ago, one of the marines who'd been assigned to watch over the prisoner came looking for Crawford, visibly distressed. But another man had redirected him down the hill to where Crawford had gone to check on the men working inside the MRAP. Now Jason was wishing he'd asked the guard if there was a problem.

If something was wrong, would Crawford have said something? Jason wondered. Studying the area around the tents, he thought: No, that stubborn jackass wouldn't say a damn thing.

Something wasn't right . . . he could feel it.

'Guys, I'll be back in a few minutes,' he called to the men in the cave.

As he loped down the steep incline, a *whump-hsssss* sound – like Fourth of July fireworks being shot up into the sky – made him stop dead in his tracks. He crouched low at the same time as his eyes locked on to a fiery orange light streaming through the night . . . on a direct path for the loitering marines.

Jason cupped his hands and yelled, 'Get off the road!'

But it was too late.

The marines had no time to react. The RPG mortar struck directly at their feet and popped, tearing them to pieces in a billowing fireball. Shrapnel spray took down three more marines posted nearby.

Jason looked over his shoulder and saw the marines streaming out from the cave. Hazo and Camel were with them. They'd clearly figured out what was going on.

'We're under attack!' one of them yelled to the others still inside the cave. 'Everyone out!'

Down below, chaos broke out as the marines tried to determine where the enemy was positioned.

Another mortar fired at the camp from a different angle. This time, Jason traced the exhaust trail and pinpointed a gunman sinking below a hummock situated fifty metres south from the camp. The grenade struck one of the Humvees and threw out a huge fireball, sending marines dashing for cover.

At the same time, automatic gunfire started raining down from elevated positions along the neighbouring mountaintop. That's also when Jason spotted trucks less than a klick south along the roadway. He scrambled down to the camp, his sights locked on to the tent.

The chaos happening outside the tent – gunfire, explosions, shouting – rang loud and clear, but Lance Corporal Jeremy Levin was unfettered as he pleaded with Crawford, 'But we can't move him now! I just told you he's infected!'

'Stand down, Corporal,' Crawford said. He turned to the two guards. 'You two go outside and make sure no one comes near this tent . . . and I mean no one.'

The marines rushed to the door and disappeared.

'Colonel . . .' Levin pleaded, grabbing Crawford's arm. 'This man is very, *very* sick! He's got—' His fearful eyes went to Al-Zahrani, whose face and tunic were pasted with bloody vomit.

'Get your mangy paw off me, Corporal. I know damn well what he's got.' Crawford's crazed eyes went wide. He forcefully shoved the medic back into the table, sending the laptop and microscope hurling to the ground.

Groaning, Levin picked himself up off the ground. The horror of Crawford's words came crashing down upon him. 'Wait. What did you say?'

Crawford looked away, calculating his options.

'What do you mean you know what he's got?' Levin's voice was tremulous.

A malevolent expression came over Crawford. 'Don't you worry about that,' he hissed. 'Just have Al-Zahrani ready for transport. This is your last chance.'

'Look at him!' Levin screamed, pointing at Al-Zahrani. 'It's too late to bring him *anywhere*! Besides, don't you hear what's going on out there! He needs to be quarantined! We *all* need to be quarantined!'

Crawford smirked. 'No *we* don't,' he replied knowingly. He noted that the notoriously cautious medic wasn't wearing his flak jacket.

The colonel's response confused Levin. 'But I *saw* what's happening inside of him! Anyone who touches him . . . anyone who goes *near* him—'

Realizing the futility of the situation, Crawford snatched the M9 pistol off his belt holster and fired a single shot into Levin's unprotected chest.

As Lance Corporal Jeremy Levin crumpled to the ground,

the tent's rear door opened. Crawford wheeled instantly and dropped to one knee. He aimed his pistol at a turbaned man who was coming inside.

The man froze and raised his hands.

Seeing the intruder's face, Crawford lowered the gun.

'Easy,' Staff Sergeant Richards said. 'It's just me.'

Crawford collected himself and got back on his feet. He holstered the pistol and waved for him to keep moving. 'Let's go, we don't have much time.'

Striding towards Al-Zahrani, Richards eyed the dead medic, sprawled face down in a pool of thick blood that was creeping over the sand. 'What did you—?'

'Just keep moving,' Crawford replied dismissively.

Richards ripped down the American flag that hung behind Al-Zahrani and threw it aside. Making a sour face, he positioned himself at the head of the bed and reluctantly hooked his arms under the prisoner's sweaty armpits. 'Grab his feet,' he told Crawford.

Crawford hesitated at the prospect of touching Al-Zahrani.

He glanced at the medic's body and, for the first time, felt doubt. What if the medic was right? What if Stokes didn't really know how the contagion would respond in a real-world setting? After all, Randall Stokes hadn't managed the scientific aspects of the project – that responsibility had been delegated to Frank Roselli. Though Frank had parlayed his military service into a top post at Fort Detrick, he'd spent the majority of his career with Force Recon running Special Ops missions throughout the Middle East. Frank was a bright, industrious guy. But he was no scientist.

Despite the fact that Frank Roselli had recruited USAMRIID top geneticists and virologists to work on Operation Genesis, the

261

scientists had been kept in the dark as to the true purpose of their engineered contagion. For all they knew, it was just one more experiment that would be packed away in USAMRIID's ever-growing stockpile of biological agents. And in typical military fashion, each team member worked on only one facet of a very complex gem.

After Frank's superiors learned about the covert cave excavation and subsequent on-site installation he'd managed here in Iraq, Frank had been forced to resign . . . before definitive clinical tests had been performed. Regardless, Crawford was highly sceptical that a controlled laboratory environment could ever simulate the countless 'what-if' scenarios that might play out in the real world. The fact that Al-Zahrani had somehow already gotten infected only proved that point.

Since its inception, Operation Genesis had been on the fast-track. With things getting sloppy, no clear objective and no way out, Crawford found himself wishing for simpler days, when conventional battles were fought using conventional tactics. *Mano y mano.*

If only Stokes – the smartest of the three – hadn't gotten his leg blown off and had an epiphany to single-handedly rewrite the rules of modern warfare. Stokes was one charismatic son of a bitch, thought Crawford – a salesman to salesmen. The question was: had Crawford himself fallen under Stokes's spell? With all of Stokes's TV-talk of Revelation and Judgement Day, there seemed a very real possibility that Stokes might well himself be the silver-tongued Antichrist.

Secreting Al-Zahrani out the back door of this tent would surely seal the fate of humankind. A new balance would be struck. Al-Zahrani would be the ultimate experiment. The ultimate 'what-if' scenario.

'Sir! Please . . . I can't do this alone,' Richards insisted.

Snapping out of his funk, Crawford rushed over to the bed and hooked his hands under Al-Zahrani's ankles. He counted to three. They hoisted Al-Zahrani from the bed, carried him out the back door, and loaded him into the passenger seat of a pickup truck that sat idling outside.

52

'I need to speak with Crawford . . . *Now!*' Jason insisted to the two marines who blocked the door to the tent. 'So step aside!' He had to yell to compete with the barrage of gunfire throughout the camp. He dared a step closer, but the marines aimed their M-16s at his chest.

'No exceptions!' the taller marine screamed robotically back at him. 'No one goes inside!'

Jason stared disbelievingly at their weapons. 'You're making a big mistake,' he warned. 'We need to get Al-Zahrani inside the MRAP! It's the only place he'll be safe!' The MRAP was a rolling fortress designed specifically to sustain high-calibre rounds and direct hits from light and medium artillery. With the ambush intensifying, the tent was an easy target. How could these morons not figure it out?

The guards stood their ground.

Jason's adrenaline was pumping hard enough to make him see stars. It was precisely this blind allegiance that he'd come to loathe about the military. Even the most intelligent minds were malleable, so that over time a soldier's thoughts and core ideals could be deconstructed and craftily reprogrammed. Successful armies relied on this group psyche to bond soldiers under extreme conditions, but he'd also witnessed how ego-driven leadership could easily exploit loyalty for purely self-serving objectives that inevitably led to unnecessary casualties. It happened often, and it was happening right now before his very eyes. Jason clenched his fists and glared at the guards.

'Sorry. We have our orders,' the shorter, less malleable one replied.

'And we have ours!' a deep voice blasted over the din.

In unison, Jason and the marines turned to the voice.

Meat, Camel and Jam stepped up in a V formation, pointing M-16s at the marines.

'Let's keep things friendly, fellas,' Meat suggested. 'Let the man inside. You know he's right. So be smart, will you please? Right now we've all got a real battle to fight.' He tipped his head towards the road where the remaining marines were mobilized, struggling to hold back the advancing enemy convoy now a half klick south.

The marines exchanged glances.

'You've got big balls, pal,' the taller one said.

'And I've got the dick to match them,' Meat boasted. 'So what's it gonna be?'

The taller man grimaced, lowered his weapon, then tapped his partner on the arm and motioned for him to step aside. 'Behave yourself in there,' the marine warned Jason.

Jason nodded to Meat, then swiftly made his way through the door.

*

Inside the tent, Jason was shocked to see that Al-Zahrani was gone and that the medic had been shot dead. Momentarily sidetracked by the miasma that covered the bed, he registered a tiny blinking red light. It was the tripod-mounted camcorder Crawford had set up to record his interrogation. Jason darted over to it and checked the device's tiny LCD screen, which flashed 'DISK FULL.' How long had the device been offline? With no time to review the footage, he hit the eject button, took out the mini-DVD disk and pocketed it.

Then his eyes caught the splotchy blood trail that began alongside the bed and snaked to the rear door.

He sprinted to the rear door and threw it open. Out back there were no guards and Crawford was nowhere to be found. In the sand, parallel tyre tracks curled around the side of the tent. Dust from a moving vehicle still hung in the air.

Jason dashed around the tent, his eyes tracing where the tyre tracks bent on to the roadway, heading north. Despite the danger from flying bullets, he ran out near the road and ducked behind the confiscated pickup trucks – now three instead of four. Looking north, he found the fourth pickup racing along the winding road-way. The driver was wearing a turban. The passenger's slumped head – also wrapped in a turban – was barely visible through the blown-out rear cabin window. He had no doubt it was Al-Zahrani.

There was no way a militant could have broken the perimeter, snuck Al-Zahrani out from the tent, and stolen the truck unnoticed. And why hadn't Crawford had guards posted at the tent's rear door? Because an insider orchestrated the grab, Jason quickly concluded. 'Crawford, you motherfucker.'

Where could they be taking Al-Zahrani? Something told him that Crawford wasn't concerned about protecting the prisoner. So what was his motive?

'Yaeger, get out of there!' a distant voice screamed. 'Grenade!'

Without thought, Jason sprang up and ran for the shallow ravine that cut along the opposite side of the road. On the periphery of his vision, he glimpsed the mortar arcing through the air on a direct line for the trucks, just before he dived for cover.

He was midair when the mortar struck. Amidst a spray of heat and glass, a tyre rim hurtled directly for his head like a frisbee. He was certain he would be decapitated. But the blast wave cartwheeled his body forward and down an instant before that could happen.

He landed on his back at the bottom of the muddy ditch. He slowly opened his eyes and assessed his body, fully expecting to see some missing parts. Amazingly, no shrapnel had touched him – not even a graze. Everything moved fine, nothing felt broken. Just some ringing in his ears.

'Google!' a concerned voice yelled.

Jason looked up and saw it was Meat.

'Dude! I thought you were dead!' He slung his M-16 over his shoulder and slid down into the ditch. 'I saw you running out here. What are you, nuts?'

'They took Al-Zahrani. Moved him out in one of the pickup trucks . . . heading north.' Jason pointed.

'Who?'

'Pretty sure it was Crawford or one of his men.'

'Why would he do that?'

'Don't know. But we've got to get Al-Zahrani back.' He raised a hand up, saying, 'Give me a pull, will ya.'

Meat clasped Jason's hand and tugged him to his feet.

'The trucks are toast,' Meat said. 'And there's only one Humvee left . . . but it's got two flat tyres.'

'So we'll follow them in the MRAP,' Jason replied hastily.

'Way too slow. That thing's not built for speed and it's a pig on gas. They might have a good head start, but I've got a better idea,' Meat said. 'Let's go.'

53

Nestled behind a hill on the camp's northern limit, the Blackhawk had yet to sustain bombardment. That indicated to Jason that the militants had concentrated on a purely southern incursion, with no artillery fire coming from the expansive western plain, or the mountains to the north and east. Most likely, the enemy scout Jason had spotted earlier had been spooked by the patrolling marines and realized that any attempt to surround the encampment would take too long and prove too risky.

Jason knew that once the hostile RPG gunners were in range, the Blackhawk would become their primary target.

'Let's go! Move it!' Meat yelled towards the camp from the top of the hill. He waved impatiently for Camel and Jam to pick up their pace. Then he ran down the hill towards Jason.

'You still know how to fly one of these things?' Jason asked.

Meat gave the chopper a sideways glance. 'No worries, bro,' he said, patting Jason on the shoulder.

Meat hurried to the chopper, opened the cockpit door, and hopped in the pilot's seat.

Camel and Jam crested the hill and scrambled down to Jason.

Seeing them alive gave Jason relief. At the onset of the attack, they'd all been safe inside the cave helping to clear debris.

'It's pandemonium back there!' Jam said.

'Where's Hazo?' Jason asked.

'He's fine,' Camel said. 'He said he'll stay here and keep an eye on things.'

With Crawford unaccounted for, Jason wasn't thrilled about the idea. But there was no time to deliberate. 'Fine.'

The Blackhawk's engines fired up. Seconds later, the turbine whined to life and the flopping rotors began turning, gathering momentum.

'You've got to be shitting me,' Camel said, with frightened eyes on the cockpit window where Meat was putting on his flying helmet. 'You're letting *him* fly?'

'We've got no choice,' Jason said. 'Meat said the pilots were inside the first Humvee that blew.'

'Mother Mary,' Jam said.

'He figured out how to turn the thing on,' Camel offered with a sigh. 'It's a start.'

Jason trotted to the chopper and slid open the fuselage door. He leaped inside, Camel and Jam coming in behind him.

While Jason settled in the copilot's seat alongside Meat, Camel and Jam each claimed a jumpseat and began buckling their harnesses. Jason looked over to Meat. The guy's eyes were nervously roving the controls, hands splayed flat on his thighs.

'You sure you can do this?' Jason asked him.

'Just like riding a bike, right?' Meat chuckled nervously.

Jason wasn't so sure. It had been eight years since Meat's brief stint with the Coast Guard. Shortly after 9/11, sea patrol and rescue missions had become increasingly dangerous as Islamic extremists used sea routes to circumvent US border patrols.

Homeland Security responded by cross-training military personnel to accompany Coast Guard crews. Most of Meat's training had been inside a simulator, and he had only logged a few flight hours inside a Sikorsky Jayhawk. The Blackhawk's instrumentation and gadgetry, though, was more complicated and he could see that Meat was mentally running through the mechanical sequences, reacquainting himself with the gauges and controls. And unlike the Jayhawk, its bigger cousin was fully outfitted with armaments and countermeasures.

Suddenly, something flashed along the hill's crest, burst bright orange and rang like a thunderclap. The chopper rocked sideways as blast debris clanged against the fuselage. Stones strafed Meat's window and fractured the glass into a web of cracks.

'Go!' Jason yelled into the helmet microphone.

Meat excitedly pushed down too hard on the collective control stick, forcing the Blackhawk to jolt upward. As if he weredriving a car, his right foot instinctively stomped the anti-torque pedal so that the nose yawed perilously to the right, swinging the mountainside into full view.

Jason grabbed hold of the grip bars, bracing for collision.

Then Meat got the feel for the pedals and used his left foot to rotate the chopper and orient the nose back towards the plain.

Camel yelled through the intercom, 'Grenade!'

Meat saw it streaming towards them. He pushed the cyclic control stick forward and left, to pitch the vector. The nose dipped and the chopper shot forward. The RPG mortar practically skimmed the Blackhawk's belly before striking the cliff face, throwing off a concussion wave that whumped the chopper like an invisible fist.

Meat fought with the controls to keep the chopper straight.

'Get us clear!' Jason yelled, pointing out over the plain. 'Then move into firing range!'

'Roger,' Meat said.

'Firing range?' Camel muttered over the intercom.

'We can't abandon the platoon,' Jason said. 'They won't be able to hold off those gunners. We've got enough firepower to take them down.'

'What about the truck? Al-Zahrani?' Jam said.

'We'll catch up to them,' Jason replied confidently. 'Don't worry.'

'You'll need to work the weapons console,' Meat said, glancing over at Jason. He pointed to the copilot controls in front of him.

Staring down at the switches, gauges and computer interfaces, Jason felt instantly overwhelmed.

Meat flipped some switches on the cyclic's grip which powered on the AGM-114 Hellfire missiles rack-mounted on the pylons. The targeting interface illuminated on the LCD in front of Jason – a camera tracing the terrain beneath the chopper with glowing night vision, overlaid with crosshairs.

'Works like a videogame,' Meat explained to Jason. 'I'll walk you through it as soon as we're in range.'

'Got it.'

Safely out over the plain, Meat banked the chopper along a wide arc and headed south to allow for the first glimpse of the enemy convoy.

'Holy shit!' Jam said. 'Look at them all!' He pointed out the fuselage window.

Jason saw what he meant. There looked to be almost a dozen trucks on the road south from the camp.

'All right,' Meat said, flipping down the helmet's night-vision lenses. He paused to study the enemy formation. 'They're bunched up pretty nicely along the road. I'll take us two klicks out so we can line up for a nice shot. I'll need to focus on keeping this thing steady. So I'll need you to send some rockets at 'em,' he told Jason. 'Use the toggle button on top of the grip to move the crosshairs over the target. Then squeeze the trigger to get a laser on it . . . you'll see it come up on the screen. Just be sure to keep the laser dot on the target until the rocket hits. Use the red button to fire the missile. Fire and forget. Think you can do it?'

'Roger that,' Jason said, focused on the targeting screen and getting a feel for the control grip. He used his thumb to move the crosshairs side to side. As he tested the forward and backward functions, the camera zoomed in and out.

'They see us coming,' Jam said, scanning the militants through his night-vision goggles. The Arabs were scrambling to target the incoming Blackhawk.

'Doesn't matter. Their RPGs are only good up to a thousand metres. And their guns can only shoot half that distance. They won't know what hit 'em,' Meat said.

Climbing higher, Meat smoothly circled along a northerly course. 'Get ready,' he said to Jason.

He swung the chopper around, gained more altitude, and let the digital stabilization system assist in hovering the chopper. Luckily, there was minimal drag from the light winds moving over the plain. 'Go for it, Jay. Give 'em hell.'

The roadway cut horizontally along the targeting display, sandwiched by the foothills on the back side, a deep ravine and dense wheat field in the front. The convoy lined up onscreen like a shooting gallery. Jason immediately knew that the Arabs' hasty attack was about to backfire horribly on them. He decided to use the same tactic that roadside bombers had so frequently employed when assaulting US convoys – strike the lead vehicle first, then the rearmost vehicle next to immobilize everything in between.

Jason felt his stomach go into a knot as he zoomed in and panned the crosshairs over one of the trucks fanned out in the front of the convoy.

'Remember to keep the laser on the target until the missile hits,' Meat said.

'Got it,' Jason said. He squeezed the trigger control and a flashing red dot appeared on the display. He adjusted the aim, held the dot steady, and the crosshairs flashed from red to green. He slid his thumb over the red firing button and pressed down on it.

The first missile hissed out from its pod, shot out in front of the chopper along a high arc, then bobbed and weaved as its onboard guidance system synchronized with the laser's coordinates. Jason kept his eyes nailed to the crosshairs, made slight adjustments for the side-to-side rocking caused by Meat's less than graceful attempt to hover the Blackhawk. Onscreen the missile struck with a brilliant flash.

'Nice!' Meat said.

'Now let's hit them in the rear.' Intensely focused, Jason panned the crosshairs to the convoy's rear, picked his target and squeezed a laser mark. Keeping the laser dot steady over a pickup truck mounted with a crude machine gun turret, he hit the fire button. The second missile hissed out from the weapons pylon, spooled and angled sharply towards the target. Within seconds, it hit – decimating the target with flawless execution.

Jam and Camel hooted and high-fived one another.

'Now pop 'em in the middle,' Meat said.

'Roger that,' Jason said. He targeted the remaining vehicles and fired a third missile.

Another explosion rocked the convoy's centre in a maelstrom of fire, hurling bodies and metal in every direction.

Meat pulled the cyclic to the left and the chopper banked. He spotted the Arabs charging north along the open roadway. 'They're on the run, heading north to the camp. Camel, you're up. I'll sweep in and you hit anything that moves with the mini gun.'

'Roger,' Camel said. He assumed a crouch position behind the six-barrel M134 Gatling gun pedestal-mounted outside the fuselage doorframe. He opened the ammunition container cover to check the supply. It was filled with 7.62 mm shells. He flipped on the mini gun's master arm switch, then adjusted the gun scope's night-vision display. Gripping the fire control handles, he tested the swivel mount's action.

'You ready, Camel?' Meat called over the intercom.

'Ready,' he replied, steadying his thumbs over the trigger buttons.

Meat manoeuvred the Blackhawk on a sharp trajectory, gliding low on approach, and hooking sharply along the road.

Camel lined the runners in the scope's crosshairs – all scrambling for cover. He opened fire at 3,000 rounds per minute, effortlessly cutting down the combatants and sending bodies tumbling off into the ravine. He even managed to strafe a trio attempting to climb over the foothill. In one sweep, he guessed that half of the fifteen surviving Arabs had been taken out.

Meat pulled up and banked out over the plain again.

'One more pass . . . then the marines are on their own,' Jason said.

The Blackhawk's final sweep eliminated all but three Arabs, whose focus had turned from attack to retreat.

'Shit, Camel,' Meat said, impressed. 'That was some nice shooting.'

'He's the goddamn Terminator!' Jam said.

As the chopper pulled away, Jason was fixated on the roadway, which in less than five minutes had been transformed into a living nightmare of carnage and fire. His nerves were buzzing with adrenaline, fingers trembling. Though he feared the emotional swirl of satisfaction, euphoria and indifference that this perfect devastation evoked, he allowed himself to embrace the primal urge awakened deep in his core – the lust for vengeance; the driving force that pushed otherwise rational men to commit unspeakable acts to exact justice. That's for Matthew. Burn in Hell . . . all of you.

But the vendetta was far from complete.

'Now let's get Al-Zahrani back,' Jason said.

54

LAS VEGAS

If there was an economic slowdown in Las Vegas, it certainly wasn't evident at the bustling work site of Our Savior in Christ Cathedral, Flaherty thought. An armada of construction vehicles commandeered the sprawling parking lot – cement mixers, flatbeds piled with steel framing and massive cable reels, and HVAC vans. Throughout the lot, building materials were organized into sectors: rows upon rows of tinted-glass panels; mountains of honey-coloured marble floor tiles; hundreds of porcelain restroom fixtures sorted by colour. And stacked three-high were clusters of shipping containers bearing various import seals.

Flaherty steered the rental car around dozens of pallets stacked with pale limestone blocks. The clear plastic wrappings were stamped: 'AUTHENTIC JERUSALEM STONE, INC.'. A forklift had just removed a batch and was heading to the building's south side where a huge glass-domed amphitheatre abutted the mountainside.

Near the cathedral's main entrance, he parked in a designated visitors' lot.

'You think it's smart to just barge in there?' Brooke said, peering out at the building. 'Shouldn't the police be here or something?'

'This place has a lot of windows. The pastor might make a break for it the second he spots a police car.'

'So how do you propose we handle this?'

'I propose we get married,' he said, deadly serious.

'Excuse me?'

'Just follow my lead and you'll get the idea,' he replied coolly.

He turned off the car, pocketed the keys and opened his door. 'Let me come around and get you.'

Baffled, Brooke waited for him to circle to her door. He opened it and proffered a hand. 'Come, darling. I think you'll love this church. I hear the wedding ceremony is breathtaking.'

Then she caught on to the ruse. 'Ah, very clever. We're posing as customers. I like it.'

'Works in the movies,' he said with a shrug.

When Brooke clasped his hand, he noted her gold Irish Claddagh ring – two hands clasping a heart and surmounted by a crown. It could easily pass as an engagement ring . . . If she wore it differently.

'First, let's fix this,' he said. Keeping her hand out of view, he pointed at her ring, explaining: 'This says you're romantically available. Not good for our charade. May I?' he said, pinching the ring with his fingers.

'Of course.'

He pulled the ring off her finger and slid it back on with the heart facing outwards. 'There we go. Now *that* says you're engaged.'

He turned and pushed her door shut. Unexpectedly, he felt Brooke's arm hook him around the waist.

Peering at him with doting eyes, she said, 'Let's make it look genuine, shall we?' She leaned in and passionately kissed him on the lips. 'Just in case anyone's watching. How's that?'

For a moment, he revelled in the magic of a first kiss. 'Good,' he replied finally, trying like hell to pass it off as meaningless. He cleared his throat. 'Very authentic.'

She threaded her arm through his and rested her head on his shoulder. 'Shall we?'

'Yeah. Of course.'

Flaherty locked the car, and they set off for the main entrance. 'Is this guy Stokes for real?' he said, trying to take in the sheer scale of the church, its opulence. 'Look at this place. Talk about excess.'

'This place makes the Crystal Cathedral look like a tool shed,' she said. A massive shallow glass dome was central to the building's architecture, and Brooke was sure it covered the building's nave. 'Looks to me like his architect borrowed this design from Hagia Sophia in Istanbul.'

'Isn't Hagia Sophia a mosque?'

'The Ottomans converted it into a mosque in the fifteenth century, added minarets and other Islamic touches. But it was originally a Christian basilica built by Emperor Justinian I in the sixth century.'

He gave her a how-in-God's-name-do-you-know-this-stuff look. 'The same Justinian that tried to reunite the Holy Roman Empire but was stopped by the bubonic plague, right?'

'That's the guy.'

They approached the bank of entrance doors, set beneath a soaring archway. Above the doors, Flaherty eyed a massive bronze placard shaped to resemble an unfurled scroll. The incised gospel excerpt read:

'COME, FOLLOW ME,' JESUS SAID, 'AND I WILL MAKE YOU FISHERS OF MEN.'

– MATTHEW 4:19

Flaherty shook his head. 'All this place is missing is the slot machines and swim-up bar.'

'Don't be too hasty,' Brooke said. 'We haven't seen the inside yet.'

55

Randall Stokes's mind was in a fog as he listened to Crawford's painful account of a siege staged against the encampment by Al-Zahrani's supporters. The death toll among the platoon was remarkable, given the fact that the militants who'd come for Al-Zahrani had only guns and RPGs. However, Crawford insisted that the squads assigned to clearing the cave were late to respond to the attack. Had the contract soldiers not commandeered the unit's Blackhawk and staged a potent counter-attack, Crawford conceded, the entire mission might well have been jeopardized.

Stokes squeezed the phone's receiver. 'And where is Al-Zahrani now?'

'I had him moved, just like you wanted. Problem is I don't think he'll make it.' His next words were tinged with dissension. 'This isn't good, Randall. You should have waited to—'

'Let's not play the blame game,' Stokes warned, his voice hoarse. A coughing fit came over him and he held the phone aside until it subsided. During the past three hours, his breathing had become progressively strained and gritty. It felt like his chest had been filled with pebbles.

'You sound like shit,' Crawford said.

'Don't worry about me. Just don't make the same mistake as Frank. Don't lose your backbone. Hear me? We stick to the plan.'

'Wait . . . what about Roselli? Did he get cold feet?'

'You could say that.' Out the window, he noticed a silver sports sedan winding its way through the parking lot.

'This plan of yours has gone to shit!' Crawford blasted. 'How am I supposed to explain this grand fuckup to the major general? I'm calling for backup.'

'You'll do no such thing,' Stokes said, his tone grave. Another coughing fit came over him, more intense this time. He snatched the square-folded handkerchief from his suit jacket's breast pocket and held it over his mouth. When he pulled the handkerchief away, he was stunned to see that the crisp white linen was speckled with red dots. As he stared at the blood long and hard, a chilling realization hit him: this was no mere physical response to stress.

'Randall? You there?'

He pressed the receiver to his ear. 'Do nothing until that cave is cleared out. Understand?'

'Let's be sensible about this. Al-Zahrani's been infected . . .'

Infected. The word lingered in Stokes's mind as he stared at the handkerchief. Infected?

'So maybe we can use that to our advantage.'

'After all our preparation and planning, there is no way in hell that I'm going to rely on one catalyst. You heard what Frank told us: rapid transmission is critical. It's the whole purpose for what we've done inside that cave. If Al-Zahrani is isolated, the whole thing fizzles out. There'll be no back-pedalling now. We've come too far for that.'

'Technically, we have no idea what the real effect might be,' Crawford challenged indignantly. 'Remember, none of Frank's scientists knew how this thing would be used. We have no guarantees. These aren't lab mice . . .'

'Fine. We're hunting with a shotgun instead of a sniper rifle,' Stokes quipped. 'So be it.'

Outside, the driver had just gotten out from the car and was making his way around to the passenger side. Stokes didn't recognize the man's face. 'There's no such thing as a perfect plan,' Stokes said. 'Now scrape your men together and open that tunnel. Anyone asks questions, you tell them you've got four more terrorists to pull out of that hole. That's all anyone needs to know.'

As the female got out from the car, Stokes did a double take. Even from a distance she looked awfully familiar.

'I'll see what I can do,' Crawford said, exasperated.

The connection went dead.

Growling in frustration, Stokes slammed the receiver back on its base. He glared at the handkerchief again before stuffing it back in his pocket.

When he directed his attention back outside, the couple were out of view. So he spun his chair to a flat screen monitor dedicated to the cathedral's close circuit security cameras. To the left of the display he referenced a schematic of the first floor and used the mouse to double-click one of the embedded camera icons in the section representing the main lobby.

The camera's live feed filled the monitor – a straight view that perfectly framed the couple. Stokes worked the zoom controls to get a close-up of the female. He froze the feed, dragged a virtual box over her face then double-clicked the frame to enlarge the image. His eyes went wide. 'Can't be,' he muttered.

He went to his e-mail screen, pulled up the message he'd sent to the Boston assassin and opened its JPEG attachment.

A perfect match.

'What in God's name is *she* doing here?' It was insult enough that the miserable prick of an assassin had botched his assignment. But this? Having her show up on the doorstep? Now?

He slid open the desk drawer, pulled out his Glock and confirmed that the ammo clip was full. Clicking the safety off, he dropped it into his jacket pocket.

The computer let out a small chirp to alert that a new e-mail message had arrived.

'Now what?' he grumbled. When he saw who'd sent the message, his heart faltered. 'It's about time, Frank,' he muttered. He opened the e-mail and read Roselli's long-awaited message:

How ironic that I'd come to your office to kill you. But as always, you were a step ahead. Congratulations, Randall! If there is justice in this godforsaken world, you will no doubt confiscate my PDA, which holds the incriminating information about your mad conspiracy to exterminate innocent people in the name of God. If so, you may have noticed the thin residue coating its keyboard. See that rash on your hand? . . .

Pulse accelerating, Stokes turned over his hand and assessed the raw, inflamed skin on his palm.

Since you're so obsessed by disease, it's only fitting that you die from pestilence. That was a highly concentrated strain of anthrax you touched. Even more potent than the Ames Amerithrax we'd field tested in 2001. When absorbed through the skin it's 100 per cent lethal, non-transmittable to others. Engineered for selective reduction, or covert assassination. If you touch your nose, eyes or mouth, its virulence will be intensified. Death comes swiftly, but not before two to three days of intense suffering as your respiratory system bleeds out and chokes you. Or maybe you'll choose to hasten your demise by your own hand? Good riddance. See you in Hell.

Stokes's shoulders slumped. He crumpled in his chair and turned to the window. On the other side of the glass, a black dove stared in at him.

56
IRAQ

'That's them,' Jason said, lowering his binoculars. From the sky, the rogue pickup truck was easy to spot as it sped along an open ribbon of dusty roadway leading west over the expansive plain.

'Where do you think they're taking him? Kirkuk?' Meat asked.

'Probably. And we can't let that happen.'

'No problem.'

'Without killing them,' Jason clarified.

'Well, who doesn't like a challenge?'

'If you get us low alongside them,' Camel cut in over the intercom, 'I can shoot out the tyres.'

'Much appreciated,' Jason said, scanning the terrain in infrared through his binoculars. 'But I think I've got a better idea. Meat, the road crosses a bridge about three klicks out. Think you might be able to set us down on the west side, block them in?'

'Hell yeah,' Meat said. 'We could just take out the bridge too.'

'That would be a waste of taxpayer dollars,' Jason said with a smile. 'Let's not be lazy, okay?'

'I was just joking,' Meat replied sheepishly.

'And if the truck turns around?' Jam asked.

'If they turn around, they've got nowhere to go,' Jason said. 'We'll just keep them moving until they run out of gas. Then we'll get on the ground and surround them. It's just the driver and Al-Zahrani. Al-Zahrani's in no condition to run and the driver certainly won't be able to carry him far without help.'

'I still think we should just blow that truck to hell,' Jam said.

'That's your retirement plan down there,' Camel reminded him. 'No body, no bounty.'

'Fuck the money,' Jam said. 'That fucker needs to die.'

A pregnant pause indicated a quiet consensus.

The Blackhawk was closing the gap fast. Meat swept in over the roadway. The truck had less than a kilometre lead now.

'What exactly is wrong with Al-Zahrani anyway, Google?' Camel asked.

'Not sure. The medic was running some tests when I left . . . was trying to figure out the problem. But whoever took Al-Zahrani from the tent killed the medic on the way out the door.'

'I liked the doc,' Meat said. 'Good guy.'

The bridge was less than two kilometres away.

The truck accelerated.

'He's going for it,' Meat said.

'Pull ahead and drop down on the other side,' Jason said.

Meat pushed forward on the cyclic and eased down on the collective. The Blackhawk swooped low over the truck on a direct path for the bridge.

Below the bridge, Jason suddenly noticed activity – Arab men scurrying out from under the trusses . . . with weapons. Jason screamed, 'Pull up!'

Through his night-vision lenses, Meat saw an RPG tube

287

aimed directly at him. 'Oh fuck,' he gasped. He pulled the cyclic hard to the left. At close range, the chopper was hopelessly caught in the gunner's sight. In anticipation of being hit, he decreased altitude.

The grenade launched in under a second, and the gunner – whether by luck or design – anticipated the chopper's movement.

The mortar struck high behind the cabin with the mast and rotors taking the brunt of the explosion. Hot metal shot through the cabin.

The Blackhawk listed hard to the left and through the cracked windshield Jason saw the moonlit horizon tilt like a seesaw. Then the chopper's nose dropped precipitously and the ground came into view – not even ten metres below.

The ensuing freefall happened so fast, Jason had no time to brace for impact. In an instant, there came a deafening crunch of metal and shattering glass. Jason's head whipped forward. For a good ten seconds, his eyes saw nothing but white.

The chopper had come to a standstill at a thirty-degree forward pitch so that the harness dug into his ribs. Knifing pain radiated across his chest. A warm, wet sensation came over his feet and legs, which he immediately assumed to be his own blood. When his vision finally came into focus, however, Jason was surprised to see that he was actually submerged in water up to his shins.

The chopper's entire front end had crumpled into a wall of gritty earth.

Over his right shoulder he saw the glowing moon. The landscape he could see was cleaved by a wide irrigation canal – reduced to a stream, thanks to Iraq's recurring drought – with steep embankments that snaked through the fields covering the plain. The water flowing through the canal churned around the downed Blackhawk.

'Fuck,' Meat groaned, rubbing his neck. 'Are we dead yet?'

'We will be if we don't keep moving,' Jason said. He tried to think how far the chopper had flown from the bridge. 'They're going to come for us.' He unclipped his helmet and tossed it into the shallow pool that covered the floor, worked the harness buckles next.

Meat did the same.

'Camel?' Jason called out. 'Jam? You guys okay?'

No answer.

Jason slid off his seat and peered into the rear to check on them. What he saw was horrifying. Both men were hanging limply from their harnesses. Camel's helmet had been blown clear off, along with half his skull. A foot-long metal rod speared through the top of Jam's helmet and out through his face. Behind them, the fuselage had been punched open by the obliterated transmission.

Feeling his knees starting to wobble, Jason fought to remain focused, called upon his training to override the threatening emotional storm. You won't survive unless you keep it together. He closed his eyes for a moment and cycled a deep breath.

'Jesus, Google,' Meat said, distraught. He gestured the sign of the cross. 'This is fucking awful. How could this happen?'

Overwhelmed, Jason didn't have an answer for him.

The distant sound of a roaring truck engine echoed through the canal, gaining in intensity.

'Now what?' Meat said.

Jason reached around his seat and grabbed the M-16s stowed there. He tossed one to Meat.

'Now we make them pay for this.'

57

Jason and Meat climbed the embankment and low-crawled into a dense barley field that bordered the canal. Fifteen seconds later a lone pickup truck made a slow approach through the canal, heading straight for the bright flames shooting up from the fallen Blackhawk.

'You've got to be kidding me,' Meat whispered, craning his head up and peeking out through the wispy stalks. 'These guys look like kids.'

Scanning the enemy, Jason counted five men – the driver, a passenger, three men with machine guns in the cargo bed. Meat was right: even with scruffy beards, none of these guys looked older than twenty. Certainly not Kurds, thought Jason. He couldn't help but wonder why an Iraqi Security Force patrol had yet to respond. Complete autonomy in Kurdistan would be slow coming if this was any indication of a US handover.

Jason felt sick to think that there hadn't been time to pull Camel and Jam from the wreck, because the chopper's engines were now fully ablaze. It wouldn't take long for the bodies to be roasted. However, with the entire fuselage roiling in smoke, it was impossible for the Arabs to notice that the cockpit was empty. This gave them a false sense of security, because when the truck came to a stop, all five men let their guard down, certain of victory. They jumped out from the truck, shouldered their weapons and gathered close to the crash site. They raised their hands to the sky and began ululating and chanting '*Allahu Akbar!*'

When they started posing for pictures, however, something inside Jason snapped. This disrespect for human life was the very cancer that was eating away at the Middle East. Without thinking, he rose up and clasped his M-16. Caught up in their jubilation, the Arabs didn't notice him trawling the top of the embankment.

Jason's impulsive move surprised Meat. Left to devise his own tactical response, he opted to sneak behind the chopper to the opposite embankment in hopes of catching the Arabs unawares, should they spot Jason.

The posse formed a tight circle around the cameraman to view the digital shot he'd taken.

Positioned directly above them, Jason's presence went undetected. He shook his head in disbelief and lowered the M-16. There'd be no satisfaction unless he could see terror in their eyes, so he whistled to get their attention. That did the trick. They turned in unison and a long moment of pure confusion paralysed the posse as they assessed his tatty Arab attire. Jason could tell that they suspected him to be one of their own.

On the opposite embankment, Meat emerged from behind the chopper's severed, flaming tail. The Arabs had their backs to him, so he readied his weapon and waited for a cue from Jason.

With dramatic fervour, Jason jabbed his fist skyward and yelled, '*Allahu Akbar!*'

Only one Arab echoed his cry, but the man's gullibility elicited only rebuking stares from the others. Trepidation had taken its hold. Two of the men exchanged calculative glances and prepared to make a play for their shouldered weapons.

'You want a picture? I'll give you a picture you won't forget.' Jason's expression turned dark. 'Everyone smile.' Finally, he witnessed the terror he'd been waiting for.

Panic seized the Arabs. Before they could scatter or take up their weapons, Jason raised his M-16 with lightning speed and opened fire in smooth sweeps.

Meat followed Jason's lead, strafing the Arabs from behind with no mercy.

Within five seconds the posse had fallen, riddled beyond recognition.

Neither Jason nor Meat stopped firing until their ammo clips had emptied.

When it was finished, the river ran red.

With no words spoken between them, Jason and Meat collected the weapons from the dead Arabs and loaded them into truck.

Jason snatched the camera from the ringleader's dead grip. He took a few steps back, snapped some pictures of his own and slipped the camera into his pocket. Then he walked over to the truck and dipped into the driver's seat. He grimaced when he saw paperwork on the dashboard that bore a familiar Arabic insignia.

Meat climbed into the seat beside him and saw it too. 'Fucking Al-Qaeda. They're like cockroaches.'

A disturbing realization settled over Jason: this ambush was no coincidence. These men who'd been lying in wait were no mere splinter group. 'These guys had been tipped off that Al-Zahrani was driven out from the camp,' he said. Contrary to his original appraisal, the enemy had cast its net wide.

'They aren't so stupid after all,' Meat said in self-recrimination.

For a few seconds, Jason mourned the engulfed chopper, burned the image into his mind and soul. This would be the last time he'd underestimate the enemy. Then he put the truck in reverse and rode up on to the embankment to execute a K-turn.

Keeping the lights turned off, he backtracked through the canal towards the roadway.

Within two minutes, the dark silhouette of the bridge came into view. As he moved in cautiously, he spotted a dark form tangled on the rocks underneath the span.

'What is that?' Meat said. 'Is that—?'

Seeing nothing moving, Jason flipped on the headlights. Now the form was easy to identify. 'Yeah. It's a body.'

Making a slow approach, Jason scanned the immediate area. No vehicles. No men.

'All clear,' Meat confirmed with a second set of eyes.

Jason parked the truck close to the bridge. He and Meat got out and slogged over to the dead man.

'Is it one of them?' Meat asked, focused on the headwrap and tunic.

'No,' Jason said. He pointed to the feet. 'He's wearing marine-issue combat boots. And that's the same turban Al-Zahrani's driver was wearing.' He crouched next to the body, clasped the shoulder, and turned it over.

The head slumped back and the throat yawned open like a grisly smile where it had been deeply sliced from ear to ear.

'Awh, Christ,' Meat said, putting his hand to his mouth. 'That's foul.'

Immediately, they both recognized the face . . . and it was no Arab.

'Staff Sergeant Richards,' Jason said, shaking his head. 'Figures.'

'I never liked that guy,' Meat said. 'What a prick.'

Jason kicked the body into the water. 'Damn, Crawford. What were you thinking?' he seethed.

'Hate to state the obvious, Google. But there must've been more of those guys under this bridge. 'Cause they killed this fuck,' he pointed at the dead staff sergeant, 'and the truck he was driving isn't here any more. I think that means Al-Zahrani is gone.'

'Not exactly,' Jason replied confidently.

58

LAS VEGAS

Brooke Thompson and Thomas Flaherty strolled up the cathedral's centre aisle, their eyes pulled in every direction by the interior's ambitious design.

Shafts of muted sunlight penetrated the gravity-defying geodesic dome and wove together above the voluminous prayer hall. The outer walls were clad in alternating blocks of polished and crenulated Jerusalem limestone. The central altar, dominating the rear wall, resembled a concert stage with its huge viewing screens, speaker clusters and spotlighting arrays.

Most impressive to Brooke was the magnificent bronze baldachin that formed a lofty canopy over the altar. It depicted the haloed Jesus with rockstar hair and flowing robe, His welcoming arms spread wide in blessing, His feet surfing a cloud. Throughout the space she noticed no other iconography: no Holy Mother; no apostles or saints; no dove nor crucifix. Simply the Saviour.

Thousands of seats arranged in tiered arcs had already been installed on the main floor, but the balcony was still an unfinished piece of curved concrete.

'I guess tithing really does pay,' Flaherty said.

'I'd say,' Brooke agreed.

'Welcome,' a cheery voice called to them from somewhere in the front of the hall.

Flaherty spotted the greeter first. 'Over there,' he said, pointing near the centre stage where a small hive of workers was busily assembling a mammoth pipe organ. Off to the left, a gaunt man with a pure white pompadour waved and headed for the front steps to meet them.

The guy shot like a bullet up the main aisle, and opened his arms as wide as the bronze Saviour overhead. 'Welcome, my friends!' He planted himself at arm's length and proffered a hand, first to Brooke. 'Minister Edward Shaeffer, at your service.'

'Hi, I'm . . . Anna,' she said, accepting his soft, manicured hand.

'May Christ's love *shine* upon you, Anna,' he said with Broadway flair, clasping his other hand over hers.

Anxious to get her hand back, she said, 'And this is my fiancé, Thomas.'

'Oh . . . *fiancé*. How exciting. Such a joyous time. Congratulations.'

'Thank you,' Brooke said. She noticed that when the minister glimpsed her modest ring, his enthusiasm diminished notably.

Shaeffer relinquished her hand and took up Flaherty's.

'Thomas,' the minister repeated, 'A name straight from the gospels,' he said. 'Though I trust you are not a doubter, Thomas.'

'Seeing is believing, but I'm flexible,' Flaherty said with a smile.

'Excellent.' The minister stage-whispered to Brooke, 'He'll make a find husband, I'm sure.'

'We've just moved into town,' Flaherty explained, 'and we were hoping to have our wedding ceremony here.'

'I'm sure we can work that out, though the cathedral won't be open for another three or four months.'

'We were thinking about next October,' Brooke said.

'That should do just fine.'

'While we're here, would it be possible to meet Pastor Stokes?' Flaherty asked.

The directness of the request caught Shaeffer off guard. 'Oh, I'm afraid he's indisposed at the moment.' The minister hadn't a clue as to why Pastor Stokes had been holed up in his office all day. Typically Stokes was a diehard advocate of 'open-door' management. But Shaeffer had twice been turned away by Stokes's assistant, even when he'd made it clear that the company who'd delivered the organ had important questions about the installation. 'Been a very busy day.'

I'm sure it has, thought Flaherty. 'But he is here today?' he delicately pushed.

'Last I checked, yes,' the minister said with growing incredulity. 'Though for wedding arrangements, you'll need to speak directly to our Minister of Ceremonial Rites, Maureen Timpson. And she's on vacation until next Wednesday. I'll gladly give you her card and some information . . .'

'That won't be necessary, Edward,' a warm voice called out.

A tall figure materialized from the shadow beneath the balcony.

Brooke immediately recognized Randall Stokes from the glitzy picture in Flaherty's file.

'Well, I stand corrected.' The minister's blushing cheeks showed genuine surprise.

'Did I hear "wedding"?' Stokes said with a well-rehearsed

smile. Striding down the main aisle, his artificial leg limped slightly on the incline. 'How exciting.'

Brooke immediately understood how Stokes had achieved celebrity status. The man had presence – tall and handsome, meticulously dressed. Though she noticed his complexion was pallid and his red eyes showed fatigue.

'I'd shake your hand, but I'm feeling a bit under the weather today,' Stokes apologized. 'Edward, I'll talk to Anna and Thomas so you can finish what you're doing.'

The minister was momentarily stumped, but knew not to question Stokes. 'Splendid. That will do just fine. It was very nice to meet you Anna, Thomas. Once again, welcome. And we look forward to seeing you on Sunday!' He put his hand over his heart and half bowed before ambling back towards the altar.

'Please, walk with me,' Stokes said, giving each of them equal attention. 'We have so much to discuss. We can talk in my office.'

'I figured I'd save you some trouble,' Stokes said, pressing the button for the elevator at the end of the long corridor that connected to the lobby. 'I'm sure you have many questions.'

Unsure of the context of his remark, Brooke and Flaherty remained silent.

'However, if we're all going to be honest,' Stokes added, 'shouldn't you use your real name, Ms Thompson?' He looked deep in her eyes. 'Ms Brooke Thompson. Isn't that right?'

Brooke gave Flaherty an uneasy glance.

Flaherty spread his hands and squared his shoulders. 'Look Stokes—'

'I must admit . . . I don't know who you really are, my good man. And I don't like that.'

'Smith. John Smith,' Flaherty replied curtly.

Stokes grinned tightly. 'Of course. Have it your way, Mr Smith.'

The elevator chimed and the doors slid open. 'Please,' Stokes motioned them inside.

'Maybe we'll take the stairs,' Flaherty said.

'Fine by me, though it's seven flights to the top.' Stokes boarded the elevator and kept his thumb on the control panel to hold the doors.

With reluctance, Brooke and Flaherty stepped in beside him.

'Good choice.' Stokes pushed the top control button, the doors glided shut, and the elevator began its imperceptible ascent. Gospel music pumped in from overhead speakers.

'How was your flight from Boston?' Stokes asked.

'Smooth sailing,' Flaherty said. In close quarters, he noticed Stokes was wheezing. And the crisp overhead lighting highlighted a film of perspiration that masked the preacher's face.

'Are you CIA or FBI?' Stokes asked.

'Neither,' Flaherty replied truthfully.

Stokes gave him an appraising stare. 'I'm not surprised. Feds love to travel in pairs and wave their credentials around. Makes them feel special. You're not the cowboy type. So let me guess . . . You've got a Boston accent' – he thought aloud – 'Bostonians prefer to stick to their own.' Simple deduction led to only one conclusion: must work for the same outfit as the mercenaries who'd found the cave. 'Therefore, I'd guess you're with Global Security Corporation.'

'Lucky guess,' Flaherty replied flatly. 'Agent Thomas Flaherty.'

'All right, Agent Flaherty. Now we're getting somewhere.'

The elevator came to a stop and the doors whispered open. They stepped out into a cosy antechamber trimmed in cherry wood and with modern leather furnishings and an empty reception desk.

Stokes led them around the desk and through a double door that brought them into his office.

'Please, have a seat,' Stokes said, indicating the wingback chairs on the guest side of his desk. 'Something to drink? Soda, coffee, tea, water? Got the hard stuff, too, if you so desire.'

'No, thanks,' Flaherty said.

'Ms Thompson?'

'I'm fine,' she said, trying to reconcile how this charismatic televangelist had sent an assassin to kill her.

Stokes sat behind his desk and folded his hands over his chest.

'You actually would make a handsome couple,' Stokes admitted. 'But why are you really here?'

Flaherty got to the point. 'Our intelligence shows that during the past twenty-four hours you've been communicating with US Marine Colonel Bryce Crawford. He's been making encrypted calls to a landline in this building. That phone there, perhaps?' He pointed to the phone on Stokes's desk.

'Perhaps,' Stokes replied.

'So you're aware that Colonel Crawford's platoon is assisting an extraction effort currently under way in the Iraqi mountains?'

'I am.'

Stokes's candour surprised Brooke.

'I assume you're also aware that Frank Roselli was killed in a freak car crash today. Not far from here, in fact.'

Stokes paused before replying. 'Very unfortunate.'

'Funny thing is, the coroner suspects foul play since Roselli died of asphyxiation behind the wheel before careering into a telephone pole.'

'Not a heart attack?' Stokes said.

'No. But I'm sure that's what you're gunning for,' Flaherty said. 'You don't seem too broken up for a man who just lost a close friend.'

'I've seen plenty of death in my day, Agent Flaherty. After a while, one gets numb to it.'

'Seems you've killed plenty in your day too.'

Keeping his composure, Stokes responded with, 'I killed lots of bad guys so kids like you could eat McDonald's, drive SUVs and have 3.2 children. Liberty comes at a price. The only thing I'm guilty of is being a diehard patriot.'

'But why did you try to kill *me*?' Brooke asked.

Not ready to completely tip his hand, Stokes grinned.

'Hold on, Brooke,' Flaherty said. 'You see, Stokes, at roughly the same time Frank Roselli was killed, an assassin tried to kill Ms Thompson in Boston. But he died trying.' He noticed that this titbit made Stokes's jaw muscles ripple. 'Our office had a tough time working through the guy's multiple identities. Naturally, his fingerprints and dental records were non-existent too. He did, however, have a marine tattoo on his arm. A tattoo common to most guys in 5th Marine Regiment, 1st Division Expeditionary Force, in fact. So we tried running his prints through the CIA database instead. Lo and behold, we found that Corporal Lawrence Massey trained at Camp Pendleton. And wouldn't you know it . . . he served under Bryce Crawford.'

'Go on,' Stokes encouraged, intrigued by Flaherty's apposite deconstruction. He steepled his hands under his chin.

Flaherty was amazed how Stokes could be so cavalier given the seriousness of the accusations. 'In 2003 Ms Thompson was hired by one Colonel Frank Roselli to assist in a covert excavation in the Iraqi mountains, a project for which the Department of Defense has no formal knowledge. The same cave, as it turns

out, that Crawford is so intent on protecting. Everyone commissioned to work on that dig, present company excluded' – he
tipped his head towards Brooke – 'has turned up dead in the past
twenty-four hours. And of course there are those bone samples
Roselli had brought back from the dig and studied at Fort
Detrick. All those teeth. Bottom line is that a common thread
pulls all this together. And it's not a cave.' Flaherty got up from
his chair and paced over to the trophy wall, pointed to the
framed picture of Stokes, Roselli and Crawford. 'You're a smart
man, Stokes. So I'm sure you see where I'm going with this.'

Then a coughing fit struck Stokes. He snatched the pocket
handkerchief and held it over his mouth. When he was done, he
stared at the bloodied linen and struggled to catch his breath.
Shaken, he shook his head and laughed.

'Are you all right?' Flaherty couldn't help but ask, trying to
avoid looking at the bloodstained handkerchief.

'Actually I'm not okay, Agent Flaherty,' Stokes said, mopping
his chin, then chucking the vulgar handkerchief in the waste-
basket beneath his desk. 'Which makes this your lucky day.'

'How so?' Flaherty asked.

'You see, I'm not just a smart man. By tomorrow, I'll be a
dead man. Which means I have no reason to hide anything from
you. So you'll get your answers. All of them. You'll hear things
you'll wish you never heard. But first I'll need to show you a few
things to help you sew your thread.' He rose to his feet, came
around the desk and hesitated. 'And you're wrong about one
thing.'

'What might that be?'

'The cave *is* the common thread.'

59

Randall Stokes ushered the two guests across the office to an ordinary-looking door centred between two floor-to-ceiling bookcases. He punched a pass code into a keypad mounted on the doorframe to disengage the vault's pneumatic locking system. He clasped the door handle, paused, and turned to Brooke and Flaherty. 'Few have ever been in this room. This is where I keep my personal collection,' he confided in a whisper.

When Stokes pulled the door open, a motion sensor activated the lights in the space beyond.

'Come and see,' Stokes said, leading the way inside.

The tantalizing possibilities had Brooke's heart beating triple-time. She could tell Flaherty's curiosity was equally piqued.

'After you,' Flaherty said to Brooke. As she slipped past him, he paused at the threshold and gave the formidable security door closer consideration. He noted the deadbolt on the door's inside face. Giving the spacious vault a cursory once-over, he detected no other doors or windows. The air in here was thin. One word came to mind: asphyxiation.

As she moved deeper into the vault, Brooke was rendered

speechless by the incredible assortment of Mesopotamian relics Stokes had amassed. Display cases and shelves filled with jaw-dropping specimens: dozens of cuneiform tablets inscribed with the same characters she'd deciphered in the cave; ancient tools from the early Bronze Age, including an axe, chisels, hammers and knives. 'Are these reproductions?' she asked Stokes.

'All originals,' he said like a proud father. He looked back to the door. 'Will you be joining us, Agent Flaherty?'

'Just taking it all in,' Flaherty said, and made his way over in small steps. The smooth soles of his loafers caught the slick surface of a wide swath of carpet in the room's centre. A trace of chemicals wafted up into his nostrils. Cleaning solution. The area had been scrubbed very recently. Flaherty had a sneaking suspicion as to why.

'Oh wow,' Brooke muttered. She stared in wonderment at the huge monolith carved in bas-relief with two winged Mesopotamian protective spirits, or *apkallu*, facing one another in profile, as if courting for a dance – each half human, half lion. Raised broad wings and intricate rosettes adorning ceremonial dress depicted their divinity. 'Is this from Babylon?'

'No. That was the seal that we removed from the cave entrance.'

'Really.' She quickly tabulated that it predated Babylonian works by at least fourteen centuries. Yet its quality was equally stunning. 'It's magnificent.'

'Indeed. Even more impressive than what came centuries after it. Just like the writing you transcribed for us – far more sophisticated than anyone ever expected.'

In the obelisk-shaped display case next to the seal, Brooke spotted a highly unusual clay tablet etched not only in writing, but schematic designs. 'This text . . . these images,' she said in awe. 'Is this what I think it is?'

Stokes nodded. 'The world's oldest map. Given to me by a dear friend.'

For a long moment, Stokes stared at the artifact. More than anything, this keepsake symbolized the incredible spiritual transformation he'd undergone after the monks had found him disfigured on the roadside all those years ago.

In the sanctuary of a hilltop monastery, it had been Monsignor Ibrahim himself who'd overseen Stokes's physical and spiritual rehabilitation. The monsignor had brought Stokes to the looming mountain that marked Lilith's ancient tomb and imparted to him a haunting tale of civilization's first Apocalypse that transformed what had once been a lush paradise. By torchlight, they'd stood side by side in the cave's entry passage as the monsignor recounted Lilith's journey, immortalized in stone. He'd shown Stokes the chamber where Lilith's victims had been buried en masse. Then he'd brought Stokes to the demon's tomb, deep inside the mountain.

'Like you, Lilith's bold venture into the unknown realm had not been in vain,' Monsignor Ibrahim had told him. 'Her predestined journey merely marked the beginning for many changes yet to come. Everything you need is here. Now it is time for your destiny to begin.'

And from that humble beginning – that tiny mustard seed – sprang Operation Genesis.

Stokes punched a code into the base of the display case, then unhinged the lid. He removed the tablet, admired it and offered it to her.

'A map for what place?' Brooke asked as she cautiously accepted the tablet.

305

'That, Ms Thompson, is the map to what later mythology would call Eden. A treasure map that points to the beginning of humanity and civilization. A thriving city in the northern mountains of ancient Mesopotamia. It is how we found the cave.'

Once again, Brooke was overcome by wonder.

'You can see here,' Stokes said, 'the river that once led to the Zagros Mountains. But the real clues are written here.' He indicated the wedge-shaped symbols.

The way the symbols repeated suggested to Brooke that it was a numbering system. If so, the established timeline of recorded history had again been turned upside down. The earliest known numeral system had been developed in southern Mesopotamia in 2000 BC by the Sumerians – a sexagesimal system that used the number sixty as its base (with ten as a subbase). With sixty being the smallest number divisible by every factor from one to six, it could easily be separated into halves, thirds and quarters. Thus it simplified common measurements, such as time, geometric angles and geographic coordinates. The Sumerians annotated numbers one through nine with Y-shaped wedges (e.g., three: 'YYY', six: 'YYYYYY'), and tens were sideways Vs that looked like less-than signs (e.g., twenty: '<<', fifty: '<<<<<').

What appeared on this tablet looked much different – much more sophisticated than the Sumerian numbering system. 'These are numbers?' Brooke said.

'Yes. Geographic coordinates based on astrological measurements,' Stokes said. 'Ingenious for its time.'

'Is that possible, Brooke?' Flaherty asked.

She considered it, then nodded. 'The Mesopotamians were obsessed with the celestial cycles. So I'd say, yes.' But without fully transcribing and testing the number system she had to accept what Stokes was saying. 'And this was what led you to the cave?' she asked Stokes.

'Yes.'

If he'd truly been able to decipher this tablet, she thought, then why would he have commissioned her – an outsider – to assist in the excavation? It didn't add up.

Flaherty was losing his patience. 'This is all very nice, Stokes. But let's talk about the other things you found in the cave. The real reason behind your excavation. We know about the skeletons. So why did you study all their teeth?'

'Yes, the teeth,' Stokes said. He reflected for a moment to choose his starting point. He directed his response to Brooke. 'As you know, the emergence of civilization was long, uneven, violent, and marked by many false starts and setbacks. And every major turning point . . . every conquest in history, was determined by nature's most potent equalizer: disease. Pestilence is the planet's survival mechanism. The means not only for maintaining equilibrium, but for genetically selecting winners and losers.'

Flaherty said, 'I thought guys like you didn't believe in evolution?'

'Creationism may make for good sermons, but it certainly doesn't make good sense or good science,' Stokes admitted. 'Ms Thompson, the story you deciphered on the wall of that cave chronicled one of the most profound events that shaped modern civilization. It told of a thriving, technologically advanced people who'd effectively been wiped out shortly after the arrival of a foreign visitor.'

'Lilith,' Brooke said.

'That's one of the names later mythology ascribes to her,' he conceded. 'Lilith was responsible for a wholesale extermination at the dawn of the earliest civilization. A theme that would play out many, many more times throughout our history.'

'But only the males died, right?' Brooke said.

Stokes raised his eyebrows. 'Every one of them. Which begged the question: how could pestilence selectively afflict only men? It seemed impossible. But the remains found in that cave substantiate the story. At that time Frank Roselli was overseeing Fort Detrick's Infectious Disease lab. His top virologists and geneticists studied specimens from the cave – traces of ancient DNA left behind from a most unusual virus. Of course, I'm not a scientist,' Stokes said, 'so the nuances are lost on me. However, I do understand the basic mechanics.' He paused to marshal his thoughts. 'The majority of conventional viruses are coded in RNA and replicate within the cytoplasm of host cells. But some viruses, like Lilith's plague, are coded in DNA and penetrate deeper into the host cell's nuclear core to replicate.'

Roselli had explained to him how the nucleus of human cells stores the entire genetic code – the genome. The genome has twenty-three chromosome pairs, twenty-two non-sex chromosomes, and one pair of sex chromosomes. The female sex chromosome is noted as 'XX' and the male's is 'XY.' At the genetic level all humans are 99.9 per cent identical. Mutations passed on from one generation to the next make up the remaining 0.1 per cent of the genetic code. These 'single nucleotide polymorphisms' recode one of the four nucleotides – adenine (A), cytosine (C), guanine (G) and thymine (T) – along the gene, changing an 'A' to a 'C' or a 'G' to a 'T'. And in those slight mutations, ancestry can be traced back along a 100,000-year genetic tree to one man and one woman in Africa – the genetic Adam and genetic Eve. 'Which means we're all distant cousins,' Roselli had explained. Roselli inevitably sided with science by refuting the notion of a truly common variant among any ethnic group. Yet Roselli's scientists clearly demonstrated that a high frequency of specific genetic variations were common among different ethnic groups.

Stokes's interpretation of the genetic data was simple: the Middle East was a hotbed of genetic variation, and Lilith's plague was capable of pinpointing the specific genetic sequences that accounted for it.

And Stokes was sure that Lilith's plague wasn't mere science – it was a mechanism put into play by God Himself to destroy the wicked early civilizations in the Middle East. He'd learned that from the man who'd given him the map to Eden.

'When Lilith's virus enters the host cell's nucleus, replication can only occur when the viral DNA successfully binds to a matching gene sequence found on the male Y chromosome. And we believe that that gene sequence is specific to males of distinct Arab ancestry. In the absence of this specific Y chromosome gene marker, the virus remains dormant. So a female, or a male of non-Arab descent, can carry the virus, but not manifest its symptoms.'

'Come on, Stokes. I'm no scientist, but that sounds a bit out-landish to me,' Flaherty scoffed. 'I've never heard of anything like that. There's no "Arab" gene. That's ridiculous.'

Stokes was undeterred. 'The Y chromosome makes up less than half of one per cent of the male genome. But unlike most other genes, the strands of the Y chromosome do not recombine over successive generations. Quite simply, that means the Y chromosome is transcribed almost perfectly from father to son with virtually zero mutation.'

'He's right,' Brooke said. 'It's how ancestral lineage is deter-mined.'

This aspect of genetics, Brooke knew firsthand, had been widely adopted even by anthropologists. Human migrations out from Africa brought ancient peoples first into the Middle East. There, climate and other environmental factors caused slight adaptive mutations. The Middle East became a nexus for successive migrations pushing out across Eurasia and eventually across land bridges to the American continent and as far south as Australia (thanks to intercontinental land bridges resulting from dramatic drops in sea level brought on by the Ice Age). And every step of the human journey brought greater diversity – including slight changes both in the paternally transcribed Y chromosomes and the maternally transcribed mitochondrial DNA.

Stokes added, 'Mapping the Y chromosome is how scientists know that 16 million men living today are direct descendants of Ghengis Khan. A distinct genetic marker unites 8 per cent of all men living in the former Mongol Empire. Similarly, the skeletons we found in that cave were among the earliest ancestors of modern Arabs. When we compared their Y chromosomes to modern Middle Eastern men, the similarities were startling. So that brings us to a most compelling crossroads.' He held out his hands like a magician. 'You're a smart man, Agent Flaherty. So I'm sure you see where I'm going with this.'

Flaherty certainly understood what Stokes was implying, though he wasn't buying it. 'You're hoping to recreate Lilith's plague.'

'Bravo,' Stokes said, grinning.

'You can't be serious,' Flaherty scoffed. 'If you're bitter about losing your leg, you might want to consider psychotherapy instead.'

'I assure you this is no joke, Agent Flaherty,' Stokes said.

Brooke, too, was incredulous. 'You're saying you've created a plague that kills only males of Arab ancestry?'

'Give or take,' Stokes said.

'Give or take?' Flaherty said, horrified. 'So you're playing around with a virus that you don't even understand?'

'It's impossible to account for every mutation. We can't anticipate every scenario,' he admitted.

'But you developed a vaccine, right?' Brooke said. 'I mean if this virus is from six thousand years ago, there's no guarantee that *anyone* will be immune.'

'There is no vaccine, Ms Thompson,' Stokes said. 'And by the time one is developed, the balance of humankind will be reset, just as God intended when he sent Lilith over those mountains so long ago. Lilith had been snuffed out before her destiny was complete. We're merely giving her another chance to finish what she started. It's a perfect solution to solve the hostilities in the Middle East. No soldiers or weapons needed. We let Mother Nature do what she does best.'

'The DNA would have degraded,' Brooke said with conviction. 'The DNA in those teeth wouldn't have been any good.'

'You're missing the point, Ms Thompson. The teeth from the skeletons in the burial chamber only confirmed the genetic profiles of the plague victims. The teeth gave us a template for the Y chromosome marker. And you're absolutely correct: the viral DNA found in those specimens wasn't well preserved. However, thanks to those brazen Mesopotamians who managed to execute Lilith, some of the viral DNA *had* been perfectly preserved. Let me show you.'

Brooke and Flaherty watched Stokes step over to the veil-covered display case in the room's centre. 'You see, it wasn't only Lilith's victims we discovered in that cave.' Stokes pulled the veil away, revealing the most prized item in his collection, which was locked within a rectangular glass case. 'It was Lilith herself.'

60

Mounted atop a cylindrical glass base inside the case was a translucent sphere, flat on top and bottom, and no bigger than a medicine ball. And frozen within it was a severed human head.

'Exquisite, isn't she?' Stokes said, doting upon the severed head without utmost adoration. '"Upon her forehead was a name written, Mystery, Babylon the Great, the Mother of Harlots and the Abominations of the Earth."' He smiled. 'Revelation 17:5.'

Cold prickles shot down Brooke's spine. Lilith's ancient head was both beautiful and ghastly. Wisps of golden hair intermingled with blood swirls spun through the honey-coloured sphere which resembled glass. The flesh remained intact so that even now, millennia later, the refined face seemed locked in time, a snapshot of death that bore testament to a most brutal execution. The morbid lips remained in a taunting smile. But it was the punishing, inescapable stare of the eyes that was most frightful. Like staring at Medusa, Brooke imagined herself being turned into stone.

'As you can see, she has been perfectly preserved,' Stokes said.

'After the executioners cut off her head, they immediately sealed it away, hoping that Lilith's evil would be trapped for eternity. Obviously, they were wrong, because it wasn't Lilith's soul that had been the source of her malevolence. It was her DNA. And you can see how we got to it . . . where we drilled through the resin,' Stokes explained, pointing to thin bore holes that extended through the resin like invisible straws, and penetrated through the skull's soft crown. 'All we had to do was extract the dormant virions and culture them.'

'So if it's so simple, why are you so concerned about the cave?' Flaherty said.

'Come now, Agent Flaherty,' Stokes said, feigning disappointment. 'A virus in a dish is useless. For a plague to have any effect, it must be spread – widely and rapidly. It needs a catalyst.'

Then Flaherty remembered Jason saying how sick Al-Zahrani had been when they pulled him out from the cave. 'You infected Al-Zahrani, didn't you? Is he your catalyst?'

'He's infected, yes. But I certainly can't rely on him. He's only one man, after all. Let's think of him as an experiment.'

'Lilith was only one woman,' Brooke countered. 'And think of what she did.'

'This isn't 4000 BC, Ms Thompson. Things work much differently nowadays.'

'So then what *is* your plan, Stokes?' Flaherty insisted. 'Sounds to me like you've got nothing to lose now. Why not just tell us what's inside that cave?'

Stokes enjoyed watching Flaherty stew the possibilities. He stepped up to the display case, pressed his hand against the glass, and stared at Lilith with deep reverence. 'The inherent beauty of plague,' he cryptically replied, 'is that once it is introduced into a population, nature itself provides the most reliable and potent delivery system. It's been that way since the beginning, just as God intended. Even the mightiest empires can't stop nature.'

For a long moment, Flaherty ruminated on the phrase 'delivery system'. 'You aren't seriously considering biological warfare,' Flaherty said. 'It violates every peace treaty. The United States can't afford to—'

'No missiles will be fired, I assure you, Agent Flaherty.' Stokes's breathing was getting shallower. 'Once the infection begins, no one will be able to stop it. In under an hour this virus rips through cells . . . gets into the blood, the lymph nodes, you name it. In less than two hours, it strikes the lungs and becomes pneumonic.'

'Nu-what?' Flaherty said.

'It becomes airborne. Someone can catch it just by breathing it in,' Brooke said in horror.

'Very good, Ms Thompson,' Stokes said. 'Suffice it to say, when all is said and done, an entire generation of Arabs will be wiped out . . . and any threat of Islamic fanaticism right along with them. And there will be zero accountability for the United States. It will be viewed as Allah's divine retribution.'

'That's not true,' Flaherty said. 'Scientists will study the disease. They'll see that—'

'When scientists study the DNA of the virus, they'll be unable to explain its origins. I promise you that. They will rule out the possibility of any scientist being able to engineer such a complex, exotic contagion. They'll attribute the plague to a mutation bred in the backwaters of the Middle East. It's been nearly a hundred years since Spanish Flu killed upwards of 50 million people – more casualties than all the soldiers and civilians in World War I. And as far as scientists are concerned, we're long overdue for the next great pandemic. You saw how excited they were about swine flu. That was a joke compared to this. The scientific community will feel nothing but vindication.'

'Why do this?' Brooke challenged, abhorred by Stokes's indifference. 'What's the point?'

'The point? Come now, Ms Thompson,' Stokes said. 'I've fought these people for almost two decades. This is no ordinary enemy. They don't wear uniforms. They don't respect innocence. They hate civilization . . . and everything we stand for. Flying planes into buildings was only the beginning for them.'

'Terrorism is a universal problem – not a Middle Eastern one,' she pleaded.

'Wars are fought one battle at a time, Ms Thompson. To spare the innocents, extreme measures are sometimes necessary. Your idealism is endearing, but fails to recognize the chilling reality we're facing. We've reached the tipping point where only one side can inevitably survive. Call it Social Darwinism.'

'You're a real nut job, Stokes,' Flaherty said. 'I'm giving you one more chance to answer my question. What's in the cave?'

'I could tell you, but that would only ruin the surprise,' Stokes replied wryly. 'Besides, it's too late for you or anyone else to do anything about it.'

'I don't have time to play games with you.' Flaherty's fuse had burned out. If there was something in the cave, Jason would need to be warned. He decided to cast diplomacy to the wind. He went for his gun. But Stokes anticipated the move and, to Flaherty's surprise, managed to draw his own gun first. And to Flaherty's horror, the pastor levelled the Glock at Brooke's chest.

'Don't be upset, I've had lots more practice than you, Agent Flaherty,' Stokes said. Another coughing fit struck, but the gunslinger managed to keep his aim true. He covered his mouth with the crook of his arm and when he pulled it away, blood and bile covered his jacket sleeve. 'Let's not make this messy. I told you, I'm already a dead man. Don't you see?' He held out the gory sleeve. 'I've got nothing to lose.'

'You don't look dead to me,' Flaherty said.

'Roselli managed to infect me with one of his lab experiments,' Stokes said. 'Some home-grown variety of anthrax, apparently. So if that's the case, I won't last another day. With that in mind, I'm determined to witness the results of all my hard work. And right about now, you're making that very difficult for me. Give me your gun.' He extended his free hand and motioned for it. 'Be sensible and, unlike me, you'll both live to see another day.'

Flaherty knew that despite Stokes's hopeless condition, the former Special Ops commando was fully capable of pulling the trigger at least once before going down – no matter how well executed Flaherty's shot might be. With Stokes unconcerned about confessing his heinous acts, Flaherty had to gamble that he'd keep his word. After all, though at the moment it seemed an abomination, Stokes was a servant of the Lord. 'Fine,' he said, lowering the gun and passing it to Stokes. 'You win.'

Stokes pocketed Flaherty's Beretta. 'Now while I attend to business, you can make yourselves comfortable.' Keeping the Glock on Brooke and his eyes on Flaherty, Stokes stepped backwards towards the door. When he'd crossed the threshold into his office, he lowered the gun and reached for the door handle. 'Behave yourselves and I'll have someone let you out after this is over.'

Then Flaherty and Brooke watched helplessly as Stokes pulled the door closed.

61
IRAQ

'You're sure these coordinates are right?' Meat asked, checking his handheld GPS unit again. 'I mean, this thing's pretty accurate.'

Fist-sized stones that littered the unpaved road forced Jason to slow the pickup to a crawl. 'Mack has yet to be wrong,' he said.

'But you said Mack is getting his information from the Israelis,' Meat reminded him.

Twenty minutes ago, the satellite trace Jason had called in to Mack had pinpointed the square paint marker he'd scrawled on the hood of the truck Staff Sergeant Richards used to spirit Al-Zahrani away from the camp. The grid provided by Israeli Intelligence led them here, to a desolate region twenty-four kilometres south of Irbil, and less than a twenty-kilometre drive from the downed Blackhawk. The perfectly flat terrain provided long-range visibility over the wheat fields extending out in every direction. An occasional ramshackle structure poked up into the landscape.

But no sign of the hijacked pickup truck.

'I don't trust Israelis, especially Mossad,' Meat said.

'Come on Meat, there's no reason to believe the information isn't credible.'

'Sure there is: no truck. That's good enough reason for me.' Meat groaned in frustration and punched the dashboard. 'Shit, Google. We can't go losing these Al-Qaeda fucks now! Not after what they've done!'

Jason felt equally frustrated. Losing Jam and Camel was a crushing defeat. He'd called Camp Eagle's Nest and requested a rescue patrol to be dispatched to the crash site.

'They must be on the move again,' Jason guessed. 'I'll have Mack request another—'

'Whoa . . . hang on,' Meat said, craning his head to see something out the side window.

'What is it?'

Meat waved his hand as if he was greeting someone. 'Stop the truck.'

'What the hell are you doing?'

'See that shit box over there?' he said, pointing out the window to a two-storey house constructed from cinderblocks, which glowed in milky moonlight.

'What about it?'

Meat grinned deviously. 'Seems someone is expecting us . . . or should I say their expecting the guys that *should* be riding in this truck.'

Jason stopped the truck and barely glimpsed an Arab man passing beneath the house's bright porch light and disappearing around the building. 'Who? That farmer?'

'That's no farmer. The guy was strapping an AK-47. Back it up. We're going in.'

*

'How do propose we do this?' Meat asked Jason, flipping the safety off his Glock and cocking its slide bolt.

'Fast,' Jason simply replied. He rolled to a stop and let the truck idle twenty metres from the house. There appeared to be no one outside, but in the second-storey window, he saw two silhouettes moving like shadow puppets behind drawn shades.

'You think they brought Al-Zahrani here?' Meat asked. 'This place is a dump.'

'Exactly. It's perfect.'

Meat's eyes went wide. 'Oh, hey . . . look over there.' He pointed to a crude overhang attached to the side of the house. 'There she is.'

Only a corner of the scratched-up bumper and a sliver of the sky-blue tailgate stuck out from beneath the camouflage netting that covered the stolen pickup. 'Good eye,' Jason said.

'Get ready. There's our host,' Meat said, pointing with his chin to the side door. The Arab leaned out from the doorframe into the porch light. The AK-47 was slung over his right shoulder. He was moving his head side to side, trying to see inside the truck, but the greasy windshield was casting nasty reflections.

Meat grabbed for the door handle, but Jason gripped his arm. 'Hold on. He can't see us through the glare.' Jason eased the truck forward and put it in park five metres from the house. 'Sit tight. We'll let him come to us.'

Looking deeply concerned, the Arab waved to them again in a hurrying motion.

'Get your knife out, then wave him over to your side. Let's see if he bites.' Jason reached down and grabbed the AK-47 he'd stripped from the dead Al-Qaeda photographer.

Meat set down the Glock and unsnapped a K-bar knife from

a sheath clipped to his belt. Then he stuck his arm out the window and made a summoning gesture.

The Arab scowled, didn't budge. He looked back into the house, as if someone was beckoning him.

'*Ta' âl huna!*' Meat yelled in Arabic, and motioned again with more urgency. 'Come on over here, stupid,' he grumbled.

Finally the man broke away from the house and made his way to the truck with hands spread in confusion.

'Put him down nice and quiet,' Jason instructed.

'Don't worry, I'll be tender.'

As the Arab drew close, Meat turned from view, pretending to get something from behind the seat.

The Arab cornered the truck's front bumper and came to Meat's window, saying in an agitated tone, '*Ista' gil*?! *Êsh çâir fik?*' He slammed his hands on the door and leaned in for a better view.

The Arab made eye contact with Jason and his haggard face blanched.

Meat wheeled, grabbed a fistful of the man's tunic and tugged him close. In the next instant, he plunged the blade through the man's Adam's apple. He felt the tip of the knife clip bone. The Arab's attempted scream was instantly reduced to a gurgling yelp. Blood spewed over Meat's hand as he turned the blade like a doorknob, then sliced upward to the jaw and into the brain. The Arab's eyes rolled back into his skull and Meat made sure to let the body drop to the ground out of view from anyone who might be watching from inside the house.

'Let's go,' Jason said, calmly opening his door and stepping out from the truck. He directed his face away from the house and clutched his AK-47 low behind the opened door.

Meat got out and stripped the AK-47 from the dead man. The safety was off and he checked the clip. Full. Gripping the weapon, he hurried around the truck, headed straight for the door. His face was knotted with determination and adrenaline.

'So much for being subtle,' Jason mumbled and fell in behind him.

At the door, Meat intercepted a second unlucky Arab who'd been calling out for the dead guy. Without hesitation, Meat levelled the AK-47 at his chest and squeezed off a quick burst that opened his torso like overripe fruit. Then he charged inside.

Jason stepped over the body and shadowed Meat with his weapon drawn. Peering in at the house's tight rooms, he was glad to have an AK-47 since the weapon's short muzzle and rapid-fire action were just what the doctor ordered for a raid in a place like this. He turned right and swept the first room. Nothing but a wooden table and two metal folding chairs.

Like a raging bull Meat stormed to a second door that led into a narrow hallway. He held his AK-47 with a straight arm, turned flat. What he liked to call 'gangsta style'.

Jason heard frenzied voices overhead. Three distinct tones. He immediately moved back against the wall just as the plaster ceiling tore apart in a hail of bullets. He dropped to one knee, raised his AK-47, and strafed the ceiling in a wide 'G', followed by a tight 'X'. In one corner, a heavy *whump* shook the floorboards, followed by a second *whump* near the middle of the ceiling. In both spots, blood dripped down from the sieve of bullet holes. The voices had gone silent, but a single set of footsteps pattered fast towards the centre of the house before Jason could line up for another sweep.

Meat also heard the runner and bolted to the base of the house's central staircase. He immediately spotted his target and opened fire. An agonizing scream rang out just before a rifle came cartwheeling down the stairs.

By the time Jason made it to the hall door, Meat had ducked into the next room and reappeared, shaking his head to indicate that it was empty. Jason signalled for him to remain still.

A perfect silence settled over the house.

Then Jason heard a small voice coming from a room at the top of the stairs. He listened intently. Someone was chanting a prayer.

'Fuck this,' Meat grumbled. 'Cover me.'

Before Jason could stop him, Meat charged up the stairs.

Jason raised his AK-47 to cover the landing, fully expecting Meat to get hit with a faceful of lead. But there was no resistance from above. At the top of the stairs, Meat popped in and out of the room to the right, then disappeared through the left door.

Three seconds later, he yelled down, 'Google, get up here!'

62

Crawford shone the floodlight up at the gaping hole the marines had opened on top of the rubble that dammed the tunnel passage.

Emerging from the other side, a grimy face capped by a sand-coloured helmet appeared in the light. The marine reported, 'It won't be easy, but we can get through.'

'Fine, Corporal,' Crawford said. 'We'll make it work.'

'Colonel, there's a lot of blood on this side,' Corporal William Shuster reported matter-of-factly. 'Some fingers and tissue too. Not pretty. I'm sure there's plenty of meat buried under these rocks. I don't see how anyone could've survived the explosion.'

Crawford remained stonefaced. 'Al-Zahrani managed to walk out of here. Let's make sure no one else does.'

Shuster scuttled down the rocks, holding a flashlight in his right hand, an M-16 slung over his shoulder. His left hand was balled up in a fist and he opened it to reveal a palm full of gum-ball-sized metal ball bearings covered in a tacky film – trademark shrapnel used in padding suicide vests. 'Found these on the ground,' he said. 'They're covered in C-4 residue. Not sure why one of them would have detonated himself in there. You'd think he'd have waited for a few of us before pushing the button . . . take a few infidels with him on his way to paradise.'

'Mystery solved,' Crawford grunted for show. None of this news surprised Crawford. It wasn't just the lingering smell of motor oil that clued him in on the source of the blast. Stokes had been quick to inform him about the clumsy gunman who'd let loose some rounds into the man who'd been strapped with plastic explosive. With the cameras knocked off line, however, even Stokes had seriously underestimated the extent of the collapse. More troubling was the quiet calm on the other side of the blockage. Crawford anticipated activity. Lots of activity. And not from the holed-up Arabs. 'Now I need you to take a couple men in there with you. See how deep that tunnel runs. Make sure it's empty.'

'We could use the PackBot,' Shuster suggested.

Crawford wasn't hearing it. 'No time for robots, Corporal. Don't think. Just do.'

Shuster was amazed by Crawford's stubborn fixation with this tunnel, particularly in light of the devastating ambush that the platoon had marginally endured (thanks to Crawford's refusal to radio for backup). With the medic having been killed by Al-Zahrani's abductors, the wounded were left to tend to one another. Every remaining able-bodied marine had been ordered back to the tunnel to finish the debris removal. No one could yet confirm if Crawford had radioed for reinforcements. That had the platoon grumbling about the colonel's motive. With Staff Sergeant Richards unaccounted for, discontent was fast brewing throughout the ranks.

Crawford turned to the six men tightly congregated in the passage behind him. 'Ramirez . . . Holt. You two get in there with Corporal Shuster and see what we've got.' The marines looked at one another in a way that clearly suggested latent dissension. More reason for swift action. 'This isn't a democracy, gentlemen. Get your lights and your weapons and get in there! And your radios won't be any good under this mountain, so leave them behind.'

The reluctant designatees took up their M-16s and light gear packs, filed past Crawford and clambered up the rocks.

'And where's that damn Kurd?' Crawford blasted.

'Here, sir,' a quiet voice called from the rear.

The four marines made room for Hazo to shuffle through.

Crawford squared up with the interpreter. He had to make a conscious effort not to react to the Kurd's appearance. The man looked haggard and feverish, his eyes bloodshot. The striking similarity to Al-Zahrani's early symptoms was alarming. Since the onset of Operation Genesis, Stokes had been forthright about the wide reach of a custom virus that would target Arab males. 'It won't be only the terrorists who fall. Know that the innocent fathers of our future enemies, too, will be sacrificed along the way,' Stokes had told him. 'If we have any survivors in there,' Crawford briefed the Kurd, 'I'll need you to talk some sense into them. Tell them to be smart and surrender. Can I count on you to do this?'

'Jesus, Colonel,' Shuster said defiantly. 'Clearly he's in no condition to—'

Crawford's chest puffed out like a rooster. He stepped up to Shuster and put his face so close, the two men touched noses. 'Corporal, you are way out of line.'

'Please,' Hazo said, putting an appeasing hand on Shuster's arm. 'I will help you.'

'I hope you're right about all this, Colonel,' Shuster warned.

Thick veins webbed out over Crawford's red face.

Shuster unstrapped the M9 pistol from his side holster and proffered it to Hazo. 'If you're going in there, take this.'

Hazo nodded and accepted the gun, though no matter what might happen, he vowed not to go against his beliefs.

Shuster gave Hazo a quick tutorial on how to flip off the safety and fire the weapon. 'And stay behind us,' he added.

'I will,' Hazo said, clumsily holding the gun away from his body.

Shuster climbed up and disappeared through the hole.

'Good luck,' Crawford said to Hazo.

Hazo offered no reply and began his climb towards the hole.

63

LAS VEGAS

The instant Stokes attempted to close the vault's door, Flaherty snatched the clay map from Brooke and bolted after him. He was only four steps away when the door stopped short from seating against the doorframe. On the other side of the door, Stokes tried pulling harder on the handle, yet the door didn't budge. It took mere seconds for Stokes to detect the problem: the deadbolt was slightly engaged so that the thick slide bolt protruded just enough to keep the door from seating. While no one had been watching, Flaherty had tampered with the deadbolt just before he'd come into the vault.

Immediately, the door swung inward.

But Flaherty was already in a wide pitcher's stance with the clay tablet cocked back above his right shoulder.

On the other side of the door, Stokes was raising his gun to prepare for a cautious re-entry. His eyes, however, went to the room's centre – not directly in front of him.

Flaherty's faster reaction time won out. He launched the five-pound tablet at Stokes's head.

The tablet whirred through the air on a direct line for the

pastor's face. Stokes nimbly bobbed sideways so that the tablet instead skimmed his right ear. In the process, he managed to fire one misaligned shot that sailed past Flaherty and thwacked into the thick security glass on the front side of the display case containing Lilith's head.

Before Stokes regained his footing, Flaherty charged forward like a linebacker and buried his right shoulder in the preacher's abdomen. The tackle lifted Stokes, brought him crashing down on to the floor with his chest catching the brunt of the impact.

There was a loud pop and Flaherty felt something under him give way. He was shocked to see a glossy wingtip sticking up over his shoulder. Flaherty realized it was the business end of the pastor's prosthetic limb – tangled under his arm.

Stokes was quick to respond and the gun came arcing towards Flaherty's face.

With both hands, Flaherty grabbed at Stokes's wrist and forced the Glock sideways. A second shot rang out and punched through the wall.

Getting into a wrestling match with Stokes was a losing proposition, Flaherty was certain. But Stokes had two things working against him: a missing leg and Anthrax-tainted lungs. With the struggle escalating, Flaherty could hear bubbling sounds coming from Stokes's chest.

Stokes responded with a head butt that caught Flaherty on the bridge of the nose and made him see stars.

'Aaaghh!' Flaherty screamed out. He managed to hold on to the gun. At the same time, he buried his shoulder in Stokes's face.

Choking, Stokes struggled to push Flaherty away.

Then Stokes let out a muffled scream and Flaherty felt the gun pinned hard against the floor. He glimpsed a chunky black clog grinding down on the gun.

'Let it go, Stokes!' Brooke yelled. She pulled her foot up again and stomped down a second time. Finally the gun fell free from his mashed fingers. A swift kick sent it skittering across the carpet.

Desperate for oxygen, Stokes flailed and bucked, trying to use his liberated stump for leverage.

Like riding a bronco, Flaherty couldn't control the crazed pastor. To regain his balance, he had to relinquish his grip on Stokes's wrist. That meant he had no choice but to pull his shoulder off Stokes's mouth.

The pastor coughed fiercely, spraying blood on Flaherty's neck.

Another forceful buck sent Flaherty tumbling on to the floor.

Stokes rolled on to his elbows and retched blood and bile on to the carpet.

It was the opportunity Brooke had been waiting for. In her hand, she clutched the nearest solid object she could find – the clay tablet. With all her might, she swung the map of Eden down at Stokes's head. It connected. The pastor collapsed on to the floor.

64

IRAQ

'Jesus Christ,' Jason gasped, standing at the top of the stairs. He had to cover his mouth and nose with his sleeve to fight off a fetid stench.

In the room to the right, he caught a quick glimpse of the two men he'd struck blindly from downstairs. In opposite corners of the room, each body lay face down and twisted on the splintered floorboards.

'In here, Google,' Meat called again.

Jason lowered his AK-47, stepped over the dead guy Meat had gunned down on the landing, and went into the second room. The horrid smell sharpened, and its source was immediately apparent.

Sprawled atop a mattress that was the room's only furnishing, Fahim Al-Zahrani lay in a gory mire of blood, vomit and tissue. Since much of the stringy red slime still draped from the corpse's blue lips, Jason assumed it to be a purée of Al-Zahrani's innards. Blood streamed like tears from the corpse's lifeless eyes – the orbs solid red. And the entire mattress beneath his lower half was completely saturated in red, suggesting that blood and liquefied organs had found their way out every possible exit.

'Man,' Meat said from the far corner, 'what the hell's going on here?'

An elderly Arab – unarmed – sat on the floor beside Meat, legs tucked to his chest, rocking back and forth. He was chanting prayers in Arabic. Every few seconds, a spate of coughing interrupted the recitation. The old guy displayed the same pallid complexion Jason had noticed in the man whom Meat stabbed in the throat.

'I mean, what did these guys do to him?' Meat said.

'They didn't do this, Meat. They *couldn't* have done this.'

'Then who did?'

As if on cue, Jason's sat-com vibrated. He dug in his pocket to find it, saw that it was Flaherty.

'Tommy?'

'Yeah, it's me.'

'Everything all right in Vegas?'

'No. Not by a longshot, I'm afraid.'

Jason listened as Flaherty rehashed the candid tell-all discussion he and Brooke had had with Pastor Randall Stokes – the discovery of an ancient contagion that USAMRIID scientists under Frank Roselli's guidance had weaponized for mass transmission throughout the Middle East. Staring over at Al-Zahrani, Jason felt his nerves turn to ice. When Flaherty detailed Stokes's sinister objective – to annihilate the Arab male population – he could feel a dark cloud settling over him. He'd had a similar response when in September 2001 his sister Elizabeth had called to report that Matthew had officially gone missing at the World Trade Center.

'Not sure if I'm buying what Stokes was saying about this

virus he and Roselli concocted. Seemed a bit out there to me . . .'
Flaherty said.

'He's right, Tommy. Trust me. We just found Al-Zahrani and
he's dead.'

'Dead?'

'Yeah.'

'But you only pulled him out of that cave a few hours ago.'

'That's right. We thought he had a fever. But now . . . God, it
looks like something minced his organs and pushed them out his
throat. We killed a few others that had been in contact with
him . . . it's a long story. But they weren't looking too good
either. If you ask me, I'd say they were showing early signs of
being infected with this virus.'

'Virus?' Meat said, looking alarmed. His eyes went wide with concern as he looked at Al-Zahrani again. 'What do mean "virus"?'

'Virus,' the elderly Arab echoed grimly. 'Yes . . . virus,' he said
holding out his hands and staring at them with vacant, yellowed
eyes.

'Shut up!' Meat demanded, kicking the old man.

Jason stifled Meat with an abrupt hand gesture.

'The others you killed . . . were they Arabs?' Flaherty asked in
a low voice.

'They were.'

A pause.

'So it's true,' Flaherty said in a grim tone. 'It only kills Arabs.'

'For our sake, I hope so.'

'Stokes was pretty proud of the fact that this virus could
specifically target Arabs,' Flaherty reiterated. 'Let's not go
making any assumptions. I hope you'll be fine. Are you okay?'

Jason wasn't so sure. 'You said this thing can spread through
the air?'

'What?' Meat said, startled by the bits and pieces he was over-hearing. 'You mean just breathing it—'

'These men you've killed . . .' Flaherty said, thinking it through. 'You've got to get rid of the bodies. Burn them or something. Until we find out what's really happening, we can't risk letting this thing get out in the open.'

'Agreed.'

'There's something else too. However Stokes was planning to spread the virus, it's in that cave. He referred to it as a "delivery system". I don't know how or what that might mean, but he implied that it somehow uses nature, not warheads. Our friend Crawford has been in on this thing all along. And he's determined to finish this, understand? So you've got to wrap things up there quickly and find a way to get back to that cave and stop Crawford.'

'I'll do that,' Jason said, ruing the fact that he didn't force the issue of calling for backup earlier. 'Hey, is Stokes dead?'

'No. But he will be soon. And not from the bump on his head. Seems there was a mutiny among the ranks. Frank Roselli, the USAMRIID guy, managed to infect Stokes with some military-grade anthrax. Talk about poetic justice. Anyway, when Stokes comes to, I'll see if we can get anything else out of him.'

'Great work, Tommy. I'll take it from here.'

65

'How long till Candyman gets here?' Meat asked, uncapping another of the five-gallon gas cans they'd liberated from the shed where the stolen truck had been hidden.

'Ten minutes,' Jason replied with little emotion. His vacant eyes fixated on the elderly Arab whose chant had come to an abrupt halt, thanks to a single shot Meat had pumped through the top of his head. All things considered, the execution was truly a mercy kill. The old man had offered no resistance.

In every way, the mission added new meaning to the phrase 'take no prisoners'. The death toll Jason had witnessed over the past nine hours was as deep as it was wide. Undoubtedly, the demise of Al-Zahrani and his militant underlings was to be celebrated – and in time, would be. After all, he reminded himself, these men were terrorists of the worst variety: extremists hell bent on indiscriminately destroying civilization; brainwashed by radical interpretations of the Qur'an and the Hadith; convinced that sacrificing innocent lives was sanctioned by Allah.

But for Jason, a disturbing truth was fast coming into focus: terrorism was a two-way street. If Stokes were to succeed in unleashing his wretched apocalypse on the Middle East, the combined acts of terror carried out by the minuscule minority of Muslim extremists would seem trivial in comparison. And the fact that evangelical fanaticism stoked the pastor's fervour was all too similar to the enemy Jason had been fighting all these years. What could have pushed Stokes over the brink of sanity? he wondered. Jason knew firsthand that war could easily blur the lines. Even as he stood over the grand trophy of this conflict – the body of Fahim Al-Zahrani – he felt no true sense of victory.

'Come on, Google,' Meat said. 'We don't have much time. Soak him really good.'

'Right,' Jason said. He uncapped another gas can and began dousing Al-Zahrani and the mattress, trying to avoid breathing.

'It's a fucking shame, really,' Meat said, motioning to Al-Zahrani.

'How's that?' Jason said, pouring out the last of the gasoline.

'We're about to light up a ten-million-dollar barbecue. We actually bagged this fucker and now we're going to destroy any proof of it. For the record, though, it's not about the money, Google,' Meat confessed. 'I'm just glad this fucker's dead. You know, for Camel and Jam.'

'Me too, buddy,' Jason said, patting him on the shoulder. He reached into his pocket and pulled out the camera he'd confiscated from the crash site. 'But don't worry, we're going to show the world this guy's toast.'

Meat smiled. 'Awesome.'

Jason snapped a dozen photos of Al-Zahrani's corpse, including close-ups of the face. 'That should do it.' He slipped the camera back into his pocket.

'Show time,' Meat said. He handed Jason one of the match-books he'd found in the downstairs kitchen. 'I'll give you the honour. I'll take care of the other room. The downstairs is ready to go. We just need to light it on the way out.'

When Meat left, Jason set the gas can down and filed the image of Al-Zahrani in his memory. He peeled back the matchbook's cover, tore off a match and struck it.

'Burn in Hell,' Jason said.

He flicked the match on to the mattress.

66

'Oh that is some nasty shit.' Disgusted, Private Miguel Ramirez aimed his light down on the slippery red goop smeared over the rocks. Seeing that some of the slime was dangling between his fingers – long strands of black hair clumped together by mocha-coloured skin – stimulated his gag reflex. So he looked away, flung the fleshy chunks off his fingers, and wiped his hand clean on his pants.

'Man up, Ramirez. We've got work to do,' Shuster said.

The pallid marine slid down the steep rock pile and cycled a few calming breaths.

'You good?' Shuster asked.

'I'm good,' Ramirez unconvincingly replied. He pulled the M-16 off his shoulder and slid the flashlight into the mounting clip on the rifle's muzzle.

'All right,' Shuster said. 'I'll take the lead. Ramirez, you're behind me . . . then Holt.' He turned to address the surprisingly resolute Kurd, whose primary concern seemed to be the hand-gun, which he handled as if it were on fire. But the man had plenty more to worry about, because up close in the glow of the flashlight, Shuster now noticed how pale Hazo looked. The tiny veins in his eyes now formed a web of red around his irises. It wasn't the most opportune time to come down with a cold. 'Hazo, you'll be in the rear. Keep a safe distance, and if for some reason we have company in here, don't wait around to ask questions. Just make it out as fast as you can. Understand?'

Hazo nodded.

'You remember how to use the gun?' he said pointing to the M9.

'I do.' The words brought a scratchy tickle to the back of Hazo's throat. He buried his mouth in his sleeve and coughed to alleviate the discomfort. He could feel a tightness settling into his lungs.

'All right. Here we go.' Shuster used his sleeve to mop the sweat from his eyes, then directed his M-16 straight down the tunnel. The muzzle-mounted flashlight cut four metres into the darkness, revealing solid rock. He felt like he was staring into the entrance to Hell itself. Even with all his military training and field experience, he wasn't prepared for a hostile encounter in this environment. Should an enemy be lurking in the shadows, there'd be no choice but to face him head on – no cover, nowhere to run. The light would provide plenty of warning to anyone hunkered down in the darkness, mark a clear target even for a novice shooter. The weighty Kevlar-lined flak jacket that covered Shuster's chest offered little solace, feeling like nothing more than tissue paper. And at close range, he felt that his combat helmet would shield his skull no better than a Tupperware bowl.

Shuster set off down the passage. The tunnel ran straight for fifteen metres and felt perfectly level underfoot. With the scuffing of boots and the clattering of gear, it was difficult for him to hear anything. So every few metres, he'd signal for the procession to stop. Then he'd listen for any sounds that might be emanating from within the mountain. When all went still, however, the only noise he detected was the wheezing sounds coming from Hazo's chest.

Fifteen minutes had elapsed since they'd left the entry point forty metres back. The ground began to gradually pitch downward as the passage narrowed and began curving in a wide arc.

As they went deeper, the cool air got thinner.

The passage straightened again, just before the ceiling seemed to disappear. When Shuster aimed his light upward, he felt like he was staring up from the bottom of a crevasse – as though a colossal axe had cleaved the inside of the mountain. Instead of opening into sunlight, however, the sheer walls tapered gradually inward until fusing once more about ten metres up.

Shuster halted the procession once more to listen for activity.

This time, he thought he heard something. And it wasn't the Kurd's stuffy chest. The lofty ceiling was amplifying a sound that seemed to be carrying up from inside the mountain.

'What the hell is that?' Ramirez whispered.

'Don't know,' Shuster said. The persistent churning sounds were difficult to place, but didn't seem to indicate a human source. 'Maybe an underground water source. Like an aquifer or an underground river.' He pressed forward.

'Wait,' Ramirez protested.

Shuster stopped and turned back to the private. 'What?'

'That doesn't sound like water to me. I don't like it.'

'Only one way to find out,' Shuster said, motioning ahead. But Ramirez wasn't moving.

'I say we tell Crawford to go fuck himself. Let him send his robot down there.'

'Hey!' Holt interrupted. 'I saw something moving up there.'

Shuster spun and took aim with his M-16. He swung the light side to side, up and down. Ahead, the passage was still.

'Oh that's it,' Ramirez said, repeatedly looking back the way they'd come. 'I'm getting the fuck out of here.'

'No you're not,' Shuster said. Shaking and fidgeting like a caffeine junky, Ramirez clearly had an extreme case of jitters. 'Pull yourself together, will you?'

Hazo shimmied past Holt, saying, 'Excuse me, please.'

Confused, Ramirez backed up to the wall to let the Kurd through. 'Where are you going?'

Hazo didn't answer. When he tried to squeeze past Shuster, the corporal grabbed him by the arm, saying, 'Hold up, Hazo.' He glanced back at Ramirez. 'I'm not about to send our inter-preter to do your job. Ramirez, be a man for God's sake.' He patted Hazo on the shoulder and motioned for him to return to the back of the line. 'We're got a plan. Let's stick to it. Stop wast-ing time.'

Shuster raised his M-16 and moved forward.

'You're a pussy, Ramirez,' Holt said, giving the dissenter a prodding push.

'Fuck you. You would've been right behind me and you know it.'

67

'Thanks for getting here so fast,' Jason yelled to Candyman over the sound of the Blackhawk's whirling blades. Once in the helicopter, he buckled his harness, tightened the chin strap on his flight helmet and adjusted the mic boom on his headset. Next to him, Meat fussed with slackening the shoulder straps to accommodate his bulk.

'No problem,' Candyman said. 'It was easy to find you. That's a mighty big fire you boys lit up. Could practically see it the second I got up in the air. Didn't even have to bother with the GPS.' He motioned to the ravaged outline of the safe house, engulfed in orange fire. A column of thick black smoke boiled straight up from the conflagration into the windless sky before melding into the night.

'Man, you guys don't mess around,' said the slight copilot with an air of admiration.

Jason wasn't about to explain why they'd set the house ablaze. The act was not something to be glorified.

But Meat felt the kid deserved to hang on to the outlaw image, saying, 'We like to be thorough.' He managed a thin smile.

'I'll say,' the copilot said. 'Who was in there anyway? Some of those Al-Qaeda fuckers?'

Jason gave Meat a stern glance. Meat said nothing.

'Even for a rookie you're an idiot,' Candyman chastised the copilot. 'Why don't you go jerk off to *Full Metal Jacket* for the two-hundredth time and leave these guys alone?' He worked the controls and lifted the Blackhawk smoothly into the air. As he banked north, the chopper's downdraught whipped up the smoke and flames.

To the west, two klicks out, Jason spotted three Humvees angling fast along the dirt roads that bisected the fields, heading for the blaze. In the glare of their bouncing rectangular head-lights he spotted Iraqi Security Force insignias. His jaw clamped tight. *Now* they were showing up?

'Don't worry about the sand cops,' Candyman said as if linked into Jason's thoughts. 'Our guys will get there first and send them on their way.' He swung the chopper a bit. 'There . . . see?' He raised his hand for Jason to see, then pointed down and left.

Down below, only a klick away, a second convoy was cutting its own path through the wheat fields on a beeline for the burn-ing house. This time, the headlights highlighted nothing but desert camouflage. Six marine Humvees.

Jason's jaw slackened.

'Two more platoons are heading for the cave,' Candyman added. 'Another unit's already handling the chopper wreck. Said they found a bunch of shot-up Al-Qaeda in a ditch. That your handiwork too?'

Jason said nothing, so Meat spoke up. 'They were taking pic-tures of the wreck, like they were at Disney World . . . probably looking to update their Facebook page. We didn't feel that was appropriate.'

The eager copilot chimed in with, 'Yeah, gotta teach these sand monkeys some manners.' But Candyman shot him a biting stare and he sank into his seat.

'By the way, Google,' Candyman said solemnly, 'sorry to hear about Camel and Jam. That's a goddamn shame.'

'Thanks.'

A few more seconds went by without conversation.

Eventually, Candyman had to ask, 'Did Crawford fuck things up as badly as you said?'

'Worse,' Jason said. 'You have no idea.'

'That guy's going to be in a world of hurt when the BG finds out what he's done . . .'

The BG, thought Jason. Despite his distaste for conspiracy theories, there was no telling if the brigadier general wasn't part of this too.

68

The inverted-V ceiling dropped precipitously once more as the passage drilled through the mountain in a wide hollow tube that reminded Shuster of an earthen storm drain. He kept the procession drumming along to a steady, furtive cadence – Ramirez, Holt and Hazo following in his wake. Sweeping his light in wide arcs over the rough stone confirmed an absence of mining or tool marks. Only time and the elements had been this tunnel's quarrymen.

The tunnel curved gently from left to right, then back again, the ground rising and falling along a general downward trajectory. The air quality was degrading quickly, and Shuster worried that if something were not soon found, he'd need to abandon the exploration. One thought kept cycling through his mind: why would Fahim Al-Zahrani have retreated back towards his enemy? If Al-Zahrani had met a dead end, they had to be nearing it – which coincided all too well with the strange sounds that were growing stronger with every step. He paused once more to try to decipher the noise.

'Goddamn it, what *is* that?' Ramirez said.

'No idea,' Shuster replied, trying to conceal his deepening anxiety.

'Sounds like something's alive down there,' Holt said.

No one challenged the idea.

'Wait here,' Shuster suggested. 'I'll go check it out.'

'Absolutely,' Ramirez said. 'That's a very good idea.'

They all watched in silence as Shuster disappeared around the bend.

With time to rest, Holt became acutely aware of Hazo's worsening health. Hazo, bracing himself up with the tunnel wall, was ashen and sluggish, and his chest heaved every time he inhaled.

'Hey, Hazo,' Ramirez said. 'You know anything about this place?'

Hazo shrugged. 'Just legends.'

'That's a start,' Ramirez said. 'What legends?'

Hazo paused. 'A demon was buried here,' he explained bluntly. 'This is what some say.' His thoughts flashed back to Monsignor Ibrahim and Michelangelo's painting of a half-woman, half-serpent entwined around a tree.

'Demon?' Holt jumped in. 'Exactly what kind of demon?'

There was no reason to keep secrets at this juncture, thought Hazo. 'Those are her pictures on the wall near the entrance. Her name is Lilith,' he explained weakly. 'Thousands of years ago, she came to this place . . . these mountains. She killed every man and boy.' The conversation quickly exhausted his lungs, forcing him to cough.

'Crazy bitch,' Ramirez seethed as if one of the victims had been his own brother.

'How? How did she kill them?' Holt pressed. He felt like he was a boy scout again, hearing haunted campfire stories. Hazo

345

reluctantly cast his bloodshot eyes to the ground. 'Come on, Hazo. If we're stuck in a demon's grave, it would be nice to know what we're up against.'

Trying to catch his breath, Hazo managed to force one tentative word from his lips: 'Pestilence.'

'Pest-a-what?' Ramirez asked, agitated.

'Disease, Ramirez,' Shuster said. 'Learn the language, will you?'

Ramirez lingered on the word, his M-16 drooping in his grip. He repeated it to himself with a sense of fatalism: 'Disease.' He pulled a gold crucifix out from under his collar and blessed himself with it.

'It's just a story,' Holt reminded him.

'A story? You saw Al-Zahrani when they pulled him out of here. Man, he was sick . . . real sick. You saw him.'

Holt rolled his eyes and spread his hands.

Then Ramirez took a hasty step back from Hazo, looking spooked. 'And look . . . now *he's* sick,' he said accusatorily. He tightened his hold on the M-16. A psychosomatic tickle came to the back of his throat and he grabbed at it. 'I don't want to catch no damn disease . . .'

'Settle down,' Holt said.

'Guys!' Shuster's voice echoed up from the mountain.

Holt cupped his hands around his mouth and shouted back: 'Yeah?'

'Get down here . . . I found something!'

Holt set off on a brisk pace through the tunnel, Ramirez and Hazo bringing up the rear. The passage essed twice and curled sharply before spilling into a cavernous black hollow. Holt stopped dead in his tracks. 'What the . . .?' he gasped.

346

'Over here,' Shuster called to him from deep within the hollow.

He spotted Shuster's flashlight floating in the voluminous darkness. The light played over the surface of a massive angular form plonked down in middle of the cave, which resembled an unhitched semi-trailer or a railroad boxcar. And it seemed that the sounds they'd been hearing – now clearly recognizable as the whirring of mechanical parts – were coming from inside it.

'Come on, Holt!' Shuster shouted. 'Get over here!'

'Am I seeing what I think I'm seeing?' Ramirez said over Holt's shoulder.

'This ain't no dream,' Holt said, pointing his light down to illuminate the ground. He was surprised to see that a section of the cave floor had been levelled into a two-and-a-half-metre-wide path, definitely not by natural means, but by some kind of excavating machine. On either side, the natural limestone formations had been left intact, looking like a moonscape. Around the cave's perimeter walls, his light glinted off enormous stainless-steel holding tanks shaped like inverted baby bottles. For a moment he felt like he was back on the tour of the local Budweiser brewery, in the fermentation room.

Holt and Ramirez trotted over to Shuster, while Hazo paused to catch his breath.

'How did this get down here?' Holt asked.

'Must have been brought in here in pieces . . . assembled on site. Modular construction. See there,' Shuster said, moving his rifle muzzle up and down so that the light emphasized one of many riveted seams connecting the container's outer steel panels.

'Looks like a shipping container,' Ramirez said.

'Sure does,' Shuster said, making his way around it.

'For what, though?' Ramirez mumbled. Thoughts of the ancient legend had his imagination running wild. The short hairs on his neck bristled.

'Take a look at this,' Shuster called over.

Holt and Ramirez kept their M-16s at the ready and angled around the hulking container. A pale purple light glowed on to a grooved steel ramp that led down from the side of the container. The container's short side was two and a half metres square, partially enclosing a central entryway a metre wide, two metres high. Beside it, a mechanical door mounted on rails had been slid open. Semi-transparent plastic flaps – like those used for meat lockers – dangled like a curtain from the top of the entryway to provide an air barrier. The flaps distorted the details of the container's interior, but provided enough visibility to suggest that there was no one inside.

Ramirez immediately spotted six identical containers lined neatly in a row behind this one. '*Seven* containers?'

'That's right,' Shuster said, backing up and aiming his light up over the container. 'And take a look up there.' He traced the beam along the tubular flex-duct leading out from the top of the container to where it joined a boxy central trunk that rose like a chimney for fifteen metres before disappearing through the cave's lofty vault. Six identical flex-ducts branched off the main feed and patched into the tops of the other containers. The gentle breeze pushing out between the entryway flaps confirmed that fresh air was being pumped in from above ground. 'It's a ventilation system,' Shuster said.

'Detainment cells?' Holt guessed.

'Maybe Saddam's weapons lab,' Ramirez said.

'Only one way to know for sure,' Shuster said, noting PVC

pipes snaking down beside the duct work. Water lines, he guessed. 'Stay here. I'll take a look inside. See what we've got.' He swung his M-16 up on to his shoulder and ascended the ramp. Bathed in pale purple light, he felt like he was boarding a spaceship.

69

While the marines were preoccupied with the strange box-like structure at the cave's centre, Hazo had just made a discovery of his own. As he'd squatted to catch his breath, his flashlight tilted towards the cave's outer wall and highlighted a most unusual anomaly, easy to miss in the enveloping blackness. Amid the cave's natural rock formations, anything man had touched stood out glaringly. And what he saw was nothing natural.

Resuming a standing position, he directed the light at the spot where the rock face had been smoothed flat around a modest arched opening burrowed into the rock maybe a metre up from the ground. It reminded him of a mosque's *qibla* niche that directed Muslims towards Mecca during prayer.

He considered calling out to the others. But he needed to conserve his energy. A profound lethargy was settling into his limbs and his fever was spiking. Perspiration was welling out from his pores.

Compared to what the others had found, this was something he could inspect alone.

Mindful of his footing on the uneven ground, Hazo made his way to the wall in stops and starts. He squared his body with the niche and directed his light inside it. It ran much deeper than he'd thought, extending maybe two metres into the rock like a small tunnel. The interior surfaces were covered in hash marks. Hewn with a chisel, he guessed. A deep lip the width of his hand had been carved around the rim of the opening. Probably meant to keep in place a seal – a *thick* seal.

Perhaps the seal had never been set in place. Or more likely: the seal had been *removed*. It stood to reason that the contents had also been looted.

That got Hazo thinking about what might have been stored inside the niche.

The implied width of a seal that would seat into the rim also downplayed the idea that the niche was intended for repeat usage. That meant the contents were intended to be locked away or protected long term, maybe indefinitely. Anything placed deep inside the niche would require someone to squirm on his belly to reach it. Therefore, the design was best suited for something long and narrow that could be slid inside.

As he thought about the cave's known mythology, the realization hit him like a wrecking ball.

'A body,' he whispered.

The niche's dimensions could accommodate perfectly a prostrate corpse, he was certain of it. With some help, he himself could slide into it and still have room to spare.

Scrutinizing the base of the niche under the light, he noticed stains and dried material on the porous rock, which also supported the hypothesis. It appeared as if decomposed flesh had left discolorations in the rock.

He concluded that this niche had been designed to be a tomb – a most legendary tomb, despite its modest appearance.

Lilith's tomb.

70

On final approach to the camp, the Blackhawk glided low and came to a hover over the roadway precisely where Jason's unit had initiated its ambush only nine hours earlier. To Jason it seemed as if he'd fired that first kill shot a lifetime ago in another dimension where certain truths and rational motives still existed – where his true enemy was an outsider.

'Jesus,' Candyman said as he surveyed the ravaged camp. 'What a mess.' On the southern perimeter, five Humvees had been rendered smouldering heaps of twisted metal. The two elongated tents at the camp's centre had fared no better – each burned bare to the ribs. Laid neatly beside the roadway, he counted fifteen body bags ready for airlift.

'I'm still not seeing any backup down there,' Meat said, disgusted by the inability of the unwieldy military machine to mobilize on-the-fly. 'What does it take to get these guys motivated?'

'They'll be here,' Candyman said decisively. 'I'd give it another forty-five minutes or so. When they radioed the camp, Crawford told them that everything was fine . . . that the camp was secure. So they were heading back to Camp Eagle's Nest. I had to convince them to turn around again.'

'Fucking Crawford,' Meat seethed. Quickly scanning the area, he couldn't locate the colonel. 'I'm gonna snap that fucker's neck when I find him.'

Candyman set the Blackhawk down on the roadway and said, 'Good luck, fellas. I've got orders to keep moving.'

'Thanks for everything, Candyman,' Jason said.

Before the Blackhawk had even lifted in the air, Jason was halfway up the slope with Meat scrambling to keep up with him.

The marines posted outside the cave weren't sure how to respond to Jason's urgency. They immediately began arguing in hushed tones about how to handle the situation. When Jason reached the top of the slope, they took position in front of the cave to block his entry and gripped their M-16s threateningly. But he could see defeat in their eyes, the telltale sign of demoralization.

Jason stopped and raised his hand to Meat's chest to stop him from bowling through them.

'We don't have time for this shit,' Meat grumbled.

'Crawford's in there?' Jason asked.

'Yeah,' the soldier in the middle said, trying to decipher his motive.

'How about my interpreter?'

The soldier nodded. 'Hazo's in there too.'

'All right. Here's the situation,' Jason said in a calm voice, making eye contact with each of them in turn. 'Al-Zahrani's dead.' He watched them exchange glances. 'And the biological contagion that killed him is contained in this cave.'

The news hit them like a slap in the face.

'Contagion?' the soldier said. He shifted his feet and looked warily over his shoulder into the cave.

'That's right.'

'Didn't I tell you!' the one on the right said. 'Shit!'

'Calm down,' Jason said, holding his hands out. 'You'll be fine. From what we know, the disease is only lethal to the local population.'

They all looked at him with puzzled expressions.

'It's . . . complicated,' Jason said. 'But our intelligence operatives in the States have apprehended a suspect who has been communicating with Crawford ever since your unit arrived here. Seems we stumbled upon some kind of weapons stash . . . in there.' He pointed to the cave. 'And Crawford is doing everything he can to salvage it. We suspect he's going to somehow release a highly lethal biochemical weapon. If he succeeds . . . if we *let* him succeed . . . countless innocent lives will suffer the same fate as Al-Zahrani.' He let them contemplate the stakes for five seconds. Then he laid it on the line for them: 'I need your help. We need to get in there and stop him. Before it's too late.'

'And if we don't?' the soldier in the middle asked.

'That's not an option,' Jason replied gravely.

'I mean why do I care if Iraqis die? Better them than us . . .'

Jason had to press his hand harder against Meat's chest to keep him from pouncing on the guy. At this juncture, the last thing he needed was a squabble with Crawford's unit. These marines had been through plenty, and straining their allegiances could prove unwise. He pointed to the body bags heaped along the road and made one last attempt at diplomacy. 'You can thank Crawford for what happened here today. This could've been avoided. All it would have taken is one call. Crawford has gone rogue and you know it.'

'We're wasting time,' Meat said, clenching his fists.

'And if you're wrong?' the soldier asked.

'I'm not. And the proof is inside this mountain. Come with us and see for yourself.'

The marines exchanged glances.

The sensible marine on the right was the first to break. 'He's right. What Crawford's been doing . . . it's crazy. Don't make no sense. I mean he had us clearing rocks away 'fore we could even help our own guys. Who *does* that?'

Jason took his hand off Meat's chest and the ringleader took a step back. 'What's it gonna be?'

71

LAS VEGAS

While Agent Flaherty was busy making phone calls to arrange for Stokes to be taken safely into custody, Brooke decided to have a closer look at the artifacts in the vault. The objects Stokes had pillaged from Iraq were pristine specimens that would surely prove to be among the most impressive ever recovered from the region – and to intimately experience them was a temptation she couldn't pass up.

First, she approached the case containing a sizable clay jar, just to the left of the case that accommodated Lilith's macabre severed head. Before commencing her analysis, she gave the head a sideways glance, certain that the demon's dead eyes were evaluating her every move.

'I'm just going to have a quick look,' she explained to the head. 'Nothing to worry about.' Best to play nice with the evil temptress, she thought . . . just in case.

The clay vessel was roughly a a third of a metre wide at its bulbous base, and stood about half a metre tall. Posted behind it was an enlarged photo board containing various pictures documenting its careful extraction from somewhere deep inside the cave.

The first photo showed one of the bas-reliefs Brooke had herself studied in the entryway. It depicted Lilith carrying this very same jar – the magical vessel the ancients believed had enabled her to destroy every man and boy she'd come in contact with; the cursed jar she'd brought out from the forbidden realm to unleash evil into the world. Pandora's misnamed 'box'.

The cuneiform beneath the relief was barely legible in the image. But with all the time she'd spent transcribing the writings, Brooke could practically recite the story from memory, word for word. The account told how Lilith protected the jar until the very end, and warned that it was the source of her evil. The passage also described how the villagers had entombed the jar with her beheaded corpse in hopes of neutralizing its destructive powers.

She was surprised that the vessel hadn't been destroyed immediately following Lilith's execution. After all, the ancients believed that the ritual breaking of clay dispelled magical spells.

The second and third photographs showed Lilith's tomb in two stages: first covered by an ornately carved seal with two protective spirits (she glanced at the real-life version standing on the plinth only a little way away); second with the seal removed to show the *in situ* contents. The tomb was simple enough: a deep, arched niche carved into a rock wall. The prone skeleton's rib cage and arm bones were barely visible behind a squat clay pot positioned at the front of the niche. The top of the jar could be seen poking up from behind the pot.

The thrill of discovery sent tingles down her spine. I wish I could have been there, she couldn't help but think. Though she herself would certainly not participate in such an act if she were privy to the dig's sinister purpose, she could only imagine how exciting it must have been for the archaeologist who'd had the dubious honour of exhuming the relics. She wondered briefly if that same scientist might also have crossed paths with one of Stokes's hitmen, but with less favourable results than her own.

Now she focused on the pot's construction. Since pottery styles and techniques evolved over the centuries – generally becoming more refined except during times of great famine – vessels such as this were critical to dating and deciphering archaeological sites, even though truly reliable methods for chemically dating pottery were still being devised.

The vessel's irregular form clearly showed that this jar had been handmade without the aide of a pottery wheel. Strange, since pottery wheels had been in use centuries before 4000 BC. And the jar's neatly painted lines and decorative slashed incisions all resembled similar relics she'd studied from Hassuna and Samarra – sites that dated to 5500 BC.

Another display case contained a reconstructed necklace, also recovered from Lilith's tomb. The necklace's beads were of two varieties: glossy obsidian, a black volcanic glass found in eastern Turkey, and smooth cowry shells, which in antiquity would have been found along the ancient shores of the Persian Gulf. Brooke had seen similar pieces from Arpachiyah and Chager Bazar, all dating to the Ubaid period, around 5500 BC.

How could Lilith have acquired a jar and jewellery from fifteen centuries earlier? she wondered.

Tantalizing possibilities streamed through her mind.

Then she had a shocking realization. The stout clay pot shown in the photo had been cut precisely in half, probably with a laser, so as to free the hardened core that encased Lilith's head. The halves had been put back together and were on display to the right of the case holding the head. Similar razor-sharp lines ran down both sides of the jar, suggesting that it had also been cut in two to study the contents.

Could the original contents still be inside the jar? Or was this just the reassembled vessel? Brooke's heart began racing at the thought of it.

She studied the glass case containing the jar. It had a hinged top with a slim release arm running down to the base. And on the base was a small keypad, similar to the case from which Stokes had removed the clay map. She'd seen the numbers Stokes had pecked to access the map. Odds were the code was the same for this box. Wouldn't hurt to try.

Brooke glanced over at Lilith's head again. The witch was still glaring at her, as if transcending space, time and death to start a cat fight. But Brooke's excitement easily trumped the perceived threat. 'Screw you, lady,' she said in a haughty tone. 'If I can open this box, I'm having a look at your goody bag. I almost died because of you. So as I see it, you owe me one.'

Brooke looked back over her shoulder towards the open door. She could see Flaherty with his phone to his ear, standing over Stokes. Stokes was still face down on the floor, not moving, with his hands cuffed behind his back.

'Here goes nothing,' she said, turning back to the case. She punched in the code . . .

The keypad changed from asterisks to plus signs, flashed three times. Then the top's locking mechanism snapped open.

Grinning, Brooke unhinged the top. She held her breath, reached into the case and pulled the cover off Lilith's clay jar.

72

IRAQ

The container's hi-tech interior baffled Corporal Shuster. Overhead, the fluorescent tubes looked like the ultraviolet lights one would find in a plant nursery – something used to mimic nourishing sunlight. The oxygen-rich air was redolent with an ammonia-like scent.

Mounted like cubbyholes along the side walls were seven levels of adjoined Plexiglas cells. Each cell was the size of a footlocker and had a clear hinged front panel that was vented with a dense grid of tiny air holes.

Cages? wondered Schuster.

All the front panels were tilted wide open by a mechanized piston so that whatever had inhabited the cages seemed to have been set free. When was anyone's guess. Inspecting one of the cages, he saw a thick wire mesh bottom with a tray liner that angled towards a slot on the side wall. Perforated tubes looping around the tray's edges were likely intended to flush away waste.

But there was plenty of waste on the floor. Liquid and grape-sized pellets – black against the purple light – oozed between the grated floor panels as he stepped over them. He crouched down for a better look, but recoiled from the acrid stench. Coating almost every surface were short black hairs, as straight as pins. Millions of them.

Along the back side of each cage, a dozen short metal tubes with rolling ball ends protruded from the wall like nipples. He used his index finger to push in on one of the tips. Milky fluid streamed out over his fingertips. He held his fingers to his nose. Oddly, it smelled like wheat beer. A feeding system, he guessed. Probably linked into the PVC supply lines he'd seen running up to the ceiling.

Air pumped in from above. Food pumped in from above, he pondered.

By all appearances, it seemed as if the whole operation was automated from the outside.

Ramirez brushed aside the plastic flaps and made his way inside. He came to a stop after two steps. 'What kind of freaky shit is this?' He buried his nose in his sleeve.

'Breeding kennels, I think,' Shuster said.

Ramirez wasn't buying it. 'For what?'

'Don't know.'

'Maybe Al-Qaeda's selling puppies on the black market to fund the jihad.'

'Funny.'

Shuster tried to figure how many creatures one cage might have accommodated, but without knowing the size of one of them, it was tough to crunch the numbers. If the other six containers were of the same design, he guessed that the mystery brood could conservatively number in the thousands.

'Who could have built this?' Ramirez asked.

Shuster shook his head. 'Got me.'

'Creepy,' Ramirez muttered. He sidestepped the corporal and paced slowly along the aisle, trying to make sense of it all.

Standing outside the container, Private Holt swept his disbelieving gaze over the sophisticated installation that had been constructed inside the cave. Definitely no small operation. Just how deep beneath the mountain was he standing, anyway?

He peered through the container's door and could see Ramirez and Shuster pacing back and forth along the centre walkway. Then he turned to see what the Kurd was up to. Not far from where they'd entered the cave, Hazo was using a flashlight to inspect what looked like a hole in the wall. The surrounding blackness made it appear that the interpreter was floating in space.

'Everything all right over there, Hazo?' he called out, his voice echoing through the cave.

Hazo signalled that he was okay.

Then the ventilation system's motor turned off with a loud *thunk*, startling Holt.

'Hey,' he called into the container. 'Did you guys switch the air off?'

'No,' Shuster called back. 'It's probably on a timer. Nothing to worry about.'

'Right,' Holt said, calming himself. But when the fan whirred to a stop, other sounds masked by the humming motor suddenly came to the foreground. It took a moment for his ears to adjust, but the sounds were definitely there – subtle scratching noises. The vast space made it difficult to discern where they were coming from, but they seemed loudest towards the rear of the cave. 'Guys, I hear something weird out here.'

No answer.

'Guys?' He peered into the container and could see Ramirez talking to Shuster, bitching loudly. The sounds persisted. Scratching. Shifting and shuffling. Holt aimed his M-16 towards the disturbance, moved the light slowly from right to left through the soupy darkness, but saw nothing.

The more he listened to the sounds, the more he tried to convince himself they were nothing at all. Probably some other piece of machinery buried deeper in the cave that was in need of a little grease.

Holt moved stealthily down the excavated path, pausing outside the door of each container and glancing into its interior. There was no movement inside any of them. What exactly were these things? he wondered.

As he cornered the final container, the noises grew louder. Much louder. He deliberated on whether to investigate or turn back. Then his light settled on a wide opening in the cave's rear wall.

He stood perfectly still and angled his right ear for a better listen.

Now he was certain that the noises were coming from inside the burrow. What if the terrorists were holed up in there waiting to make a move?

He looked back and saw Ramirez coming out from the first container, Shuster right behind him. When Ramirez didn't see Holt, he got nervous and began hunting the darkness with his light. 'Holt! Where'd you go?'

'Over here,' Holt called out quietly, reluctant to draw attention to himself so close to the tunnel.

Ramirez shined his light directly into Holt's eyes. 'What are you doing?'

'Hey! You're blinding me!' Holt said in a loud whisper.

The light diverted away.

'Sorry.'

'I hear something over here,' Holt said, rubbing his eyes. 'I'm gonna check it out.' He blinked a few times, but Ramirez's light had spotted his vision.

'Go ahead . . . I'll be right over,' Ramirez said, peering into the other containers as he drew closer. He waved agitatedly for Holt to move on.

Reluctant, Holt levelled his rifle and advanced towards the opening. Once inside, he hesitated and shone the light into the tunnel. The passage looked similar to the one that had brought them into the cave – a wide conduit cutting through rock with a quarter of a metre to spare overhead. The ground pitched steadily downwards into a sharp bend that curved out of sight about ten metres from where he was standing. Whatever was causing the disturbance was definitely in there.

'Damn.' Despite the subterranean chill, he had to wipe sweat from his forehead. Wait for Ramirez. Not safe. Wait for Ramirez . . . his mind kept repeating.

Ramirez's shrill voice called out, 'Keep going, you pussy . . . I'll be right there!'

Holt groaned in frustration. Overriding his inner alarm, he pressed onward.

This isn't smart. You're being stupid. Turn around . . . he thought.

The ground was tricky underfoot with lots of jagged edges that pushed upward like petrified fingers. Holt tried his best to dismiss any notion that they would suddenly come to life and grab at his boots.

There are no such things as demons, he began repeating over and over again in his mind. That Kurd is whacko. There are no such things as demons . . .

As the light rose and fell over the rough walls, Holt's eyes began playing tricks with him, thanks to Ramirez shining the light right in his eyes. Circles of floating colours drifted like phantasms over his field of vision. He flicked his eyelids rapidly, hoping to make them go away. They didn't.

As he followed the bend, he raised his M-16 higher on his shoulder, stared down the muzzle. Whatever was making the noises, he was certain of one thing: there were no friendly targets in this godforsaken underworld. So if anything moved – anything at all – he would shoot first, ask questions later.

The sounds intensified, throwing his senses into high gear.

Definitely didn't sound like a machine. Or terrorist, either.

Sssst.

Chssst.

Fffffsss.

Sssssssssst.

He paused to crank his courage up a notch. Instead, his anxiety ballooned. The walls seemed to constrict around him as if he'd been swallowed by a gargantuan snake. His chest started heaving. He fought to catch his breath. He lowered his weapon and used his sleeve to blot more sweat from his spotty eyes.

Something tapped his shoulder from behind and he let out a bloodcurdling scream. In the same instant, he whirled fiercely and tweaked his ankle. When he tried to bring the rifle up for a shot, the muzzle hit the wall hard enough to shatter the element in his light.

'Whoa! Relax!' Ramirez yelled out, holding out his hand. 'Calm the fuck down. You scream like a girl. I'm not the Boogeyman.'

'What the fuck!' Holt screamed. 'Why are you sneaking up on me like that!'

'Sorry,' Ramirez said. 'Sorry. Geez, you sound like my niece when I take her on a roller coaster. Take the skirt off, Sally.'

Holt took a few seconds to compose himself.

Ramirez couldn't help but laugh.

Holt laughed too, and it felt good. 'Scared the crap outta me, you—'

The droning from deep within the tunnel suddenly whipped up like a raging tempest.

Ramirez's smile went flat. He took a step back and brought his rifle up high. 'What the . . .'

Before Holt could turn to see what was emerging from the shadows, he saw Ramirez's eyes go wide with terror. 'Holy shit! Get out of the way!'

Fully panicked, Holt refused to look back. He scrambled towards Ramirez, clumsily barrelling into him when he tried to squeeze past. Both men went down.

'What the fuck!' Ramirez shouted, scrambling to his knees and reaching for his M-16.

Holt's frantic hands swept the ground, probing for his weapon. His fingers registered something. But it wasn't steel – it was spongy. And it bit him. Then came another deep bite on his thigh. 'Ahh!'

Ramirez was back on his feet and shone the light on Holt. His blood went cold as thousands of eyes glared back at him.

73

Anxious to share his discovery of Lilith's tomb with Shuster, Hazo made his way towards the cave's centre and along the row of containers. Arranged side by side, two metres apart, the containers reminded him of railroad boxcars.

Glancing into the interiors, he spotted Shuster milling about inside the fourth container. Best not to disturb him, Hazo thought.

He waited outside.

He aimed his light up the ventilation stack that rose directly above the fourth container straight through the cave's lofty ceiling. He traced the light down the stack to a truck-sized motor housing mounted on a sturdy steel platform atop the fourth container, directly above the door. Round amber lights blinked on its control panel. Having heard the buzzing fan come to an abrupt stop a few minutes ago, he presumed that the system had gone into sleep mode. He noticed that other critical systems hardware had been installed on the platform too; clearly, the brain centre for the installation. Bolted alongside the container's doorway was the platform's access ladder.

A shrill scream rang out and Hazo spun towards it, sweeping his light side to side.

The corporal responded in an instant, bursting through the dangling plastic slats and bounding down the short ramp with his M-16 at the ready. 'What the hell was that?' he asked Hazo.

'Back there.' Hazo pointed to the cave's rear.

'Stay here,' Shuster told him then bolted off to investigate.

When the corporal disappeared around the container that sat at the end of the row, Hazo decided to climb up to the control platform for a better view. Gripping the ladder rungs, he began his ascent. Halfway to the top, he paused to catch his breath.

Off in the distance, he heard Ramirez laughing; Holt joining in shortly thereafter.

Must have been a false alarm, he guessed, continuing his ascent, slow and steady.

The wheezing in his lungs had given way to something much worse. Suddenly something ruptured beneath his breastbone. Within seconds, he felt like he was drowning. He coughed violently and a hot viscous liquid swelled into the back of his throat, bringing with it the taste of copper.

Blood.

Fighting the dread that threatened to paralyse him, he spat out the vile phlegm and managed to catch his breath. Clambering topside, he was overtaken by a bout of dizziness that forced him to his hands and knees. He cleared his lungs again, spat up more blood. If he'd been sickened by the same disease that afflicted Al-Zahrani, he realized it wouldn't be long before the lethargy would give way to complete immobility and delirium. And after that . . .

Hazo remembered what Karsaz had told him at the restaurant: 'Maybe it's not so bad that you don't have a family of your own. Less grief and worry.' Death was far worse for those left behind.

Hazo had learned that firsthand with the loss of his father, mother and brothers.

He shone the light down at the bloody puddle glistening over the platform's metal floor panel. Am I dying? he wondered.

When Ramirez and Holt stopped laughing and began screaming again, Hazo came to his senses. Getting to his feet, he was able to clearly see shifting light coming out from the tunnel they'd gone into. But he could only see the top of the opening.

'Get out of there!' he heard Shuster yell.

Hazo saw Ramirez's helmet bob in and out of view, Holt's next.

Three seconds later, all hell broke loose as the cave filled with the deafening *clack-clack-clack-clack* of machine gun fire and strobing muzzle flash.

Then Ramirez bolted zigzag up the path through the frames of violet light. His weapon was angled low, practically to the ground. He was yelling, 'Get the fuck away from me, you motherfuckers!'

Hazo leaned over the platform's safety rail, trying to discern what he was shooting at. At first, he couldn't spot the enemy.

Then the threat became all too clear.

An undulating black wave spilled out from the rear of the cave, curling, twisting, spreading fast over the ground, as if a colossal oil drum had been tipped over to flood the space. With it came unearthly squealing that filled the cave. In the darkness the pulsing crests twinkled with countless ruby specks that shimmered like sequins.

Screaming bloody murder, Ramirez kept firing indiscriminately at the swell, but the bullets did nothing to hinder its advance. As the marine's light traced wide arcs over the mass,

Hazo's skin crawled at what he was seeing from the top of the platform: a churning sea of eyes protruding from wedge-shaped heads; whiskered snouts; slithering, fleshy tails; rubbery bodies covered in black hair. Layers upon layers of them, fighting to the top, swallowed beneath, rising again.

Rats.

Hazo gasped. Thousands upon thousands of black rats. Their incalculable numbers were increasing by the second.

Hazo had seen plenty of vermin scavenging the waste dumps on the outskirts of his hometown, but none as large or aggressive as these. These rats seemed to be attacking Ramirez – mobilizing against him like an army.

'Up here!' Hazo screamed down to him. 'Come!' He coughed up more blood. 'There is a ladder!' But his weak scream was lost to the brood's high-pitched squealing.

In less than fifteen seconds, Ramirez's ammo clip ran dry. Wasting no time with a pointless reload, he unclipped the light from the weapon's muzzle and whipped the M-16 like a boomerang at the advancing horde. Then he broke into a sprint, whisked below Hazo, and headed for the entry tunnel. The determined rats weren't far behind him. Hazo watched Ramirez's light moving swiftly through the darkness. It looked as if Ramirez might outrun them.

More screams came from the rear of the cave. Hazo hunted the darkness with his flashlight and spotted Holt knee-deep in the squirming black mass.

74

LAS VEGAS

'Stop snooping around,' a gruff voice whispered over Brooke's shoulder.

Caught red-handed, Brooke flinched. Her fingers lost their grip and the jar's lid clattered back in place, fortunately not with enough force to cause any damage. Spinning around, she was face to face with Flaherty. He'd silently entered the room and was standing directly behind her.

'Caught ya,' he said, pointing a finger like a gun. 'Hands up.' He winked and flashed a mischievous smile.

'Jesus, Tommy,' she said, clutching her chest and letting out an anxious breath. She eyed his swollen nose, the bloodstains on his shirt collar. 'You nearly scared me to death!'

'You're alone in a vault with a demon's severed head, and *I* scare you?'

She bared her teeth and curled her fingers like talons. 'Oh, you are such a—'

'Whoa, slow down.' He held up his hands in surrender, saying, 'Just thought I'd tell you that we can't leave here until the infectious-disease folks come and scrub us down, prep Stokes for transport. We'll all need to be quarantined. Then the FBI drones will swing by and have their way with us. So best get comfy.'

'Great.' Rolling her eyes, she huffed and turned her attention back to the jar.

'What are you looking at?' he said, stepping up beside her.

'This. It's the jar Lilith was carrying just before she was executed. It's supposed to have some kind of magical power.'

'Spooky.'

'I just thought I'd take a look . . . see what's inside it,' she confessed.

'And?'

'I haven't gotten that far yet, thanks to you.'

'So what are you waiting for? Let's see if there's a rabbit in the hat.'

She shook her head. 'This isn't tampering with evidence, right?'

'I'd say it's gone through plenty of tampering already. I'm sure it'll be okay if we take a peek.'

'All right.' She rubbed her fingertips together, then reached into the case for a second attempt at unveiling the jar's interior.

With utmost finesse, Brooke curled her fingertips around the lid's thick rim. She lifted away the plate-like clay disc and gave it to Flaherty. 'Hold this.'

Hesitant, he said, 'What if it's cursed or something?'

She shot him a chastising look. 'For real? You're a Catholic, not an occult freak.'

'Fine.' He begrudgingly took the lid from her and held it at his side like a discus.

Brooke and Flaherty peered down at the uncovered jar.

'Looks like one of those jumbo candles from Pottery Barn . . . without the wick,' said Flaherty.

'Kinda does,' she agreed. Brooke tapped a fingernail on the solid glossy layer that levelled off just below the jar's rim, and it made the *clink-clink* sound of glass.

'I'm not seeing anything inside it,' Flaherty said. 'You?'

'No.' But her hopes weren't dashed, because if the ancient Mesopotamians had preserved the jar's contents employing the same method used on Lilith's head, then deep inside the jar, something had been trapped inside a viscous substance that over the centuries had hardened like glass. They just couldn't see it yet.

'Maybe we can shine a light in there, or something,' he suggested.

'I've got a better idea.' Closely studying the cut lines that split the circular rim into two equal arcs, Brooke could see paper-thin slivers of light squeezing through the fine gaps. 'I don't think this is glued.'

'Oh. Well maybe we could . . .'

Reaching in with both hands, she pinched the top of the rim at the middle of each half and applied gentle outward pressure on the opposing sides.

'. . . crack it open, or something.'

It was sticky at first. She bit her lip and put some more push behind her fingers. The pottery yielded with a gritty creak, yawned open along its front side from top to bottom like a giant pistachio. 'Hah . . . there we go.'

Flaherty tilted his head sideways for a better look, but refused to get any closer to the relic. With the bulbous core still masked in the jar's shadows, he couldn't yet decipher the contents.

Thrilled, Brooke was grinning ear to ear. 'Oh, this is amazing.'

Flaherty's eyes twinkled with admiration as he watched how she worked the pieces apart with patient dexterity. There was an endearing childlike innocence lurking beneath Brooke Thompson's sophisticated exterior; that wide-eyed wonderment that seemed to exist only on Christmas morning. And in this intimate moment, her passion for archaeology and discovery burned like the sun.

Brooke spread the pottery halves so that their crescent-shaped bottom surfaces slid out from under the solidified inner mass. The liberated core clunked down against the bottom of the display case. 'My God, Tommy . . . look at this!' she gasped

Setting aside his irrational superstitions, he stepped up to the case and peered in at what she'd found. He cringed at the frightful sight. 'Mother Mary.'

'It's beautiful,' she said.

'Beautiful?' Flaherty said. What had been inside the jar resembled a solid, honey-coloured crystal ball, much the same as the one containing Lilith's ghastly head. And coiled up inside the opaque mass was a considerably large snake whose jaws were hinged open and frozen in place, as if it had been drowned. Like its beheaded charmer, the snake's malevolent eyes were wide open in a threatening glare. Its hooked fangs were easily five centimetres long. The black, ropey body – thick as a beer can – was covered in scales the size of his thumbnail. He guessed that if he could stretch the thing out, it would be nearly two metres. 'That's a bizarre choice for a pet.'

'Sure is,' she said.

'Think it was poisonous?' he asked, fixated on the fangs.

'Sure looks like it,' Brooke said, slowly circling the case to see the snake from all angles.

'Why the hell would she be carrying this thing around?'

'I don't know. But think about it, Tommy . . . a snake is one of the central figures in Creation mythology, just like in the story of

Adam, Eve and Lilith.' Then halfway around the case, she froze. 'Wow, look here,' she said, waving him over.

Tommy stepped around to have a look. She was tapping on the glass to indicate a huge bulge in the snake's wide midsection; something caught inside and ballooning the body outward.

'Looks like the snake's last meal wasn't fully digested,' Brooke said.

'Not to change the subject of this fascinating discussion, but speaking of meal . . . I'm starving,' Flaherty said. He checked his watch. 'Seeing as we're going to be here awhile, I'm thinking we should raid that vending machine out in the hall. You like chips? Pretzels? Candy bars? The sky's the limit.'

'I could eat.'

'You, uh, like the Celtics?' Flaherty said with a polite cough.

'Huh? What? Yeah, I love the Celtics,' she said.

You're the woman of my dreams, he thought.

'Why do you want to know?' she asked.

'Stokes has a big-screen TV in his office, rigged for satellite. Supposed to be a great game tonight – playing the Lakers. Starts in about ten minutes. You, ah, interested?'

'Are you asking me out on a date, Agent Flaherty? I thought you were abstaining from gambling in Vegas.'

He blushed. 'Not sure if taking you into a room contaminated by anthrax, with a shot preacher lying on the floor, would qualify as romance. But I'm looking for a safe bet. So yeah, let's call it a date.'

75

IRAQ

Ramirez blazed like a thunderbolt through the cave, determined to return to the outside world in record time. Doing his best to keep the light directed towards the dodgy ground, he pumped his arms and legs like pistons, remembering how it felt to sprint the fifty at high school track meets. Normally he'd be looking over his shoulder for anyone sneaking up in his wake. For this race, however, he wasn't looking back.

He could barely stomach the idea of his niece's caged gerbil, Felix. The hell with Felix. Felix was nothing but a pimped-out mouse.

But rats? A cave full of huge, filthy rats? Repulsive. Made his nuts pull up into his stomach. And these rats seemed to be out for blood. The way they came at him like that? Pursued him? That couldn't be normal. Rats didn't eat live meat, did they? he wondered. But they sure liked the taste of Holt. The poor bastard was covered in the things. And there was nothing Ramirez could've done about it. It's not like he could've swatted them away or shot them off Holt's chest. There were so *many* of them.

There was only one option: run . . . *hard*.

Back in the cave, when he'd discarded his M-16, he'd barely glimpsed Hazo marooned on top of one those sadistic breeding kennels where some twisted psycho nurtured those flesh-eating-rodents-from-Hell. He'd be sure to send some guys with flamethrowers and grenades back inside to fry the critters and pull Hazo out – assuming he didn't die from demon pestilence first.

As Ramirez tore through the tunnel, the squealing din faded and he became confident he'd make it out from the mountain unscathed. In fact, it sounded as if the rats had stayed inside the cave.

Ramirez's relief, however, instantly withered when up ahead in the tunnel's dark throat, a series of bright flashes coincided perfectly with the metallic hammering of automatic gunfire delivered at point-blank range.

The bullets struck him low – one shattering his left kneecap, six more to the groin and thighs. His legs instantly went out and his face slammed into the ground like a pile driver. It was so fast, so shocking, that he didn't even scream. With all the adrenaline pumping through his system, even the pain was slow coming.

But when the gunman emerged into the glowing cone of his fumbled flashlight, the sting of treachery came instantaneously.

'Crawford?' he groaned, blood streaming into his right eye from a ragged gash that split his forehead. 'Wh – why?'

There was no answer. The colonel simply pressed the M-16's muzzle against Ramirez's head and delivered the kill shot.

76

The huge rodents – bodies as large as eggplants – were teeming over Holt, clawing their way up his legs, chest and back. Hazo watched in horror as the marine flailed his arms violently, flinging rats in every direction. Blood covered dozens of tattered holes in his sleeves where he'd been bitten (though his flak jacket had protected his torso). A sickly-looking thing squirmed up on to his shoulder and sank its teeth into his ear. Holt screamed in rage, tore it free, hurled it into the darkness like a football. By then, another horde of rats was grappling up his pant legs. Trudging through the knee-deep brood, it looked as if Holt were slogging through wet cement.

'Up here!' Hazo screamed again. 'Up—'

The coughing seized his voice again. Spitting up more blood and bile, Hazo watched helplessly as Holt tried to quicken his pace. Then desperation and frustration got the better of Holt and he raised his knees to try to run. It was a costly mistake.

Trampling the spongy rats underfoot caused Holt to lose his footing. He faltered, caught himself, faltered again. The rats piled on to him. He got back up again and shook some of them free, before slipping and going down a final time.

Hazo shined his light on the spot, praying that Holt would get up.

He didn't.

The rats swarmed over their prey.

Holt's arms thrashed a few more times, as if he were drowning. Then he disappeared beneath the roiling current.

'Hazo!' a voice called out over the maddening squeals.

Hazo turned and saw Shuster pulling himself up over the edge of the neighbouring container. He'd lost his helmet and his pant legs were torn up and bloody. Otherwise, he seemed unharmed. 'Are you all right?' Hazo called back.

Breathless, Shuster rolled on to his back. 'I'm okay,' he said, panting.

Hazo looked towards the entry tunnel and saw that the glow of Ramirez's light seemed to be growing stronger again – coming back towards the cave.

77

Years had passed since Bryce Crawford last walked these tunnels, yet he still recognized every oddity and anomaly inside the mountain as if they were the birthmarks of a former lover. Even the familiar loamy smell invoked fond memories of the extensive time he'd been stationed here – like grandma's turkey roasting in the oven on Thanksgiving Day.

Once Frank Roselli had declared the installation 'complete' the previous spring, the single entrance to Operation Genesis's self-sustaining breeding facility had been sealed. Every mechanical part of the gnotobiotic isolator cells that housed the rats had been designed for remote operation, thanks to technology borrowed heavily from NASA's unmanned space stations. Similarly, the facility generated its own power from a state-of-the-art compact nuclear reactor capable of continuously churning out electricity for ten years before needing refuelling.

Even replenishment of the feeding tanks was handled by a cleverly concealed pipeline to a dairy farm situated a kilometre to the west. The milky nutrient solution manufactured there was a potent brew infused with plague virions and gonadotropin hormone that stimulated the brood's pituitary development (to promote aggressive behaviour).

What they'd built inside this mountain was the most sophisticated installation of its kind. Such a pity that not long from now, not a trace of it would remain, Crawford thought.

As he neared the cave, his apprehension intensified with the sounds of squealing.

These are no ordinary rats, he thought.

He remembered Roselli saying that the proper name for a brood of rats of was a 'mischief', and how the Chinese revered the rat for its cunning and intellect, so much so that it earned top rank as the first of the twelve years in the Sheng xiao zodiac cycle. But this genetically enhanced batch of vermin would add a whole new meaning to 'Year of the Rat', thought Crawford.

In one year, the typical female black rat – sexually mature at three months – gestated every twenty-four days, gave live birth to twelve pups and spawned 16,000 offspring. But thanks to Roselli's ingenious breeding technique, the birthing rate had been increased to an average of sixteen pups. Therefore, the growth algorithm for Operation Genesis conservatively assumed that each female in the initial set would account for an astounding 24,000 descendants in the first year alone. Naturally, the descendants would carry that trend forward exponentially.

Much of the epidemiological detail was lost on Crawford. But he remembered Roselli referring to the rats as a natural 'intermediate host' for plague transmission. Stokes preferred to call them a 'delivery system'. All Crawford knew was that once the brood had reached critical mass, they'd be released from the cave into the Zagros Mountains.

Once unleashed on their new habitat, the rat population would spread out in all directions. And all the while, they'd rampantly breed; just like they'd been doing in this cave – just like their cousins, the Asian black rats or 'ship rats', had done before spreading out from China centuries earlier to transmit the Black Death throughout Europe.

Highly intelligent survivalists by nature, the rats would evade capture by burrowing underground, hiding in the mountains' nooks and crannies, and building hidden nests inside the walls of homes and buildings. Even if they were to be spotted out in the open, the rats were virtually impossible to catch, because for their body size they were among nature's best athletes: able to sprint at nearly forty kilometers per hour, swim half a kilometre, climb vertically up walls and jump up to over a metre, even squeeze their rubbery bodies through a hole smaller than a quarter. Trapping them was no easy task either since their chisel-like teeth, with more crushing force than a crocodile, could gnaw through metal and wood. At the genetic level, rats were 90 per cent identical to humans – the reason they were favoured for clinical laboratory testing. But a rat's most important physiological similarity was its brain – nearly identical to a human's in its ability for spatial memorization.

These rats will be impossible to contain or destroy.

Throughout history, rats had been the carriers and transmitters of over seventy diseases lethal to humans, including typhus, salmonella, parasitic trichinosis and, of course, *Yersinia pestis*, commonly known as bubonic plague. Similarly, according to Roselli, there'd be numerous ways the rats would transmit the Genesis Plague virions to humans. Crawford could only recall the top three: contamination of food and water supplies via blood, urine, faeces, or saliva; primary contact through a bite (less likely); or most potently, through blood-sucking sand flies and mosquitoes (prolific throughout the Middle East), that would feast on the rats, then relay the virus to humans and live-stock through bites. The perfect transmission vector.

Rats provided everything Stokes had wished for: efficiency, cost-effectiveness and anonymity.

At first, Crawford thought Stokes's plan to settle the score in the Middle East sounded insane. Now that the mission was nearing completion, however, he felt nothing but reverence for the man. Stokes was a visionary; a crusader; a *saviour*. Stokes would rewrite human history.

And Crawford was determined to play his part – to make history right alongside Stokes. During the past critical hour, however, Crawford had been unable to establish further communication with Stokes. Yet like every operational detail of Operation Genesis, there was a failsafe for this dilemma – a manual workaround. At this juncture, the mission's success hinged upon getting the rats out from the cave. Crawford had hoped that despite their neophobic tendencies, the rats would have already made their way outside. But the two blasts that had decimated the cave's entry tunnels had likely forced the rats to seek an alternative exit; the very survival mechanism that would account for their staying power in the outside world.

At this juncture, all Crawford needed to do was act the role of the Pied Piper and herd the critters out the front door. Though he wasn't counting on that being the easiest of tasks. With the rats having been down here breeding for over a year, he could hardly imagine just how many there might be inside. And since he recalled that rats evolved three times faster than humans, he wondered what effect the hormone infusions might have had on their behaviour and physiology.

If rats felt threatened, they would defend themselves. These rats, however, were likely far more unpredictable – exactly the reason Crawford had brought along the rodent repeller that had been designed for just such a snafu. The transmitter had been cleverly integrated into Crawford's walkie-talkie. After all, the simple technology could easily piggyback on the radio's circuit board. With the touch of a button, he powered on the transmitter and a steady ultrasonic signal began transmitting in the 45,000 Hz range. For the rats, the high-frequency, pulsing waves – inaudible to the human ear – were like Kryptonite to Superman.

On approach to the cave, he could hear the horde's high-pitched drone. He wondered what the rats might be trying to communicate to one another. Were they coordinating an attack on Holt, Shuster and the Kurd?

The tunnel walls fell away from his light, giving way to the cave's soupy black void. Without pause, Crawford stormed inside, machine gun raised high on his shoulder, ready to cut down any moving target larger than a rat.

78

'Don't worry, Hazo,' Shuster yelled over the squealing rats. 'Ramirez made it. He'll get help. Just stay where you are.'

But Hazo didn't respond because he was still watching the light intensifying inside the entrance tunnel. He estimated that Ramirez had only gone into the tunnel less than a minute ago. Definitely not enough time to have assembled a rescue team. So why would he be coming back inside now?

The light flashed inside the cave and caught Shuster's attention. He turned, scowled at the light, shouted, 'Ramirez! Get out of here!' He motioned for him to retreat. 'Go and get the others!'

Hazo watched the sharp luminescent beam sweep side to side. Against Shuster's order, Ramirez advanced closer. If Ramirez didn't hear Shuster, he should certainly have understood the overt hand signals. Certain that the light would attract the rats, Hazo was confused when the writhing brood cowered back and curled into itself like ebbing surf. It looked as if an invisible wall were pushing out in front of the light to press them back, like some kind of fantastical force field.

'Ramirez!' Shuster shouted in an angry voice that echoed through the cave. 'Go back!'

But the corporal's plea quickly went silent as the swell of rats continued to retreat from the light. Like Hazo, he was trying to figure out how this was happening.

Advancing to within fifteen metres of the containers, the light stopped and swung up to spotlight Shuster. The corporal shielded his eyes from the glare while trying to discern the identity of the man holding the light. It was impossible. His frustration grew. 'Ramirez, what are you doing? Get that fucking light out of my face!'

No reply. The light remained fixed on Shuster.

'Ramirez?'

The rats' squealing cries were suddenly drowned out by the clamour of automatic gunfire, and beneath the light, Hazo saw tiny white flashes spit in rapid succession.

In the same instant, Shuster's face ripped open and the back of his head exploded in a spew of blood and brain matter. The force from the impact threw him backwards and he tumbled off the container.

Dropping to his knees, Hazo flashed his light down at the body. The rats responded instantly, swarming over it.

Then the light shifted to Hazo.

There was nowhere for Hazo to go. He was penned in by the platform's railings. He scrambled for the handgun that Shuster had given him and sprang to his feet. Squinting in the light, he failed to make visual confirmation of a target, but blindly fired three shots. The light didn't budge.

'Drop the gun, Hazo!' the gunman yelled up at him.

Hazo wasn't surprised that it was Crawford's voice. 'No!' he replied.

'I'll shoot you dead right now if you don't drop the gun,' Crawford threatened in a menacing tone.

'Fine! You do what you must,' Hazo screamed. 'I'm already dead. Don't you see?'

A pause.

'Get off that platform,' Crawford yelled.

Get off the platform? Hazo repeated to himself. Why would Crawford want him to come down? If he had no problem shooting Shuster off the container . . .

'Get off . . . now!'

Having witnessed Holt's horrible demise, there was no way Hazo was willing to sacrifice himself to the rats. Best to take a few bullets and avoid the suffering, albeit the rats or the plague. Hazo turned his back to Crawford, raised his arms and shut his eyes tight. 'Shoot me!' he yelled out. 'Shoot me in the back like the coward you are!' He gritted his teeth and waited for the end – waited for Crawford's bullets to finish the job his microscopic assassins had already started.

No shots came.

Confused, Hazo eased his eyes open. 'What are you waiting for!' But directly in front of his face, he saw the answer to his own question. There, in plain view, a peculiar sticker was plastered on to the sheet metal housing covering a huge, tubular machine. The ominous symbol – a circle cut like a pie into six alternating yellow and black slices – carried a universal warning.

Radiation.

'This is your last chance!' Crawford screamed.

Hazo ignored him, as he tried to process this new information.

He quickly assessed the huge machine. Why would there be radioactive material down here? Unless . . .

Could this be a nuclear reactor? Normally a nuclear reactor was a huge thing that powered cities. And they were always shielded with thick concrete to protect against radiation leaks. But Hazo quickly determined that a radiation leak so deep inside a mountain probably made such safety precautions a moot point. Clearly, if Crawford wanted him to back away from the reactor, it could only mean that he feared a stray bullet might pierce its volatile core.

'Fine,' Crawford yelled. 'I'll come and pull you down.'

Hazo turned and pointed the gun directly at the reactor, the way an executioner might – the way a Saddam loyalist might threaten a Kurdish carpet retailer from Mosul. 'I don't think so,' he said. 'You move, I shoot.'

For ten seconds there was no response.

Then the light beam shifted.

Hazo hesitated.

Still no reply from Crawford.

Hazo called down to him: 'This is a nuclear reactor, is it not?'

Again, Crawford didn't answer.

Without warning, something hurled out from the light – glinting in fast bursts as it pinwheeled directly towards Hazo. Before he could react, it struck him in the chest like a fist, pushed him back against the reactor. He crumpled down on to the platform. All feeling to his right hand instantly turned to pins and needles. Involuntarily, his fingers went limp. The gun slipped out from his ruined grip and skittered to a stop, close to the edge of the platform.

This time, Hazo found it impossible to catch his breath. He looked down and saw a black handgrip, buried to the hilt, sticking out beneath his right clavicle, close to the shoulder. When he tried to move towards the gun, bolts of pain shot down his arm and over his chest, making him see pure white. He screamed out in agony.

Then he could hear Crawford's boots clanging up the ladder rungs.

79

It hadn't taken much effort for Jason to persuade Crawford's disenchanted marines to step aside so that he and Meat could get into the tunnel.

After squirming through the opening above the debris pile, they'd progressed quickly through a series of interconnected tunnels. Tight winding passages had widened into a subterranean corridor with a lofty ceiling joined at a point, which in turn, fed them through a tunnel that looked as if it had been dug by a huge gopher. Halfway through the gopher hole, where a sharp bend yielded to a lengthy straightaway, Jason abruptly dropped to one knee with his M-16 directed straight. He immediately signalled to Meat to halt his advance.

With no words exchanged between them, Jason leaned sideways and shone his light low to the ground less than ten metres ahead to emphasize a contorted body in desert camouflage blocking their path. The dead man was on his stomach in a pool of blood that looked purple against the dark limestone. Though the face was turned away from them, a glinting gold crucifix dangling from the corpse's neck left little doubt as to the marine's identity.

'It's Ramirez,' Jason whispered softly to Meat.

Meat's face gnarled with disgust.

Jason eased back to a standing position, listened intently for any activity. He turned to Meat. 'Hear that?'

Meat nodded. 'Sounds like rusty wheels.'

Jason proceeded forward and Meat followed close at his heels. As he stepped over the body, he caught a glimpse of the dime-sized red hole drilled through Ramirez's temple.

Crawford, you bastard. You're going to pay for this. All of this.

The tunnel curved yet again. After cautiously rounding the bend, Jason saw the slightest trace of light softening the darkness. He also heard screaming over the growing din of tinny squeals. One of the voices belonged to Crawford; the other, tinged with an accent, unmistakably Hazo. The exchange wasn't pleasant. It sounded as if the two were arguing about something.

Jason looked back at Meat and said in an urgent tone, 'Let's do this.'

80

Hazo was amazed how quickly Crawford had made it up to the platform. It seemed like mere seconds had elapsed since the colonel threw the knife into his chest. Not enough time for Hazo to muster the strength to make a play for the gun. But even the slightest movement tweaked the blade against nerves and zapped him like a taser.

Sneering and wild-eyed, Crawford gave the handgun a swift kick and it sailed off into the darkness to disappear below the rats. 'Nice try, Haji. But your aim was lousy.'

Hazo's gaze burned with contempt. 'You are an evil man,' he said. Wincing, he tried to prop himself up against the reactor.

'Don't be such a bad sport. You're no match for me. None of you Arabs is a match for me.'

'I am a *Kurd*,' Hazo couldn't help point out.

Crawford shrugged. 'You all look the same to me – Kurds, Saudis, Egyptians, Palestinians, Kuwaitis, Jordanians, Iranians, Afghanis . . . Call yourselves whatever you want. But you all popped out of the same fucked-up mould.' He reached out and gave the knife a good twist and Hazo screamed out. 'Don't take my word for it, though. That virus inside you knows the difference . . . only likes A-rab DNA. And it looks to me like you're one dead A-rab.'

Just when Hazo looked ready to pass out, Crawford relinquished his grip on the knife's hilt. He reached into his pocket, pulled out a foot-long plastic zip-tie. Tugging at the Kurd's limp arm, he strapped the wrist snugly to the rail.

Hazo screamed in agony, coughed up a wad of mucus and blood.

'Sounds like you've got a hairball in there. Oh, sorry . . . that's just the plague. Same plague these rats are going to spread to every one of your Arab brothers.' Crawford stood and eyed the huge generator. 'You aren't as stupid as most Arabs, I'll give you that. You see, this sure *is* a nuclear reactor. World's most efficient battery. But a couple of puny bullets won't do it much harm.' Then he squatted beside a luggage-sized olive drab box bolted to the base of the reactor, saying, 'But this baby, here, can pack enough punch to vaporize everything inside this mountain.' Crawford patted the boxy shell that protected the W54 Special Atomic Demolition Munition, feeling both affection and respect for what was inside it: the plutonium equivalent of twenty-two tons of TNT. 'Before that happens, I'm going to push these rats out of here, using my little whistle here.' Crawford tapped his walkie-talkie. 'That way they can swarm over this godforsaken sandbox you call a country to set things straight once and for all.'

Horrified, Hazo watched the colonel unhinge the bomb's lid to access a control console. When Crawford inserted a keycard into a slot on the panel, a digital display illuminated.

'Please, think about what you are doing,' Hazo pleaded. 'Destroy the cave . . . me . . . That is fine. You can leave this place and no one will ever know. But you can't spread this disease.

Please. Think of all the innocent people. Even *you* can't do such thing.'

'I can do anything I damn well please,' Crawford replied coyly, entering an eight-digit code on the console's number pad to override the remote arming system linked to Stokes's computer halfway around the world. 'And don't you worry about my conscience. After all this is done, I'll sleep like a baby.' He pressed a button and a digital display illuminated with numbers: 00:20:00. He looked at Hazo and grinned.

'Please. Don't.'

'Let the games begin.' Crawford hit another key and the countdown began. 'You've got less than twenty minutes. Plenty of time for some fond memories and a few prayers. Then it's off to reunite with your papa. In the meantime, I've got some work to do.'

'Crawford!' a deep voice bellowed out from the darkness.

The colonel's bravado instantly turned to alarm. He wheeled and drew his M-16 – all in one motion. His light lanced the darkness and found the target near the entrance tunnel: one of those damn mercenaries; the Goliath-sized guy they called 'Meat'. 'Don't you assholes know when to die?' He opened fire before the man could raise his weapon. But Meat managed to duck for cover into the tunnel. 'Fucker,' he grumbled.

Meanwhile, with Crawford's attention focused on Meat, Jason crept up the ladder leading to the platform. He glanced down at the unbelievably huge brood of rats – all those gleaming red eyes filled with malice staring back at him. Crawford's tirade filled in many of the blanks as to what Stokes's master plan entailed, making it perfectly clear that the rats themselves were to be what Flaherty had dubbed the plague's 'delivery system'. All this sophisticated equipment Stokes had installed was no doubt designed to increase the rats' numbers, while pumping them full of virus.

As he'd advanced through the shadows, Jason had seen Crawford tap the device on his belt and refer to it as a 'whistle' – the tool he'd be using to drive the rats out from the cave. Judging from the way the rats stayed far away from Crawford's position, he guessed it was a variant of an ultrasonic transmitter commonly used by the marines to ward off critters and pests from camp provisions. He could see that the rats were trying to break through the invisible barrier that kept them at a distance of ten metres. A wave of rats would spill into the void, cower against the ultrasonic blast and scrabble back in retreat. Then another bunch would test their mettle with the same result. Fortunately, the natural bottleneck at the cave's centre contained the rats. But they needed to be destroyed – every single one of them.

Near the top of the ladder, Jason peeked up over the edge of the platform. Crawford was facing sideways, using his light to probe the entryway for Meat. Though Crawford was wearing a helmet and a flak jacket, Jason could easily put a bullet through his face. However tempting that might seem, he'd need to try to take him alive. With Roselli and Stokes out of the picture, Crawford was the lone survivor of the twisted cabal who'd masterminded Operation Genesis. And there were plenty of questions still unanswered.

'You are finished, Crawford,' Hazo whispered, smiling grimly.

'Not even close, Haji,' he said, turning to face Hazo. Glowering, he pressed the M-16's muzzle against Hazo's head.

It was exactly what Hazo expected Crawford to do. And it drew all the attention away from Jason, who was now quietly stepping up on to the platform.

At the last instant, however, Crawford was alerted to Jason's presence by the subtle shift in the metal grating under his feet. By the time Crawford turned, Jason had lunged forward like a linebacker, burying a shoulder into Crawford's abdomen and thrusting him back against the safety rail that looped in front of the reactor.

Jason drove his elbow up into Crawford's jaw, then landed a smashing head-butt on the bridge of his nose. Blood sprayed everywhere. Jason grabbed for Crawford's right forearm and pushed the M-16 away. Shots sprayed wildly into the cave's vault. Then with all his might, Jason pressed the forearm longways over the metal rail – kept pushing down until he heard bones snap. Dazed, Crawford yelped in pain, thrashing viciously. The M-16 slipped out from his grip, tumbled over the railing and disappeared.

Crawford brought his left elbow down between Jason's shoulder blades directly on the spine. He followed it up with a knee to Jason's face.

Jason reeled, stumbled backwards and collapsed on to the platform.

Crawford used his left hand to yank the knife out from Hazo's shoulder. Hazo screamed in anguish as blood began spilling out from the unplugged wound.

Jason sprang to his feet and squared off with Crawford.

'Still got some fight left, eh?' Crawford said, grinning deviously. His misshapen right arm dangled limply at his side, and he clutched the defiled knife in his left hand.

'Plenty,' Jason said, wiping blood from a gash over his left eye.

'You're gonna need it, boy,' Crawford warned, with a menacing thrust of the knife. He eyed the spinning numbers on the nuke's console. 'You can't stop this now,' he said. 'Even I can't override the countdown.'

'I'm not asking you to stop it,' Jason replied, crouching in a wrestling stance.

'You're a cocky son of a bitch, aren't you?' Crawford said. 'But tell me, Yaeger . . . when you found Al-Zahrani drowned in his own filth, didn't you just love it?'

Jason didn't answer.

'Must have been thrilling to see him go like that.' Crawford kept low and shifted side to side. 'All that horrible suffering. After what he did to your brother, it must've tickled your dick.'

'You don't know shit about my brother.'

Crawford tested Yaeger's reflexes with another thrust of the knife. Jason pulled back nimbly. 'But I know plenty about *you*, Yaeger,' he said. 'You want revenge. You want blood. And here I am handing you retribution wrapped in a bow . . . and you're fighting me? You want this just as bad as me. These rats . . . this plague . . . it's the answer to all our problems.'

'A plague won't stop fanaticism. It's not a solution. Nothing that can kill so many innocent people is a solution.'

'That's not the way I see it,' replied Crawford.

Jason tipped his head towards the nuke. 'Time's fleeting. Best make your move now if you think you might have a chance at saving your pets.' He could see in Crawford's frenzied gaze that a bleak realization was taking hold.

Crawford stepped closer, forcing Jason to back-step to the open edge of the platform near the ladder.

Then something popped up over the lip of the platform and a bright light suddenly flashed in Crawford's eyes, making him raise his left hand to shield them.

Jason sprang at Crawford, grabbed his flak jacket with both hands and planted his right foot in Crawford's stomach. He tugged the colonel forward while dropping his back on to the platform in a somersault and using the momentum to flip Crawford upwards. He thrust his legs and the colonel launched over the edge of the platform.

Clinging to the ladder with the flashlight in his hand, Meat ducked as Crawford went airborne.

'*No-o-o-o*—!' Crawford yelled as he did a full twist. He landed hard on his back. His head smacked against the rocky ground, but the helmet spared his skull from being split open. The rats immediately retreated from the repeller so that a wide circle opened up around him.

Meat pointed the light down at him. The colonel's body was contorted into a pretzel shape. The left leg was bent completely sideways; the right arm pinned beneath the torso. With his left arm, however, he was struggling to retrieve the M-16 that had landed just out of reach. There was no movement below the waist. 'That's gonna leave a mark.'

'Thanks,' Jason said, holding a hand out for Meat.

'What are friends for?' Meat said, clasping Jason's hand and stepping up on to the platform.

'Aaaaaaah!' Crawford screamed in frustration, his outstretched left arm still half a metre from the rifle. He glared at his ruined legs, trying to will a response. But there was zero movement. 'Damn it, Yaeger! You broke my fucking back!'

'What's the matter . . . colonel's got a boo-boo?' Meat cajoled.

'We can't mess around, Meat,' Jason said. 'We don't have much time.'

81

'Hey, buddy,' Jason said, kneeling beside Hazo. He used his knife to cut Hazo's wrist free from the railing. Hazo's complexion was sickly and trickles of blood were dribbling from his nostrils and ears. 'Looks like you've had a tough time since we've been gone.'

'I do not feel so well, Jason,' Hazo muttered, his eyes distant and cloudy.

'We're going to get you out of here. Are you able to stand?'

'No. I'm too dizzy.'

'I'll carry you.'

'No . . . no.'

'Fine,' Jason said. 'Meat will carry you.'

Hazo managed a thin smile, waved his hand dismissively. 'Is it true that Al-Zahrani is dead?' he asked, looking directly into Jason's eyes.

Jason couldn't lie. 'Yeah, buddy. He's dead.'

'This disease killed him? This plague that is inside me?'

Jason hesitated. 'We didn't find him in time. We weren't able to treat him.'

'*Is* there a treatment, Jason?' Hazo asked, his voice weak.

Jason didn't know what to say. The medic was dead and according to Tommy Flaherty, Stokes had indicated that there was no vaccine. Finally, with his heart in his throat, he shook his head.

'Can I spread this to others?'

Jason swallowed hard and felt a surge of emotion fill his chest. He could tell that Hazo already knew the answer, but needed him to make peace with it. 'Yes.'

'Then I must stay here. You know that.'

A feeling of utter helplessness wrenched Jason, made his head numb. He'd already lost two men today.

'Jason, we've got a problem,' Meat said, monitoring the scene below. 'The rats. They're moving closer.' He also noticed that the tiny yellow light on Crawford's walkie-talkie that had been blinking in a steady rhythm had now turned to a sporadic pulse. 'I think Crawford's gizmo got a good jolt when he hit the ground. Looks like it's fading out.'

Jason glanced at the nuke's digital counter. Fifteen minutes, eight seconds. There was no way they could carry Hazo outside in time. And with a broken back, Crawford wouldn't be making it out either. Unfortunately, there'd also be no time to interrogate the colonel.

'Hazo's right,' Meat said. 'We don't have much time. And there's no way we can allow these rats to get out of here. Let the nuke do its job. It's the best option we've got to stop this thing from spreading.'

Jason nodded and turned his attention back to Hazo. 'You're a great man, Hazo. Your family will be very proud when I tell them what you've done.'

Meat peered down at Crawford again and his eyes went wide. Though the colonel had given up on the M-16, he was now using his good arm to make a play for the apple-sized grenades clipped to his vest. 'Oh you fucker,' Meat hissed, baring his teeth. 'Don't even think about it!' He raised his rifle, took careful aim at Crawford and squeezed off three rounds. One of the rounds split the colonel's wrist, the other two sank deep into the bulletproof flak jacket.

Crawford bellowed out in pain and spewed a string of obscenities at Meat.

'And that goes double for you too,' Meat replied, grinning.

'Thank you, Jason,' Hazo said. 'Thank you for showing me hope when I saw nothing but despair. When I meet my father again, it will be with dignity. Now you must go. Please.'

82

Meat descended the ladder while monitoring the scene directly below: rats streaming up and down the ramp leading into the container, as if staging a raid.

'Make sure you don't get bit,' Jason warned, as he gripped the ladder's side rails and swung his foot out on to the top rung.

'Duh,' Meat muttered. Reaching the lowest rung, he leaped out over the horde and landed safely in the shrinking circle of clear ground that surrounded Crawford.

When Jason looked over at the colonel, he couldn't believe what he saw. Crawford was now hammer-swinging his mangled hand at his walkie-talkie, trying to smash it. 'Meat! Stop him!'

Meat dashed over to the colonel and grabbed the thrashing arm with both hands. 'Give it up, Crawford!'

'Fuck you!' the colonel seethed, grimacing from the pain.

Cranking the arm down, Meat dropped his knees on to it, pinning it hopelessly to the ground.

Jason jumped down off the ladder and came up behind Meat.

Crawford's entire body quaked from the adrenaline coursing through his system. 'You don't know what you're doing!' he ranted madly. 'Don't let *them* win! It's them or us! Don't you see?!'

'Yeah, yeah . . .' Meat said, snatching the blood-covered walkie-talkie from Crawford's belt. 'I'll take this, thanks.' He tossed it to Jason.

Crawford spat in Meat's face. 'You're a disgrace!'

Using his sleeve to wipe the saliva from his cheek, Meat replied sarcastically, 'And aren't you just sweet as a cupcake?'

'Take his grenades too,' Jason said.

Meat plucked the three grenades from Crawford's flak jacket and clipped them to his own belt.

Meanwhile, Jason went over to retrieve Crawford's fumbled Bowie knife, which had landed within inches of the advancing wall of vermin. Crouching to grab the knife, he stared at the mind-boggling infestation – a sea of beady eyes filled with unnatural bloodlust. He was certain that plague DNA alone couldn't account for the rats' wild behaviour. What had Stokes been feeding them? He stood and paced over to Crawford.

'You're responsible for quite a few deaths today, Crawford,' Jason said. 'Mostly good men who believed in you . . . trusted you. That's a lot of blood on your hands. As far as I see it, it's high time for you to pay for what you've done.' He dropped the knife on to Crawford's chest. 'You can keep that, tough guy. See how well you do against them.' He motioned to the rats. '*Capeesh*?'

Crawford's jaw jutted out, his eyes boiling with rage and defeat.

'Come on, Jason. Let's get outta here,' Meat said, motioning to the entry tunnel.

'Just a sec,' Jason said. He unclipped the light from Crawford's M-16 and set it on the ground to illuminate the spot.

'Wh— . . . what are you doing?' Crawford demanded.

Slowly backing away, Jason grinned while holding up the sputtering walkie-talkie. With each step, the ultrasonic barrier retreated from Crawford and the hungry rats encroached a few inches more into the circular void – countless hungry eyes glinting red in the light.

The colonel tried desperately to grip the Bowie knife with only the limited function of a thumb and a pinkie. The blade slid off his chest and landed just out of reach. '*Aaaaaaah!*' He propped himself up on his good elbow, and tried to drag his crippled body away from the rats. That didn't work either.

'Hazo!' Jason called out.

'Yes, Jason. I'm still here,' came the Kurd's weak reply from high up on the platform.

'Can you see this?' He glanced up at the platform and saw Hazo's head pop into view.

'Yes.'

'This is for you, buddy. Godspeed, my friend.' Jason took another step back. The rats spilled over Crawford's paralysed legs and began feeding.

Crawford screamed bloody murder. 'Damn you, Yaeger!'

Holding the flashlight to his watch, Meat reported, 'We only have twelve minutes left.' But he could tell that Jason was determined to make the colonel suffer.

Jason paused for a long moment to let Crawford wallow in terror. Then he took another step backwards. The rats scurried up the colonel's thighs and genitals, clawing viciously, gnashing and tearing away flesh in chunks. Crawford couldn't yet feel the pain, but the sheer horror that showed in his eyes consumed the last ounce of his bravado.

Jason counted slowly to ten. Another step backwards brought

the rats over the colonel's chest. They chewed wildly at his flak jacket, digging for flesh. When they attacked the mangled arm still trapped under his torso, the ungodly pain finally registered. Shrieking in agony, Crawford swatted madly at them with his other arm, but the effort was futile.

After another ten-count, Jason took a further step back.

Now the rats fought for the tender flesh of the colonel's neck, ears and face. Crawford's thrashing arm, thick with clinging rats, was now useless. When he screamed one last time, a rat buried itself in his throat, while two more clawed at his eyes. The body went into spasm.

Satisfied, Jason dashed towards the tunnel where Meat stood anxiously waiting.

The black wave crashed over Crawford's body.

'Feel better now?' Meat said.

'Much,' Jason said, setting the transmitter on the ground just inside the narrow entryway. 'That should hold them back long enough. Now let's get the hell out of here!'

83

'What's going on in there?' one of the marines outside the cave entrance asked. 'I heard explosions . . .' He was clearly shaken by the urgency with which Jason and Meat were making their exit.

Jason hooked him by the arm as they passed, pulled him towards the slope. Meat grabbed the guy's partner by the shoulder and goaded him along right behind them.

'I need you to help me get everyone down to the MRAP . . . right now,' Jason said.

'Why? What's—'

Jason quickly conveyed the seriousness of the situation. He verified the elapsed time on his wristwatch then said, 'There's a nuke inside this mountain that's going to blow in less than four minutes.'

'A nuke?' Hearing his own words rattled the marine even more. 'Get outta here!'

'A really big nuke,' Meat said with extreme drama.

'Now go!' Jason said, prodding the marine down the slope. 'Everyone needs to be inside the vehicle!' He took a moment to survey the camp and confirmed that the backup platoon still hadn't arrived. For once, he was grateful for their inefficiency. Down below, six more marines were in plain sight, including the wounded.

'You too,' Meat said to the second marine, who was showing signs of disbelief. 'Get going.'

'But where's Crawford?' he asked.

'Dead. Same as Holt and Ramirez,' Meat told him. 'Same as us if we keep standing here.' Meat wasn't about to debate the issue. He turned and started down the slope. If the guy was smart, he'd follow.

'Dead?' the marine muttered in disbelief. He stared at the cave for a long moment wondering if he'd just been fed a line of bullshit. Then he came to his senses and hurried after Meat.

Jason secured the MRAP's rear doors the best he could since the massive indentations made by the earlier boulder collision had misaligned the hinges. 'All clear. Go!' he yelled to the driver.

The engine roared and the hulking troop carrier lurched forward.

'How much longer?' Meat asked.

He glanced at his watch again. 'Less than a minute.'

Jason hoped that the walkie-talkie had enough juice left in it to hold back the rats for just a little longer. But even if the brood managed to break through the ultrasonic barrier, they'd have a tough time squeezing through the rubble pile Meat had plugged up using Crawford's three grenades.

He scanned the worried faces of the marines huddled tight along the side-wall benches. One of the soldiers had his left arm in a sling, two others had bandaged heads, and the cute robot operator with the pageboy haircut had a makeshift splint wrapped tight over her right shin. 'Everybody all right?'

Some nods, some affirmative responses.

'Sergeant Yaeger,' the driver called back. 'I just received confirmation that 5th Division has turned around again and is returning to base camp. They're about three klicks to the west.'

'Good,' Jason said.

The MRAP gathered speed as it climbed on to the roadway and headed south.

'Jesus, what happened in there?' one of the marines asked.

Casting his eyes to the floor, Jason wasn't sure how to respond. Would anyone really believe the truth?

Meat answered for him: 'A weapons stash. *Huge* weapons stash. It was booby-trapped. Crawford must've hit some kind of tripwire that activated a timed detonator.' He looked to Jason for corroboration.

Jason nodded.

'But you said there was a nuke in there,' the second marine who'd been guarding the cave entrance challenged. 'How are we supposed to believe—'

'Hey, wise guy, I think you should shut up and grab hold of something,' Meat advised sternly, counting down the final seconds in his head.

The testy marine wisely clammed up and clasped the handle hanging over his head, tight enough to turn his knuckles white.

The others also hunkered down. Tension and anticipation filled the air.

Nobody spoke.

Five seconds later, a brilliant white light flashed through the rear window, accompanied by an earsplitting explosion on par with a thunderclap. There was a deceptive delay that preceded the shockwave. When it hit, the MRAP groaned and bucked, jostling everyone inside. Arms and legs flailed and bodies rolled. The hull filled with screams and expletives.

A barrage of heavy debris pounded the roof, clanging the vehicle's thick armour plating like a gong. The white light dissipated and a second wave of pelting debris came raining down over the truck's exterior.

Then came an eerie calm.

The intensity of the blast had Jason feeling confident that even if some of the rats had managed to escape before the nuke detonated, either the searing heat wave would have vaporized them, or the crunching pressure wave would have pulverized them.

'Told you it was a nuke,' Meat said to the sceptical marine.

EPILOGUE

LONDON, ENGLAND
TWO MONTHS LATER

'I feel like I'm hanging from a noose,' Meat grumbled as he tugged at the starched white collar that strangled his eighteen-and-a-quarter-inch neck. The rented black tuxedo paired a size 46 long jacket with a pair of 34 × 34 pants. But it all felt too restrictive, particularly at the shoulders and crotch. The shiny black patent leather 14 EE shoes were no great shakes, either; he hated the way they clicked along the marble tiles of the museum's Great Court. 'God, I hate playing dress-up.'

'What do you mean?' Jason said, fixing his own bowtie and taking extra-long strides to keep up with Meat. 'Dressing up is all we've been doing for the past five years,' he reminded him. 'Except this time we get to shower and shave, even smell nice. Nothing wrong with looking classy once in a while.'

Jason gazed up to admire the deep cerulean sky coming through Norman Foster's glass and steel canopy – a segmented dome of triangular glass panels which covered the hectare Great Court that was the heart of the British Museum. At the court's centre, he scanned the mingling VIPs who sipped champagne in front of the circular Reading Room. Still no sign of Flaherty.

'Doesn't look like Tommy's here yet,' he said, claiming a spot beneath a life-size statue of a Roman youth riding a horse, in search of conquest. Giving the statue only a cursory glance, he couldn't help but draw a parallel to Randall Stokes's lofty ambitions to chart a new course for human history.

A tuxedoed waiter carrying a tray of long-stemmed glasses brimming with bubbly immediately came to them. 'Champagne, gentlemen?'

'Cheers,' Jason said to the waiter as he took a flute by its stem.

'Yeah, thanks,' Meat said, grabbing his own glass by its narrow bulb as if were a chopper control grip.

A lithe brunette wearing a skimpy cocktail dress and high heels strode by, gazed at Meat appraisingly, then flashed him an approving smile. Meat smiled back, and miraculously the tuxedo felt comfortable. He reconsidered his position, saying, 'I suppose classy isn't so bad.'

'That's the spirit.'

'I'm just not used to getting all dressed up like some rich socialite.'

'Funny you should say that,' Jason said. He slid his hand under his lapel and pulled out a white envelope.

Meat looked at it suspiciously. 'If that's another goddamn subpoena—'

'Calm down . . .' Jason said.

There'd been plenty of court requests over the past weeks since they'd returned home from their mission. The Department of Defense had begun what would surely prove to be a lengthy inquiry into the events that had transpired in Iraq. Accompanied by an army of counsellors from Global Security Corporation's

Legal Affairs division, Jason and Meat had endured exhaustive questioning at a Congressional hearing. They'd quickly been absolved of any formal charges, thanks largely to the tell-all video captured on the disc Jason had recovered from the camcorder in Crawford's tent. The footage corroborated everything Jason and Meat had described in their testimony. It showed Crawford's crude interrogation of Al-Zahrani, Jason's unheeded demand to Crawford to call for backup, Al-Zahrani's rapid decline in health as proof that the Genesis Plague was a very real threat, plus a chilling offscreen altercation between Crawford and Dr Jeremy Levin just before a gunshot rang out to silence the medic. The video's grand finale, however, was when Crawford and Staff Sergeant Richards (dressed in nomad garb) appeared onscreen to hoist Al-Zahrani off the bed while Crawford barked orders to secrete the terrorist out the back door for a clandestine escape. Scathing testimony provided by the surviving troops of the 5th Marine Regiment, 1st Division Expeditionary Force, also empha-sized Crawford's schizophrenic behaviour, as well as the lifesaving air attack staged by the GSC mercenary unit.

The day after he'd been taken into custody, Randall Stokes had suffered a miserable and poetic demise, choking to death on his own blood in a quarantine ward at Nellis Air Force Base. Shortly thereafter, NSA cryptographers succeeded in cracking the sophisticated encryption on Stokes's computer hard drive, and retrieved all the operational details for Operation Genesis, including schematics for the breeding facilities installed beneath the Zagros Mountains and gene sequencing data for the Genesis Plague. There were even simulation models that forecast the spread of the disease – an expected 90 per cent kill rate of the Middle Eastern male population in just the first three months of the contagion's initial introduction.

Auditors had forensically reconstructed the money trail for the project's financing to reveal a complex web of twenty-seven phantom accounts in Switzerland, the Cayman Islands and Bermuda, all funnelled into a numbered account held by Our Savior in Christ Cathedral. The majority of funding had been misappropriated from defence money earmarked for biochemical research at Fort Detrick shortly after the 2001 terror attacks. The balance of funding came from charitable donations to Stokes's evangelical mission made by a veritable 'who's who' of wealthy donors. Every contractor and benefactor associated with Operation Genesis was being vetted for complicity in the plot.

Just last week, both Jason and Meat had been recommended for the highest commendations for their heroic actions in averting what might have been the most egregious act of bioterrorism ever documented. But the kudos didn't end there. There were other rewards too.

'Calm down, it's not a subpoena,' Jason said in a taming voice. He held the envelope out and waited for Meat to accept it. But Meat just stared at it.

'What is it?'

'Just open it. Come on . . . it won't bite. Trust me, you won't regret it.'

Meat reluctantly snatched it away from Jason. After confirming that his name and address appeared in the small window on front of the envelope, he began tearing at the seal.

'After that fire at the safe house burned out,' Jason explained, 'six skeletons were recovered from the ashes. Five were unidentifiable. But one of the skeletons had a very unique dental implant, as well as a titanium pin implanted surgically in the left ankle to correct for an old soccer injury.'

'All right,' Meat said, not grasping the connection. He peeked into the envelope and saw the backside of what looked like a cheque.

'Turns out the FBI matched the dental work with records already in its database,' Jason explained. 'The serial number on the titanium pin came up too.'

Meat froze before fishing out the contents from the envelope. He looked at Jason in disbelief. 'Al-Zahrani?'

Jason grinned widely and nodded. 'The only positive ID. Of course, those photos I took before we set the place on fire helped too.'

Suddenly the piece of paper pinched between Meat's fingers felt impossibly heavy.

'Go ahead, look at it,' Jason said, pointing at the paper.

Meat squared his shoulders and cleared his throat. Slowly he flipped the cheque over. His mouth dropped open when in the numeric field he saw nothing but two threes and five noughts separated by two commas. For once, he was speechless.

'Your cut of the bounty. Three-point-three million. A bit bigger than expected since Lillian had GSC match our share.'

'I always liked her,' Meat said.

'And you're about to like her even more ... because she agreed to send Jam's and Camel's widows their cut. Hazo's sister, Anyah, got his share. I've got an envelope for Tommy, too. How's that for classy?' He patted Meat on the shoulder.

Finally Meat raised his eyebrows and said, 'Whoa. Now *that* is a nice payday.'

'Sure is.' Jason raised his champagne and made a small toast. 'Here's to living to fight another day.'

'I'll drink to that,' Meat said, clinking his glass, then gulping the champagne.

'Hey, Google!' a distinctly Bostonian voice called out.

Jason turned and saw Flaherty strutting towards him with a confident swagger. When he saw the beauty on Flaherty's arm, he almost swooned.

'Hubba hubba,' Meat said. 'That the archaeologist?'

'That's her.' Wearing an elegant evening gown that accentuated nothing but toned curves, Professor Brooke Thompson looked like she'd taken a detour off the red carpet at the Oscars.

'She single?'

'Flaherty's already staked a claim,' Jason replied flatly.

'Luck of the Irish.' Meat took another swig of champagne.

'Hey, fellas,' Flaherty said cheerily. He shook hands with Jason and Meat in turn, then formally introduced Brooke.

'Really great to finally meet a pair of modern-day heroes,' she said.

'We could say the same for you,' Jason said.

Flaherty cleared his throat and raised his eyebrows.

'Yes, and, of course, you're a hero too, Tommy,' Jason added with the utmost sensitivity.

They all had a laugh as the attentive waiter delivered two more champagne flutes for Brooke and Flaherty.

'By the way, Tommy,' Jason said, taking another white envelope out from his pocket, 'I've got something for you.'

'Looks important.'

'You could say that.' Jason grinned and held it out for him.

'It can wait, though, right? I mean, this is Brooke's night.'

'Sure.' Jason pocketed the envelope.

Flaherty raised his glass for a quick toast. 'To the vanquished foe and the heroes we know.'

They clinked glasses and sipped champagne.

'This must all be pretty exciting,' Jason said to Brooke. 'To be the honorary guest at the world's foremost museum for ancient artifacts. The press, the glitz . . .'

'It's all a bit nerve-racking, actually,' Brooke admitted readily. She spotted the film crew from National Geographic shooting exclusive footage of the gala.

The evening's main event would be her highly anticipated dedication speech that would retell an ancient story of mysticism, betrayal, and retribution written in what proved to be the world's oldest documented language. The feature-length documentary, tentatively titled *The Queen of the Night*, would premier on IMAX screens before being broadcast round the world in a two-hour National Geographic special. Included would be Brooke's in-depth analysis of the cache of Mesopotamian tomb relics on display here tonight that bore testament to elaborate funerary rituals predating Egyptian mummification by over 1,500 years. Inevitably, she'd be pressed on rumours concerning the relics' mysterious procurement, but she'd stick to her story that her client wished to remain anonymous and had provided explicit directives to return the collection to its rightful home in Iraq as soon as the political situation permitted.

'I'm finally going to get to tell my story,' Brooke said. 'I'm just not sure if the world is ready to hear it.'

'Speaking of telling your story,' Flaherty said, reaching into his pocket. 'I've got an envelope too.' He handed the envelope to Brooke. 'I received a Fed-Ex at the hotel this morning. But figured I'd surprise you.'

'What is this?' she asked.

'Your carbon dates,' Flaherty replied.

Anticipation glinted in her eyes as she stared at the envelope. 'Dates for what?' Meat asked.

'The organic stuff we found in Stokes's vault,' Flaherty

explained. 'Lilith's head, of course . . . plus the snake and the rat it ate.'

'I've had my share of rats, thanks,' Meat said.

'Actually, the rat wound up being the key to everything,' Brooke explained. 'We found out that the rat was also carrying the plague. In fact, it was the primary host. So we theorized that while Lilith was feeding infected rats to her pet snake, she was bitten and caught the plague . . . became a carrier, too.'

'That is gross,' Meat said. 'Sounds like Lilith was a real prize.'

'So let's hear those dates,' Jason said, before sipping more champagne.

'Go ahead . . . open it,' Flaherty said to Brooke.

'Right,' Brooke said, her pulse drumming. She fished out the papers, unfolded them and scanned the report. 'Okay, Lilith dates between 4032 BC and 3850 BC. Just what we expected. And her DNA matches closest to . . . ancient Persia,' she said, feeling a chill creep over her skin. Persia, where Lilith and Samael became lovers. She flipped to the next page. 'The rat . . . is in about the same date range. And the snake—' Her face blanched. She shook her head. 'No, this can't be right. This is impossible . . .' she murmured.

'What is it?' Flaherty asked.

'They couldn't date it. Came up with an error.'

Flaherty shrugged. 'Okay. I guess that can happen, right?'

'Shouldn't,' she said. 'Any organic substance from 4000 BC should have plenty of carbon-14 in it.'

'But isn't there an age limit for those tests?' Jason said.

'Yeah, but—'

'Well, what's the limit?' Flaherty asked her.

She drew her lips tight and raised her eyebrows. 'Typically the test is good for up to 50 or 60,000 years. After that, whatever carbon-14 is left in the specimen is usually too minuscule to measure.'

It was Meat who cast rationale to the wind, saying matter-of-factly, 'So maybe the snake is over 60,000 years old.' Then he grinned and made his eyes go wide, saying in his best spooky voice, 'Or maybe the demon snake was never alive to begin with.'

ACKNOWLEDGEMENTS

Kudos to my wife, Caroline, for her diehard patience and encouragement, plus her keen guidance during this story's conceptual development. Special thanks to my friends Greg Meunier and Gary Stephens for their technical input on all things military. Deepest gratitude to my uncompromising agent and publishing guru, Charlie Viney. Thanks to Doug Grad for his masterful editing skills. Cheers to Ian Chapman, Julie Wright, Jessica Leeke, Amanda Shipp and everyone at Simon and Schuster UK for their continued support. My stories would only be read in English if it weren't for the global marketing savvy of International Literary Agency, so thanks to Nicki Kennedy, Sam Edenborough, Mary Esdaile, Jenny Robson, and Katherine West.

Turn the page
to read an extract from
The Sacred Bones,
also by Michael Byrnes
and available from Pocket Books . . .

POCKET
BOOKS

1.

Salvatore Conte never questioned his clients' motives. His many missions had taught him how to remain calm and keep focused. But tonight was different. Tonight he felt uneasy.

The eight men moved through the ancient streets. Entirely clothed in black, each was armed with lightweight Heckler & Koch XM8 carbines equipped with 100-round magazines and grenade launchers. Padding along the cobblestone in soft boots, every man scanned his surroundings with infrared night-vision goggles. History loomed all around them.

With an abrupt hand signal to hold position, Conte paced ahead.

He knew that his team was just as apprehensive. Though Jerusalem's name meant 'City of Peace', this place defined turmoil. Each silent road was bringing them closer to its divided heart.

The men had travelled separately from a handful of European countries, convening two days earlier at an apartment leased in a quiet part of the Jewish Quarter overlooking Battei Makhase

Square, their accommodation booked under one of Conte's numerous aliases, 'Daniel Marrone'.

On arrival Conte had played tourist to familiarize himself with the web of alleyways and winding streets surrounding the thirty-five-acre rectangular monument in the centre of the fortified Old City – a massive complex of bulwarks and retaining walls standing thirty-two metres high that resembled a colossal monolith laid flat upon Mount Moriah's steep ridge. Easily the world's most contested parcel of real estate, the Islamic *Haram esh-Sharif*, or 'Noble Sanctuary', was more familiar by another name – Temple Mount.

As the cover of buildings gave way to the towering western wall, he motioned two men forward. The wall-mounted floodlights cast long shadows. Conte's men would blend easily into the dark pockets, but then so could the Israeli Defense Force soldiers.

The endless dispute between Jews and Palestinians had made this the most heavily guarded city in the world. However, Conte knew that the IDF was rife with conscripts – teenage boys whose sole purpose was to fulfil three-year service requirements and no match for his hardened team.

He peered ahead, his night-vision goggles transforming the shadows to eerie green. The area was clear except for two soldiers loitering fifty metres away. They were armed with M-16s, donning standard-issue olive-green fatigues, bulletproof vests, and black berets. Both men were smoking Time Lite cigarettes, Israel's most popular – and, to Conte, most offensive – brand.

Glancing over to their intended entry point at Moors' Gate, an elevated gateway on the platform's western wall, Conte quickly surmised there was no way to gain access to the Temple Mount without being detected.

Shifting his fingers along the barrel, he flicked the XM8 to single-shot mode and mounted the rifle on his left shoulder. He targeted the first green ghost with the red laser, aiming for the head, using the glowing butt of the dangling cigarette as a guide. Though the XM8's titanium rounds were capable of piercing the soldier's Kevlar vest, Conte found no sport – let alone certainty – in body shots.

One shot. One kill.

His index finger gently squeezed.

There was a muffled retort, slight recoil, and he saw the target buckle at the knees.

The scope shifted to the remaining man.

Before the second IDF soldier had begun to comprehend what was happening, Conte had fired again, the round penetrating the man's face and cartwheeling through the brain.

He watched him collapse and paused. Silence.

It never ceased to amaze him just how token the expression 'defence' really was – offering little more than a word to make people feel secure. And though his native country had a laughable military competence, in his own way, he felt he had become its equalizer.

Another abrupt hand signal ushered his men onto the sloping walkway approaching Moors' Gate. To his left, he glimpsed the Western Wall Plaza nestled along the embankment's base. Yesterday he had marvelled at the Orthodox Jews – men separated from women by a curtained partition – who gathered here to mourn the ancient temple they believed had once graced this holy place. On his right lay a small valley littered with excavated foundations – Jerusalem's oldest ruins.

A substantial iron gate sealed with a deadbolt denied access to the platform. In less than fifteen seconds the lock had been picked and his team funnelled through the tunnelled entrance, fanning out across the broad esplanade beyond.

Slipping past the stout El-Aqsa Mosque abutting Temple Mount's southern wall, Conte turned his gaze to the esplanade's centre, where, just over tall cypress trees, a second and much grander mosque stood on an elevated platform, its gilded cupola illuminated like a halo against the night sky. The Dome of the Rock – embodiment of Islam's claim over the Holy Land.

Conte led the team to the esplanade's south-east corner, where a wide opening accommodated a modern staircase, cascading downward. He splayed the fingers of his gloved right hand and four men disappeared below the surface. Then he signalled the remaining two men to hunker down in the nearby tree shadows to secure a perimeter.

The air in the passage became moist the further the men descended, then abruptly cold, giving off a mossy aroma. Once they had assembled at the base of the steps, rifle-mounted halogen lights were switched on. Crisp, luminous beams bisected the darkness to reveal a cavernous, vaulted space with arched stanchions laid out on neat avenues.

Conte remembered reading that twelfth-century Crusaders had used this subterranean room as a horse stable. The Muslims, its latest occupants, had recently converted it into a mosque, but the Islamic décor did little to mask its uncanny resemblance to a subway station.

Running his light along the room's eastern wall, he was pleased to spot the two brown canvas bags his local contact had promised. 'Gretner,' he addressed the thirty-five-year-old explosives expert from Vienna. 'Those are for you.'

The Austrian retrieved them.

Slinging his carbine over his shoulder, Conte took a folded paper from his pocket and switched on a penlight. The map showed the exact location of what they'd been charged to procure; he didn't favour references to 'stealing' – the term demeaned his profession-alism. He aimed the penlight along the wall.

'Should be just ahead.' Conte's English was surprisingly good. To keep communications consistent and less suspicious to local Israelis, he had insisted that the team converse only in English.

Securing the penlight between his teeth, he used a free hand to unclip the Stanley Tru-Laser electronic measuring device from his belt and punched a button on its keypad. A small LCD came to life, activating a thin red laser that cut deep into the darkness. Conte began to move forward, his team trailing closely behind.

He continued diagonally through the chamber, weaving between the thick columns. Deep into the space Conte abruptly stopped, verified the measurements on the LCD and swung the laser till it found the mosque's southern wall. Then he turned to face the northern wall, the gut of the Temple Mount.

'What we're looking for should be just behind there.'

POCKET
BOOKS

Michael Byrnes

THE SACRED BONES

Jerusalem is a ticking time bomb . . .

An ancient artefact is stolen from beneath Temple Mount. With
thirteen Israeli soldiers dead, and the Palestinians outraged over
the desecration of the sacred ground, tensions are running high.
Detectives must work against the clock to identify the stolen relic
and the thieves, before civil unrest escalates to deadly
proportions.

In Vatican City, American scientist Charlotte Hennesey and
Italian anthropologist Giovanni Bersei have been secretly
summoned to analyse a mysterious discovery that could prove to
be history's darkest secret: a human skeleton, approximately
2,000 years old, and bearing the unmistakeable marks of
crucifixion . . .

With the malevolent eye of Vatican security expert Salvatore
Conte watching her every move, Charlotte must work against the
clock to uncover an astonishing truth that threatens the very
foundations of belief. And there's a more immediate question to
face: whether the Vatican will allow this information – and
Charlotte – to see the light of day . . .

ISBN 978-1-84739-012-7
PRICE £6.99